Enjoy !

Will "Mecca" ~~Elmore~~

MW01167268

Prison From The Inside Out

One Man's Journey

From a Life Sentence to Freedom

William "Mecca" Elmore

Susan Simone

Inkosi !... my pleasure to
gift you with my Journey
... peace & Freedom to you
my BROTher ... will !

Visit our website www.PrisonFromTheInsideOut.org

First printing 2021   ISBN 9780961444488 (paperback)

Published by the Human Kindness Foundation, www.HumanKindness.org
Incarcerated persons may request free copies by writing to the Human Kindness
Foundation, PO Box 61619, Durham, NC 27715, subject to available funding.

The authors and publisher offer discounts when ordered in quantity for special
sales and customization is possible.

Typeset and formatted by "Tofu Dave" Bellin (tofudave@tofudave.com) in Caslon Pro, a
derivative of the serif font designed in London by William Caslon I (c. 1692–1766). Jacket
design Chris Eselgroth. Cover photograph Tom McQuiston.

Library of Congress Cataloging-in-Publication Data

Names: Elmore, William, 1973- author. | Simone, Susan, 1948- author.
Title: Prison from the inside out : one man's journey from a life sentence
  to freedom / William "Mecca" Elmore, Susan Simone.
Description: Durham, NC : Human Kindness Foundation, [2021] | Summary:
  "Prison From the Inside Out is both a book and an act of trust: A black
  man from New Jersey and a white woman from New York meet in a workshop
  at a North Carolina prison. They decide they have something to tell the
  world about incarceration, self-esteem, personal growth, survival, and
  the power of trust. Together they have created this book. "Being in
  these situations for a quarter of a century let me know what I'm made
  of. I'm not invincible. I'm a mere man of flesh and blood. But let me
  tell you something: if we wanted to, me and my family, my friends, we
  could go through this struggle again. We're built like that. And
  everybody is. That's what we want to tell everybody. You are wonderfully
  made. You just don't know it. It took twenty-five years and a natural
  life sentence in prison for me to figure out that I was wonderfully
  made. How can I help you figure that out without the stick across your
  head? Please help me figure that out. 'Cause everybody don't survive the
  stick across the head. They just don't." - William "Mecca" Elmore"--
  Provided by publisher.
Identifiers: LCCN 2020039371 (print) | LCCN 2020039372 (ebook) | ISBN
  9780961444488 (paperback) | ISBN 9780961444488 (epub) | ISBN
  9780961444495 (ebook)
Subjects: LCSH: Elmore, William, 1973- | Prisoners--United
  States--Biography. | Ex-convicts--United States--Biography. |
  Prisons--United States
Classification: LCC HV9468.E56 A3 2021 (print) | LCC HV9468.E56 (ebook)
  DDC 365/.6092 [B]--dc23
LC record available at https://lccn.loc.gov/2020039371
LC ebook record available at https://lccn.loc.gov/202003937

Justice is what love looks like in public.

Cornell West, Bernie Sanders Rally, March 7, 2020

Table of Contents

Introduction

"Being in these situations for a quarter of a century let me know what I'm made of. I'm not invincible. I'm a mere man of flesh and blood. But let me tell you something: if we wanted to, me and my family, my friends, we could go through this struggle again. We're built like that. And everybody is. That's what we want to tell everybody. You are wonderfully made. You just don't know it. It took twenty-five years and a natural life sentence in prison for me to figure out that I was wonderfully made. How can I help you figure that out without the stick across your head? Please help me figure that out, 'cause everybody don't survive the stick across the head. They just don't."

William "Mecca" Elmore

Prison From The Inside Out is both a book and an act of trust: A Black man from New Jersey and a white woman from New York meet in a workshop at a North Carolina prison. They decide they have something to tell the world about incarceration, self–esteem, personal growth, survival, and the power of trust. Together they have created this book.

On March 30, 1991, William "Mecca" Elmore fired a gun toward a parked and occupied van in an attempt to protect a friend who he thought was actively involved in a drug deal gone bad. In court two years later, that same friend testified that Mecca had aimed directly at the van's occupants, one of whom died of his wound before reaching the hospital. Mecca admitted to firing the gun, but he did not plan to kill anyone, so although the public defender urged him to take a plea bargain, he insisted on taking the stand. Today, Mecca sees giving that testimony as a turning point in his life.

On the stand, Mecca described the shooting in exact detail, just as he would repeat it to me twenty years later: he did not fire directly into the van; he fired in the direction of the van, in defense of himself and his friend; the van's occupants had their shotgun aimed and were ready to shoot. But the coached and coordinated statements of the two prosecution witnesses, one of them the friend Mecca had been defending, prevailed. On May 20, 1993, the jury pronounced Mecca guilty of murder in the first degree. The court record states: "The defendant intentionally and with malice killed the victim with a deadly weapon."[1] Mecca was sentenced to "mandatory life," a sentence that meant he would spend the rest of his natural life in prison with no possibility of parole.

Prison From The Inside Out tells the story of how that sentence was served[2], using the tools of oral history. Mecca and I are collaborating writers. I am the narrator, but I am not a mediator or modifier. *Prison From The Inside Out* tells difficult and very personal truths about mass incarceration as it is experienced by the convicted and their families. What we've written down comes directly from each of the participants.

How did this book evolve? In 2009 I began working as a teaching volunteer at the Orange Correctional Center (OCC) in Hillsborough, North Carolina. Initially, I was to come to that prison camp once a week and meet with men who had been taking an African American literature course. After a few years, the workshop became a creative writing class. Then it morphed into an

---

[1]   Trial Proceedings, *The State of North Carolina v William Elmore*, Recorded August 20, 1996.

[2]   Appendix 1 provides a list of the prisons where Mecca was incarcerated.

open format where the men would suggest a topic, any topic: Donne's poetry, how to read music, how the stock market works, Renaissance art. Because attendance was voluntary, the men heard about it mostly by word of mouth – sometimes as many as twenty men came, sometimes three or four.

In the winter of 2013, Mecca arrived in my classroom at the instigation of his friend Scott-so, a Muslim man with roots in Brooklyn. I assumed Mecca, too, was a Muslim. Lesson number one with Mecca: never assume. It turned out that William Elmore had gotten his prison name while he was in jail in Raleigh, where a fellow prisoner recognized him from the streets. As Mecca tells the story:

"When I was in jail, a guy from Brooklyn said he had seen me a lot of times in Harlem, which is called the Black Mecca. He named times and dates and places and outfits I had on, so I knew for a fact he had seen me. When he saw me in jail he said, 'Hey man, I saw you on 125th Street, 116th Street. You not from Harlem?' I said, 'No. I'm from New Jersey.' He said, 'Man, far as I'm concerned, you Mecca.' He was a real huge, loud, boisterous, aggressive, intimidating guy. So once he called me Mecca, everybody called me Mecca. Even the correctional officers called me Mecca."

Every year I volunteer at the Full Frame Documentary Film Festival in Durham, North Carolina. After the festival, I show some of my favorites to men in the workshop and talk about my own work in documentary photography and how I use oral history to narrate my projects. I also bring in photo/documentary books such as *In This Timeless Time*[3] by Bruce Jackson and Diane Christian, with photographs of men on death row in Texas and a section called "Words" with comments from the men in the photos. Another book we look at is Morrie Camhi's *The Prison Experience*.[4] Camhi asks the subjects of his photos to pick a location and direct the creation of their portrait. Most of the men

[3] Bruce Jackson and Diane Christian, *In This Timeless Time: Living & Dying on Death Row in America*, (Chapel Hill, NC, University of North Carolina Press, 2012)
[4] Morrie Camhi, *The Prison Experience*, (Rutland, VT, Charles E. Tuttle Company, 1989)

who come to the workshop are "old heads," lifers or men with a long sentence, and they often trade stories, compare themselves to the men in the books, and talk about what they would and wouldn't be willing to show to the camera or write down on the page.

In early 2014, Mecca approached me after one of these discussions and asked, "Can we do that?" I wasn't sure what he meant, so he elaborated by saying, "Can I tell you my story?"

In the two decades since Mecca's conviction, none of the facts that led to his verdict had changed, but in the interim the state of North Carolina had recognized that there were people in prison for long sentences, many for life, who may have been disproportionately sentenced and had shown, in good faith, that they had changed and were ready for release. To assist them, the state created the MAPP or Mutual Agreement Parole Program, and made it available, by petition, to prisoners who were convicted under "old law," the pre–1994 Fair Sentencing laws.

In 2012, Mecca had been granted a three–year MAPP contract. The first year required that he reside in an honor grade/minimum custody facility. The second year he would be allowed to go out of the prison for up to five hours two times a week with a trained community volunteer. In the third year, he would be required to participate in a work release program and hold a job in a business outside of the prison, returning to the prison nights and weekends. On January 1, 2014, my husband, David Bellin, and I had the honor and the responsibility of taking Mecca out on his first community pass, his first experience outside of prison, unshackled, without a guard in over twenty-one years.

It was just after this initial outing that Mecca came to me with his proposal. Could we record him talking about his incarceration while he was out on one of these passes? I arranged for a sponsor, Bill Cook, to bring Mecca to the Chapel Hill Public Library, where we made our first recording. To be honest, neither of us knew where this would lead. People in prison guard their personal information closely. Mecca was very clear about that and told me early on, "In prison there are so few ways to improve your situation that everything is currency. Friendship can be your solace or your undoing." I had a digital recorder and he had a story, but we were still working out our boundaries.

Mecca began his prison life at the age of twenty-two. By 2014 he was a seasoned lifer who had spent more than half of his days on earth getting a closeup view of mass incarceration in eleven different prisons. As we talked, our interchanges became more personal; we signed a written "commitment" agreement and brought Mecca's mother, Bessie Elmore, and his sister, Cheryl McDonald, into the project.

That commitment gave us a sharper sense of purpose. Instead of just talking for the sake of talking, we were working to build a story that could capture the internal work, personal growth, and emotional struggles that make the difference between stagnation and growth, between misery and consolation inside prison.

In our talks then and still today, Mecca and I do not spend a lot of time focused on the violence, on the underbelly of prison life. We are more concerned with what goes on in the hearts and minds of the men and women who are, as Mecca likes to say, *managing* themselves in that hostile environment. What does it mean to be told you can never be allowed to live in freedom again? Is it possible to recover your balance, to live a moral life, if you are incarcerated? What does mass incarceration look like when you are the person sitting in the cell? What did it take for Mecca to preserve and grow the generous side of himself, to nurture self worth while keeping an eye out for the temptations presented by the cynicism that is justified by a life sentence? The two of us are dedicated to providing cues rather than answers: cues to people in prison for successful survival techniques, to friends and family outside about the power of empathy and support for people inside, and cues for reforms to a society that has forgotten that justice must offer some road to solace and recovery to those it convicts.

These ideas motivated us to take on the challenge of creating this book. We think they will bear fruit when those who read Mecca's story and meet the people who are part of it decide that prison reform on the outside and self respect on the inside are two sides of one fight for a society in which safety and justice are not rivals but partners.

Prison From The Inside Out is organized in three parts. In part 1, Getting into Prison, I have given the story over entirely to Mecca and Bessie and Cheryl. It is important that the circumstances that preceded Mecca's incarceration be presented unfiltered. They are recorded here along with all of the difficulties and contradictions of intent and action that were at work in the world in which his crime and conviction occurred.

In part 2, Doing Time, I enter the story as a narrator, orchestra conductor, and maybe a character too. I am learning as we go, asking questions and reinforcing or revising my own understanding of the story. The voices in this part of the oral history expand to include: two of Mecca's closest friends in prison, Scott-so and Frank; his boss at his job in the clothes house at Piedmont Correctional, James Leone; his employers at his work release job at Neese's Sausage, Andrea Neese, her son Tom, and Chris, the plant manager. The objective in part 2 is to explore how Mecca *manages* and *settles* himself – or sometimes fails to – as he grows from a very young man into a mature man under the weight of his natural life sentence. Bessie likes to say that re–entry begins on your first day in prison. Mecca affirms that and shows how it is done.

Part 3, Freedom, employs the same mix of narration and oral history, but it opens up the scope of the book to look at what happens when Mecca gets out of prison. Incarceration guarantees that a person will spend a lot of time thinking about freedom. *Doing* freedom is something else. On the plus side, Mecca finds work that builds on a commitment he made in prison: never forget the people who are left behind. He also finds a place as an advocate for prison awareness and prison reform. He works with people in re–entry. He builds a life. But he must also work through some important unfinished business when he visits old haunts in New

Jersey and travels to Missouri to see the father he has not spoken to for thirty years. Freedom is not a free ride.

Mecca has had many advantages in life. He and his family are well educated and highly motivated. Friends and family provided steady support while he was in prison. He is a thoughtful man who looks back on his prison frustrations and says, "I like to entertain myself with thinking about things. I like to puzzle it out."

Whether seen through a reflective and philosophical prism or not, prison is still prison. The cells, the rules, the food, the cold showers, the unanticipated shipping from prison to prison – that's real. The details of your daily life are controlled by the state; the complex system of regulations and physical constraints plays with your mind. The outside world needs to understand this and to help, not hold back, the 2.5 million human beings currently in the hands of the criminal justice system in the United States.

I'll pass the microphone to Mecca for the last word: "When I met you and you came up with the idea for a book, even if my mother and sister said, 'Naw, we gonna stay anonymous. We not gonna participate.' I still would have wanted to give my story away to the world. Not to shame anybody or put my finger in their face, but to kind of challenge people, to say, 'What do you value? What would you go all out for?' Like my mother says about Rocky: What would you go the distance for? What do you believe in or love enough to put it all on the table for? I want my story to be about hope, about support, about family, and about self value and second chances."

Susan Simone, October 2020

Part One: Getting into Prison

Chapter 1: "One Bad Decision"

My name is William Elmore. People call me "Mecca." I'm Christian but back on the street someone dubbed me "Mecca" for my steady presence and clear head. I take my time to scope out my surroundings. My Rule Number One *Don't do nothin' before you look it over.* This book is about what happened the time I broke my rule. The night of my crime, I made one of the worst decisions of my life.

I live in North Carolina, and you could say I came here as an illegal immigrant. I was arrested in Georgia at the age of twenty-one, extradited to Raleigh, jailed, tried, convicted of murder, and sentenced to "natural life." Born in New Jersey, I had no intention of migrating south, but by the cards dealt to me, I spent twenty-four and a half years exploring the North Carolina prison system. I have been a "resident" in eleven different prisons. This book is the story of how I survived that journey.

I talk to you now as a free man. That's because of the MAPP, Mutual Agreement Parole Program. It's available to people convicted under what we call "old law," the pre–1994 Fair Sentencing laws. A MAPP is a contract between me and the state, an agreement to comply with specific requirements as proof of my rehabilitation. On December 21, 2015, I walked out of prison and became a legal citizen of North Carolina, with parole and probation until December 2020. So technically, for that period, I was still "in" the prison system. I was allowed to drive, hold a job, and, with the permission of my parole officer, do some travel out of state. One slip up, one parole violation, and I could be returned to full custody.

Sentenced to Natural Life

What I want to talk to you about is my life as inmate[5] #121079, but the first thing you are going to ask me is what did I do to earn that number? Who died? Why? And when? These are not questions I like to answer. I began dealing drugs in and around Newark and Orange, in New Jersey, at the age of thirteen. We had money problems at home and drug deals turned out to be an easy answer for me. I never smoked, drank, or used drugs. If I had an addiction, my drug was risk. I loved the edge. Dealing, gambling, speeding, but always just under the edge, in control. Quiet inside. Mecca.

After high school I started to branch out, traveling down to Atlanta, Raleigh, and small towns down south. But that time, the night of my crime in Raleigh, I wasn't even there to do business. I was visiting a friend, Barry, who went to Saint Augustine College. He really wanted me to go to college, so he would invite me down hoping I would switch tracks. I was actually thinking about it. I would walk on the campus and get that feel of being in college. When I got out of prison, my favorite thing was to go to Duke and walk around the campus. Look at how I dress, and you'll see I should have been a college guy! No hoodie. Baseball hat and khakis, sweats and running shoes.

So that weekend, the time of my crime, I was not doing business, but one of these guys I have worked with, a friend of mine – let's call him James, because later he becomes part of my case so better just say he's James – James needed a ride from "the block" where we did business to his hotel. It's raining hard and he can't get a taxi. I'm at Barry's apartment, and he doesn't know these guys. Doesn't hang

---

5   There has been some discussion about how to refer to the incarcerated. I have chosen to go with inmate when that is the word used by the interviewee.

out with these creeps. They are not his circle of people. Barry wants me to break out. So when the call comes, he says, "Don't go. You don't owe these guys anything and it's raining and awful out there." But this guy, James, pulls out the friend card. We have known each other since we were kids. He plays on my affection, and I fall for it.

I said, "Barry write down the directions from your house to such and such street and then to the hotel and back to your house." And Barry said, "Don't do that. You shouldn't go out." And I said, "I can't leave my friend in the rain." I went out, and when I came back my life had changed forever.

I get out to where they have this little store, kinda like a bodega, the Chicken Shack, this little juke joint that has a video game and they sell fried food. The guys I'm looking for sell drugs in this area. I circle the block a few times, but I can't see anything; it's raining cats and dogs. I park the car far away, start walking to the store, 'cause I know that's where James and them will be. About halfway I see some commotion to my left out of my peripheral, in like a wooded area. I look over there at this silhouette, this body language. I say, "Okay, that's James." So I yell to him, "James, James," and he looks back and says, "Hold on a second." And I know what he's doing. He's making his last transaction. So I say, "Hurry up!" My instincts are working, so I look left and right for the police. That's just what you do in that situation.

But he's takin' way too long. Voices are rising. Some kind of conflict is going down. So I start to approach this van they're in. James is standing outside. I think maybe they're trying to rob him. I see the van, but I can't see inside. James is talking to the window. And the closer I get, the more I hear James saying, "What you want to do? It's rainin' out here. Do you want it or not?"

I see James getting nervous. Something is going wrong. So here's what I do. I make a decision that is way out of my regular game plan. When I first got to Raleigh people were kinda showing me around. Showing me who's here, what's what, because this is gonna be our terrain. This gonna be the area where we do what we do, so I gotta know. I gotta know which backyards don't have dogs, so if I run from the police, I'm not worried about getting bit by a dog. This really has a science to it, believe it or not.

As James is having this commotion, I remember there's this recreational center not too far away and behind it under some rocks, there's a pistol. I was told about this pistol from someone else doing business in the area. I've never shot a pistol before except when I went to the Poconos on vacation. I don't like guns. In the business I was in, you come across them all the time, but I keep my distance. But this time, because the pressure is on, I go to this area and I pull up the rock and there's the gun in a plastic bag. A thirty-eight. So I put it in my waistband. I don't even know how to hold the thing, but I tuck it in there.

I'm worried about the whole setup. I'm out of my element. I don't know any of these people in the van, but my friend is in a situation and for some reason he won't pull out. It's dark and it's raining, and I never get close enough to actually see anybody's faces. That's important for me to tell you. I did not know these guys. I had no personal business with them. No premeditation. No reason to kill them.

James doesn't know that I left to go get this pistol. As I get halfway back, I slow my gait down, and I see him start to back up away from the van, and I see something shiny sticking out the van window. Turned out to be a rifle that they pulled on James. He darts away without looking back. (That is going to be important later, because James is going the other way. He cannot see me anymore, but in court he is going to describe all of this as if he was looking right there, seeing everything.) He runs and the rifle is now pointed at me. I don't know if they can see me, but I turn around and run. I am scared. It's raining cats and dogs. Then I pull the gun out of my waistband, and as I'm running, I get a shot from them, and I fire one, two, three, four rounds as I'm running.

Then the van cranks up and pulls off. I keep running. I put the pistol back where I got it from, and I go back to the car. There's a place we all park. A safety zone. As soon as I get in the car, two seconds later, James is knocking on the window. He gets in and the other two guys get in back. They musta been hanging in the bushes. James says, "Man I'm so glad you came. Man, I thought they was going to kill me. They tried to rob me! As soon as they took the gun off me, I ran. What happened?" He said, "I heard some shots. Did anybody get shot?"

I said, "Don't think so, because the van cranked up and pulled off." So you should check this out: he heard the shots. He was running away, looking for the car. He didn't see nothing of what was happening back at the van.

So I take James and his guys to their hotel rooms. I go back to Barry's house. I'm soaking wet. I pull on some dry clothes. I play it back in my head a couple of times trying to be sure of what happened, seeing the van pull away, thinking nobody got hurt. It takes a while, but I finally fall asleep. Next morning I wake up. I'm thinking, "Nothing ever happened." Next day, nothing happened. I go out.

Close call, I thought. But later, the police come to Barry's and start asking about me. Barry tells me the police were there, but they didn't tell him anything. We don't know it yet, but somebody died. One of the guys in the van died from a gunshot wound. I don't know how I could have hit the guy in all that rain in the dark, but I find out later he died before he got to the hospital. It looks bad for me. I never had to face something like a gun charge before. This is not my game. I panic, all my cool thinking is gone – I run.

I find this guy who is driving out of town, and he takes me to Greensboro. I don't really know where I am, but now, looking back, I think I was across from A&T University. I call my mom, who's moved from New Jersey down to Georgia. I must have sounded bad, because she said she was getting in the car and I should stay put. I didn't say what was going on – just told her I needed a ride bad. And that's how it begins, the life that is going to be prison.

I go on the run for a year and a half. And once I run, I go into another world. I am all over the place, sleeping everywhere. I'll go somewhere, rent an apartment, and right away I'm peeking out windows, seeing Feds everywhere – because now I'm across state lines. I'm delirious because I'm hemorrhaging money trying to fund that lifestyle of being on the run. And I'm so paranoid. I would get an apartment, first month's rent and a down payment, and I would be there a week, then look out the window and... somebody's *watchin'* me. So I just walk out, never come back. The same thing with rental cars. Pay someone to rent me a car in their name. And then I'm gone, and I just leave the car somewhere. I'm twenty-one years old, and I'm scared!

While I'm on the run, the Feds get James and them under the RICO[6] act. You might think that's for gangsters, racketeering and that, but it applies to drug trafficking, selling drugs across state lines, which is what's going on with them. They say, "We got everything you guys done, up and down the highway. We got surveillance. So, is there anything you want to tell us that will help yourselves?"

And James says, "Hey, guess what – I know about an unsolved homicide in North Carolina."

Remember James never saw anything. He ran. Never saw... all he knew is what I told him, but when he testifies at my trial, he gives it all firsthand, like he witnessed it. Describes me pointing a gun into the van window, crazy stuff like that.

But we are still in the time before court. James is in prison, and I'm on the run. James gives them my whole profile, my likes, my dislikes. So they know I like fishing. One morning... I'm in Georgia... I drive out to fish. I'm sure nobody's tailin' me. So I'm standing there with my pole in the water like nothing is happening, and two guys dressed like fisherman come up to me, and they say,

---

[6]   Passed in 1970, the Racketeer Influenced and Corrupt Organizations Act (RICO) is a federal law designed to combat organized crime in the United States. It allows prosecution and civil penalties for racketeering activity performed as part of an ongoing criminal enterprise. Such activity may include illegal gambling, bribery, kidnapping, murder, money laundering, counterfeiting, embezzlement, drug trafficking, slavery, and a host of other unsavory business practices. (NOLO.com)

"Any bites today?" And I say, "No." They say, "Oh."

Look around like they are thinkin' about the fishin'. Then they pull out their badges and their guns – quick, all at the same time – and one of them says, "This is the FBI." I just looked at them and I turned around, hands behind my back. To tell you the truth, I was relieved. I had only one thought: "It's over."

They handcuffed me. Nothing rough. They took me to where my mother lived, without asking me. They knew where she lived. I guess they knew a lot. They let her see me, that I was safe. Even let her hug me. Then they took me to a holding cell in Atlanta. I had to wait for an escort so they could take me to Raleigh. Up in Raleigh I spent more than a year in jail, including the trial.

Now what's important to them is not looking for the facts. What's important is clearing the case. The district attorney, Susan Ellis (Susan Sterling... she got married), she can't get anything on me for drugs, so she's determined to get me for this murder charge. She gives my lawyer, Joe Knott, a public defender, this plea bargain to sign, and he is supposed to bring it to me. We meet in this small room, and he puts the paper on the table and tells me how blessed I am to be shown so much favor and I should sign this plea bargain. The plea bargain is for thirty-five years, second degree murder. I looked at it and all I saw was second degree murder, so I slid it back to him.

He said, "What's wrong with it?"

I said, "I told you time and time again, murder is not what happened."

He said, "What makes you so sure?"

I had been in the county jail for about eighteen months. They had a law library, and I went to it every day. I defined by their books what murder was. Murder, that's a premeditated crime. I told my lawyer, "That's not what happened. I've been telling you that the whole time."

And he said, "Listen son, you are a good kid, you're young. You take this plea bargain, you'll do twelve years at the most. You'll still be young enough to get out and be somebody." I said, "I'm not signing."

In the midst of that, the DA busted in. She said, "Joe are you done?" And he said, "No." And she said, "What's the problem? You telling me he doesn't want to sign that?" And Joe said, "Naw, he doesn't want to sign it." And she looked at me and she said, "What is wrong with you? You don't understand what's going on here, do you?"

And I said, "I really don't."

And she said, "You better understand fast, because here's the deal: I went against myself, and I can't do this plea bargain to spare your life if you don't want to sign it. I can't believe you. This guy that died, he's a robber, he's been in and out of prison all his life, he's a drug head. Personally, I don't care about this guy. This guy meant nothing to society. But I ask myself, what did you decide to do with *your* life? As a result, you're in a situation now and you don't have a lot of room to decide what you want to do. Take this plea bargain; that is your out. If you go to trial, I'll make sure..."

Now, as she's talkin', I'm lookin' at my lawyer, like, are you hearin' this? "I'll make sure that I get the max out of you. Do you understand that? And I know you understand that, because I researched you. I know your background. You went to good schools up North. Why are you in here?"

And she kept implying that I had no business being stupid enough to be in this situation, because I was much smarter than that. She said, "If you don't take this plea bargain and you go to trial, you gonna lose and be found guilty and you gonna get life. You've never been in trouble before. You are smart enough to have run this drug ring, and I tried to get the FBI to indict you, but they couldn't because they didn't have you under surveillance. I think you got away with that, but I won't let you get away with this. I'll make sure you don't get away with this."

Now remember, to take that plea I had to plead "guilty with intent." I didn't intend to kill anybody. I was in a situation and I had a gun. I shot the gun and I take responsibility for that, but I did not plan that situation, and I did not aim that gun to kill anybody. At the trial the forensics expert even said that under those conditions a person would have to be very lucky to actually hit a target. In my case very unlucky. But I had those guys, James and them, testifying differently. They told a different story, and in that story, I am the one with the deal going bad, and I am the one shooting a gun, leaning in the window of the van.

With the case going that way, my lawyer was sure I would take a plea. But in my spirit, I couldn't sign that plea bargain. Maybe now it looks crazy, but I believe, I know that *if I signed that paper, I would not be the person I am today.* I know my Self and I know that. I thought, "As a man, I cannot take that plea bargain. I have to go to trial. I have to speak my piece. I have to tell the jury what happened that night. Whatever they do is on them from that point on."

And I tell you today, I don't regret it. Never have I said to myself one night while layin' on any bed in any prison, I should have took that plea bargain. There is a part of me that rests in peace every night that I am in prison, knowing that I did, on my gut level, spiritually, what I needed to do. Oh yeah, I blew my trial. I could have been home long ago had I taken a plea, but a part of me would have been so shaky and so unsure about life. A part of me would have been quick to take the plea bargain forever, whether I was right or wrong, I could manipulate the system. That would have set me on a trajectory that's not my personality. It would have damaged me personally. It would have got me out of prison, but I would have been embattled.

That DA did her homework. When we got to court, she told that jury everything about me. She had stuff I forgot about me! Seriously. She described who I was and my potential – that if I were to take that intelligence to criminal behavior, I'd be dangerous. In the eyes of the jury, I was the kind of guy who could kill. She stuck to the murder charge and the jury convicted.

When I heard my sentence, it was probably the most surreal thing, the most devastating moment in my life. The judge, J.P. Allen, says to me, "Can the defendant please rise."

He looks at some papers that he got from the foreman of the jury. And he reads – I can hear that voice in my head now – he says, "I have no other choice, as the representative of the state of North Carolina, but to sentence you to life in prison."

In this sentence "life" does not mean life eligible for parole, some unspecified chunk of time until you get a parole. The sentence is natural life, until you die. The judge says a bunch of stuff I can't remember. I'm standing there and it's as if all the blood left my body. It was like I went underwater. Everything was muffled. I could hear the sound of his voice but nothing he was sayin', like I was in a state of suspended animation.

Everything froze. I could feel my heart – not racing, just a slow, heavy pounding. And Mom and Cheryl were behind me, and I just couldn't bring myself to look back. In that moment I was more concerned how they took the sentence than how I took it, and I didn't want to face them. I didn't want my last memory of them to be their faces, what they looked like, because, mind you, in this time, my relationship with my mother is strained. And my relationship with my sister is strained. I am thinking I'll never see them again. I don't think they'll be there anymore. I am headed to prison for my natural life with a murder charge over me. Part of me even wanted them to leave, to get back to whatever they dropped to come down South to my trial. They gave it all up for me, and once I lost the trial and got sentenced, I felt like they deserved to just do their best to forget about me, go on with their lives.

The bailiff comes, and he puts the cuffs on me and touches me sort of gently. He knew me from being in the jail so long. He takes me to the holding cell and says, "Sorry to hear that sentence."

And my lawyer comes and sits beside me. My head is down, and

Mr. Knott puts his hand on my shoulder and says, "I think you're a great kid. I'm sorry, man. I'm sorry."

And I don't even look up. I don't say anything. And he sits there for a moment, for a long moment with his hand on my shoulder. And I'm dazed. I'm empty. I'm numb. I don't know what's going on. Then he finally leaves, and I'm still sitting there for about ten more minutes. Then the bailiff takes me upstairs to the jail, and I take off my street clothes and put on that jail uniform, and off I go to Central Prison. I will not wear street clothes again until January 1, 2014, when I go out on my first community pass.

Now before we go any further, I want to say that my bullet did kill a person. When people ask me, I get right to it. I'm in prison for first degree murder. I discharged a firearm at an occupied vehicle and a guy died. So even before I went to trial that motivated me to write a letter to the widow, to the wife that I made a widow by my choice, and the daughter who I made fatherless. And I wrote about that. I said that the details in between don't matter. At the end of the day, I made a choice that left you without your husband and left your daughter without a father. That's what I was part of. We don't care about all that stuff the trial might bring out. The end result is the same. When I finally grasped that, I was motivated to write them. I actually wrote it to the DA, 'cause I didn't know their information. I asked her to give that to them.

This is important, because in my time I'm going to meet lots of guys who have stories about what they did and didn't do, but I can tell them from my own situation that you have to step up and speak to the people who are hurt by your crime. I would not plead guilty to the charge of premeditated murder, but I did kill a man, and he had family.

Doing Time: "Look at me, Son, and promise me..."

So now the trial is over and I'm in prison. I never been to prison before. The room where they process you at CP (Central Prison) is horrible, dirty with vermin. I'm thinking probably rats, cockroaches.

Real stale. They move me to a cell, but it's still bleak. I'm in this place where there is no sky. I could only stand on my bed and look out and see this little bit of sky and the people on the street. After a visit, I could see my mom there. I would wave a white cloth, and she could stand across the street and see it was me.

At CP I am deep inside and all around me are these men with all sorts of injuries and illnesses. CP is where they process you in the first time. I don't know it then, but this is also a medical area. People are there in wheelchairs. No legs. No arms. Those bags where they go...colonoscopy bags. . . and crutches...and dying of AIDS and cancer. All in one place. There's the guy beside me on the bottom bunk dying of AIDS who can't even control his own bowel movements, and he can't even ask for assistance from the officer.

When I entered Central Prison, that's when I crossed over in my thinking and realized: I don't want to see this through. I want to die. I went over it in my head, and I began to rationalize: I'm not going to give the state of North Carolina the satisfaction of keeping me here my whole life. I'm going to figure out how to die. I want it to be painless. I want it to be immediate. I want it to be in my sleep. And I was like, how you gonna pull that off? I don't do drugs. What drug you gonna take to do that? How you gonna get drugs to do that? I'm not gonna have pain. I'm not gonna cut myself. I'm not gonna do that. But I am ready to die. And that's the way I was.

Well, it didn't turn out that way. That's because of my mother, Bessie Elmore. She's a force to reckon with. I had refused to look at her or talk to her in the courtroom, but she came to CP to visit me anyway. When they said I had a visitor, I thought it was my lawyer. I go into the visiting room, it's about six feet by eight feet with mesh and I see my mom and she's got shades on because she's been crying. She tries her best to sound upbeat, but I'm not going to sound upbeat. I'm who I am. I'm not going to pretend like I'm strong. I'm weak, and I'm empty inside. I'm saying to her in my head, "What do you want? It's depressing enough. Now what do you want?"

Out loud I say, real flat, "What do you want?"

"I want to see how you're doing."

"I'm not doing good."

I'm very, very non-responsive. I'm not mad at her. I'm not mad at anybody. I just want it all to be over.

She says, "Say something."

"There's nothing I want to say.'"

"Well, say something for me. Say something for me."

"Mom, don't do this."

I drop my head.

"Do that for me."

"Mom, don't ask me that!"

"Do that for me."

She starts talking, "I remember when you were five," and stuff like that, trying to get a laugh out of me. And I'm thinking, oh, boy, don't start that.

"So you're not going to say nothing? You just going to sit in here?"

"Mom, I'm not happy here. I don't want to be here no more. I'm tired of it all. I want to give up."

"Don't say that. Come on!"

I'm kind of looking down, so I can't really see her, but I feel her. I say, "Look at me, Mom. I'm through. There's nothing left."

And she says... Her voice changed, and she pulls off the sunglasses and looks right through the glass and says, "Listen, listen. Promise me that if I stay here with you..."

"Oh boy, Mom, don't start that."

"No, *look at me!*" in that mother tone.

And I look at her. It's like instinctive. You don't have to want to, but you respond to that. I look at her, and she says, "If I fight for you, you promise me that you won't give up."

"I'm not goin' to promise you that."

"*Look at me*! If I say that I'll fight for you, you promise me that you won't give up!"

And I pause. I'm looking down, so I can't see her tears, but I can hear them moving on her face. And I say, "I don't know."

"Yes, you do. You know. Answer me!"

"Okay, I promise you."

"You said it, and I know you: when you say something, you know that's what it is, right?"

"Yeah, Mom."

And I thank God that she had the strength, the courage to say that to me. Because I had made my mind up, but now I know I have to keep my word.

No matter how mad I've been with my mother, I've never been disrespectful. And she figured that out. I don't know where she got these ideas from, but for twenty-four years she brought me materials to keep my mind stimulated, to keep my hope aroused, to keep me challenged, and she did everything necessary for me to be what I am in mind and spirit now. It was like I was back in my mother's womb and she was reading to me. She was sharing herself with me in a nurturing way that had got lost when our home got crazy with her and my dad. That was the payoff for her and for me. It's not all about me. She benefited herself, because this has taken her on her own journey within.

Know Yourself: Playing chess: opening moves

So I have made my word to my mom. When the yard is open, I go outside and find me a little place to just sit down and have these conversations with myself that I have every moment of the day, trying to make sense of things. Central Prison at that time was one of the most violent in the state, so there's a constant group of officers running this way or running that way and sometimes the violence goes on right beside you. Fighting, yelling, even killing.

I see that if I want to live this out and keep my word to my mom, I am going to need to play chess. Now, in my line of work, on the street, you had to play chess. So I begin to see that in prison it isn't about how strong you are but about how mighty. It's about how crafty and savvy you can be. Another thing about prison is that you have to *know yourself.* You start playing those games, being someone you think you should be, and sooner or later it's going to catch up to you. So this person, Mecca, he got lost at first, but now he's coming back. He's calm. He's watching, timing it, waiting to see how he can make this work. He's banking knowledge.

That's how I'm working this out in my mind for six months at CP, waiting. They don't tell you nothin'. You don't know if you might ship or if you might not, and you don't know when. That's how they play with your head. At six months and one day they shackle me up and put me on this bus and ship me to one of the blocks at Caledonia.

Whew! Caledonia is like going back a hundred years in time. Feels like I am a slave or something. Officers on horses; seventy-five hundred acres – fifty-five hundred acres of fields. Men out in those fields picking tobacco. Rifles and shotguns. It's totally extreme. At Central Prison everything is a door, and it slides and it closes behind you. Boom. Boom. Boom. Like chambers. Caledonia is like, "Look here, Boy, you can run all you want to run, because you got nowhere to go." It's a circle of buildings on a land mass that dwarfs the buildings. You can't even see the end of it. They have horses and the horses are trained. If you got on one, the horse would stop at a certain point and then turn around.

Off the bus, I go in the sergeant's office. He leans back – just like in one of those movies – and says, "William Elmore, New Jersey." Big pause. "Long way from home huh, Son?" More pause. "Life sentence. How did that happen?" Another pause. "That's all right.

You don't have to talk about it. First time?" Long look. "You gotta get you a knife, Son."

I don't say anything. I think it's a trick. If I say okay, then he's going to put me in the hole or watch me. I say, "So if I get one, you put me in the hole?"

He says, "No, I'm serious. You need to get you a knife. We got more stabbings and rapes and robberies here than probably any other prison. It's Caledonia. I don't know if you heard about it, but you will hear about it. You need to get you a knife."

I could see immediately Caledonia was going to be a game I had never played. I don't know about fields and farms and I don't know about prison. I have this sentence, natural life, but I don't know anything about prison. So I begin trying to figure it out. Somebody did give me a shank – a handmade weapon. I might have carried it for maybe a week before I said, "This is not for me. I cannot become this."

Because the way I think, if I tarry too long this way, I'm going to keep going that way. That's one reason why I never got into the hustle and bustle of prison. I had to do my time my way. Once I set my mind to a certain course, I'm there. I'm fully there, and I'm with whatever comes along. It's part of the arc – not taking that plea. Standing by myself.

This is where I start to grow my chess game. I did not carry a gun outside, and I am not going to carry a shank inside. But coming in from the prison transport, everybody's lookin' at you like you are fresh meat, so I am going to have to make a move. I head into the dorm. I am carrying all my stuff – got my blanket, got my personal bag, books and letters from my mother, got the prison clothes on my shoulder. I'm looking for the bunk.

One or two guys say, "Where's your bunk?" I give them my number and they point, "Oh, it's right there in the back."

And I get to my bunk, and lo and behold, they call chow. I look and the locker is so small I can't even fit half my stuff in it! What am I going to do? I gotta play chess. Critical thinking. Quick, Quick.

Here's one of the boldest moves you can make in prison: leave all your stuff on your bunk and go to chow! That says one of two things: You are an idiot! Or you are tough! I leave all my stuff on my bunk and go to chow. I say to myself, "This is gonna make or break my time at this prison." Got back and nothing was touched!

Okay. Next move. I'm gonna take a shower before I fix my locker up. Where I sleep and where the shower is, I can see my stuff. If someone takes it, at least I will know who. Back from the shower. Nothing touched.

Okay. I'm gonna catch the news. I'm gonna use the phone. All of that worked in my favor. It was a great move, because without me saying a word that let everybody know I'm not worried by anybody touching my stuff because I can handle myself. In prison they size you up that way.

So now my stuff is in my locker and the days start to pass.

Basketball. Everyone in prison gotta play. Somehow, growing up, I hadn't played any basketball. I played little league baseball. I was always athletic. I just didn't know the game of basketball. I do now! I can play guys half my age. But even back then, day one, some moves came to me – I didn't know nothing about how to shoot, but rebounding the ball and passing the ball, or blocking the shot, laying the ball doesn't require a lot, just coordination. I was only a hundred sixty-five pounds, but real quick, good balance, good agility.

The guys identified those things in me and they wanted me to play some more. So here's another smart move: when these guys play real aggressive, I don't cry foul. I knew aggression from the neighborhoods that I was in for my business. It's pretty much the same way that people relate to each other everywhere. Only the strong survive. So if you want to go in the corner store where there's like forty guys loitering in front, you can't be a wuss. There's a time to say, "Excuse me," so I can get in the door, and then there is the time – and you better know that time – to walk right past a guy and brush him a little bit. That's the energy of those environments. It's chess. So I play basketball, and I don't cry foul and I don't get pushed around.

Another problem with Caledonia is that it is a work camp and there's real cotton fields. Now, pickin' cotton, I never heard of it. Never. On TV, maybe. Didn't know cotton fields still existed in the world. I'm riding in the bus to Caledonia and I'm like, what is that stuff? Snow? Cotton field? You gotta be kidding me!

So here's another chess move. They have this GED program, and I sign up. The GED teacher, Ms. Williams, she's from Ireland. I hear over the P.A., "Any new participants for GED report to room so and so." I get there, and she's doing a roll call orientation.

She calls me to the desk and says, "You don't need no GED. I looked you up. Your scores are blah blah blah. Why did you sign up for this?" I said, "I'm bored." She said, "I tell you what, you want to tutor?" And I said, "Sure."

So she signed me up as a tutor. No cotton fields.

Here's one more thing to tell you about that time at Caledonia. Place showed me right away that prison is a serious game. I was tutoring this guy named Alejandro Guzman. He was from Ecuador, and he spoke very bad English. He told me he came over here to do construction for a guy who had this house and nothing but Spanish speaking people living there. Alejandro befriended a Spanish girl who also worked there; he called her his wife. One day, she told Alejandro the guy, the employer, had supposedly, allegedly, raped her. Alejandro murdered the guy and got a life sentence.

I had gotten into jogging, and Alejandro would ask me, "Um, can you jog in other prisons?" Was he trying to puzzle something out about how prison works, maybe whether jogging looks suspicious? I said, "Some you can and some you can't." I wanted to know why, and he said, "I'm going to escape." I said, "You serious?" And he said, "Yeah."

That was just when I left Caledonia. The next week, he was on the news as escaped. They put him in the field to work and he ran. They never found his body – Roanoke Rapids River, they say it's very turbulent. They say you can't survive that. Now you might think he escaped, but there would have been talk about the search and all that. He was just... gone.

Why would a man do this? Knowing he probably won't make it? Because prison is relentless. You feel: what is this all for? You go numb.

Chapter 2: Bessie's story

My name is Bessie Elmore, I moved to North Carolina when William was arrested. When he got his sentence, I made a promise. I kept that promise. I spent almost twenty-five years driving to different prisons and learning the rules for visiting, packages, phone calls, and working with the law to secure his freedom. My daughter Cheryl came down for the trial, and she moved here too. I call us the Three Musketeers. We became a team dedicated to the goal of getting William out of prison.

Before you get too lost in William's story, I want you to know a little bit about where he comes from, his people. I'm proud of William. He's done his time in an honorable way, in a manner that stands up to the kind of people he comes from. It's true I married his father, Willie Elmore, with rose colored glasses on my face. He was a good breadwinner, a long distance trucker who supported his family, but he was also a drinker, a gambler, and an angry man. I had to leave that man and that put my children out of their home. It is important to me that my children know that they are Johnsons first and Elmores after that.

I was raised in New Jersey, but I was born in Hardaway, Alabama. My father was named Roosevelt Johnson and my mother Rosa Della Steel. She moved to Hardaway from White Hall, Alabama.

My mom actually worked for my grandfather, Raspberry Johnson, cleaning his house. My grandfather was a very prominent person in Hardaway. The house my grandfather lived in – he bought it from a Caucasian. He didn't live back off the road where the Black people lived. Now, when we would visit and my cousins talked about this, I thought it was so strange because I lived in the North. But my cousins brought it to my attention that Raspberry Johnson's property touched white people's property and there was no fence!

My great grandfather was a free man and my grandfather was definitely a businessman! He didn't have stores, but he grew cotton and corn. He had a mill where he ground his own corn. He had cows and chickens. He had pecan trees and he would hire people to pick the pecans and sell them. He made his own cane syrup from sugar cane and he sold that. And he was a carpenter, so he built homes. Some people thought my grandfather was a penny pinching miser, but that's because he managed his money so well. He owned an automobile and a truck. He always had two vehicles.

So my mom, Rosa Steel, would come and clean up the house for Raspberry Johnson. She met my uncle and she met my dad, Roosevelt, but he was not interested in her for a long time. I guess he liked the single life.

My grandfather was about six feet two, and his mother was Indian – either Chickasaw or Cherokee because they settled along the Alabama River. I know a lot about my history because I researched my roots and I wrote a book. Raspberry Johnson was light with hazel eyes. Very tall and very handsome. William looks like him except for the color. My grandfather married a dark skinned woman, Bessie, and her family had money also. Bessie was an only child. They had money and owned property in Birmingham, Alabama. My grandfather was ten years older than my mother. I used to tease him saying: you married a little girl. But he said it was okay because she had finished school.

My grandfather was also a minister. He built two churches in Hardaway and he pastored at two other churches outside of town on the way to Union Springs. And on one of the churches' grounds he and another gentleman, named Wesley Carter, built a school.

Now my dad, Roosevelt, did not follow the white rules in Hardaway, period. And because of the relationship that my grandfather had with the white people in town, they came to him and they said, "Raspberry, you gotta do something about your boy. He doesn't say, "Yes, Sir' and 'No, Sir,' and he's just unruly."

My dad was in the service, but that's not where it came from. He just was not one to take stuff from white people.

The last event that happened with my father in Hardaway – the sheriff came to arrest him. This man had filed a complaint saying that he harassed him all the time. Now my father is not the kind of man that caused problems. You had to do something to him. He was very mild mannered. When the sheriff came, my father already had his own house and I was already born. He used the GI Bill to have a house built in walking distance from my grandfather's house.

That sheriff was notorious for kicking people's doors in, but not at our house. He came, he asked my mom, "Where is Lil' Buddy?"

Everybody called my dad Lil' Buddy.

And Mom said, "He's in the bedroom." So the sheriff says, "Tell him to come out here, because I have a warrant for his arrest." My dad can hear all this and yells back, "I'm not going anywhere tonight! You can come back tomorrow."

The sheriff does leave, but he comes back and arrests my dad and takes him up to Tuskegee to court. One of the gentlemen who was at the courthouse – happened to be white – knows my grandfather and my father, so he asks my father, "What are you doing in this line?"

My father's telling him what happened, and he says, "Don't worry about it, Lil' Buddy. I'm going to talk to the judge, and you'll be out in no time." So the guy does do that, and my father is out.

My dad was – I call him a militant. He did not follow the white rules in Hardaway, period. After that arrest the sheriff comes back to my grandfather and says, "Look, we can't guarantee that your boy is not going to get killed. He needs to leave."

We are in Alabama in the nineteen fifties, so this is a serious threat. My uncle Arthur is already in Jersey, so my grandfather calls him up and says, "Your brother needs to leave."

But dad doesn't want to go to Jersey, so he says, "I'll first go to Florida and see how it is; and if I can't make it there, I'll go to Jersey. Take Bessie and Roosevelt (that's my brother) to Jersey."

And that's how I got to Jersey. I was three years old.

Now, I knew we were moving to New Jersey, but I didn't know what New Jersey was. I was sad because I was very close to my grandfather, closer to my grandfather than I was to my parents. The day of my birth was this big thing, because Raspberry Johnson's first grandchild was being born in his house. It was a big to–do! A hog and a fifth of liquor! Wow! I was an expensive kid. I was named after his wife, Bessie, and he told me how heartbroken he was when she died. Leaving him, I remember how sad I was. When I was little, I would spend a lot of time with him during the day.

Now, my mom's family was not as prominent. Rosa Steel married up. She only went to the sixth grade, but she was not illiterate. She used to go up to the Tuskegee Institute and compete with all the college students and win all the spelling contests. When I married William's father, Willie Elmore, we lived with my parents before we bought ourselves a house, so my mom had a lot to do with William when he was small. He was her first grandson and Raspberry Johnson's first great grandson. My mom was very close to her father–in–law. She was like a daughter to Raspberry, because all of the time my father was in the service, it was my Mom and my grandfather in the house. My dad was missing in action for a long time, and they didn't know if he was alive or dead.

So William was spoiled. Mom watched him and I went to work. I told her, "He has to go to school. He needs to be around other children." But William didn't like that. Even at school he was always with the teacher, because the teacher reminded him of my mother, and she favored him. That's his gift and his curse, that charm. I know it helped him in prison, but it also helped him get in trouble.

William was always smart, ahead of himself. When he was about eighteen months, he was in the hospital and one of the nurses called me up. She said, "Mrs. Elmore, I'm a little concerned." And I said, "What's goin' on?" And she said, "We gave William a bottle, and he looked at it and said he wanted people food." I said, "Oh yes, he doesn't take a bottle; he doesn't eat baby food."

So they would bring him food from the children's ward. William reminds me of myself because I was always around adults as a kid. My babysitters, even when I lived in Alabama, were adults. And I was talking at an early age, and I still talk a lot!

Now my dad was also smart. When he was in the service he was stationed in Japan and he and my cousin, they learned Japanese. We didn't think much of it. Thought it was annoying because we didn't understand what he was saying, but looking back I think, "Isn't that interesting!" My cousin would come over and he and my dad would be talking in Japanese. I thought that was so funny, but now when I look back on it! Wow!

My dad came up from Florida, and we moved a couple of times but ended up in Whippany, New Jersey. He found work with a company called Rowe Manufacturing that made cigarette machines. He was a welder. And we went to integrated schools. Even though it was the nineteen fifties, we were not around racism, and my father never bowed down to any color line. I remember I was in the second grade when Perry Koristis told me I was black! Perry Koristis was from Czechoslovakia, and when he came to our class, the teacher told us that he couldn't speak good English and our job was to help him. Perry sat next to me. One day he couldn't do something, so he took out his paper and I took out my paper so I could help him. We had those thick pencils, and Perry was just doing this on his paper, moving his pencil real hard. And after he finished, he picked up his paper which was covered in thick black pencil and he pointed to me. He was trying to tell me I was black! It confused the heck out of me because no one had told me I was black!

I went home and I waited for my dad because my mom was much lighter. Her dad was a mulatto. I was the darkest kid in the house. I asked my dad if I was Black, and he told me I was, but I still didn't know what that meant. It puzzled me. How could this kid... how is he telling me I'm Black! What did that mean? I can still describe Perry to you. He had hair like Peter Lorre, and he had on a blue top and blue short pants and yellow socks. No kid at that time wore shorts to school. I wasn't helpful to Perry after that.

I also remember the summers when we went to Alabama. That's when I really got to see segregation. But I still did not understand that either. The signs when we would stop would say colored only, and I would ask my dad, "What's that mean?" And he would say, "Don't pay that any attention."

We never went into a back door. We always went in the front door. I remember the time my brother Larry and I jumped out of the car and just ran into a store and the lady in the store stopped us and said, "What y'all think you are doing?" She was bending down talking to us and then she stood up. I remember her expression. And the next words out of her mouth were, "Can I help y'all?" because my dad had come in dressed in a suit and a hat. My father was always well dressed.

When we were driving to Alabama, we went to Howard Johnson's a lot. For some reason I thought Howard Johnson was related to us because we had the same last name. We ran into the restaurant and we jumped on the stools and we were playing around. In the back you can see the Black people working and they're smiling at us. Oh! The people are looking at us and we're just rolling around and nobody has taken our order because we're kids and then my father comes in. Whenever my father would appear, people's attitude would change. So they would serve us. Normally, at that time, Blacks were not being served. You could work in the kitchen, but you had to go around the back to eat. I don't know if that was a good thing or a bad thing, because we all could have gotten killed, but my dad never backed down and he never rolled over for anybody.

In a funny way, the Johnsons are part of civil rights history. In 1963 my father took my brother to the People's March in Washington, D.C. I was visiting my grandfather in Alabama. I watched it on TV, and while I was watching, my mom called me and asked, "Did you watch the TV? Your brother got lost in D.C. He was on TV!"

I had missed Larry getting interviewed on TV because he was the first kid to get lost at the march! The reporter asked him, "Well, Larry, what do you want to be when you grow up?" And my brother said on national TV, "President of the United States!" When Barack Obama became president, I got so overwhelmed, because I felt like Larry should have been here. He didn't live to see that.

My dad used to have us listen to Martin Luther King's speeches. Every year, when we went to Alabama dad would take us up to Tuskegee to the museum where the airmen were. He used to work there, and he would take us to the square where they filmed *To Kill a Mockingbird*. I mean every year!

In New Jersey things were changing for my family. My uncle Arthur, he was more of the upper–upper. He stayed in Morristown and my aunt Violet worked at the country club, so they introduced a lot of things to their kids like golf and Toastmasters. My uncle Taylor graduated from Miles College in Fairfield, Alabama, and he was the first Black supervisor at Western Electric. My aunt Cora moved to Connecticut. There was a conversation, because Uncle Arthur wanted my dad to move out of East Orange. He could see East Orange coming down, down, down, and it wasn't a good influence on us.

It was a progressive time for my family. That's where I got my values. I kind of married outside of those values or that's how it turned out. Willie Elmore lived in Alabama. I knew him practically all of my life from visiting. So I thought, "You know what. I'm going to marry someone from the South."

I'm not a party girl, but I did go to New York discos where everybody checked out everybody. I was eighteen, and I thought he had that southern quality, and he thought that I was a party girl from the city. It was in a time when everyone was getting married – Vietnam War and the draft. So I thought, "Oh, I want to get married."

It turned out we both wanted something different, but not the same different. When we were dating, I would take him over to the Village Gate. He said, "I want what you have." He wanted my teenage life. The life I had had. I said to him, "You can't have that. You are an adult. That's past." That's not what I want when I'm married. I don't want to stay out until three o'clock in the morning anymore. What I wanted was a good life for my children.

Willie thought I wanted everything just to be "better." He would say, "You are spoiled." No, I wanted nice things but not fancy. You get married and get an apartment and then you get a house. We did get out of Orange and moved to Irvington into our own house. I did my research. Good schools but not private schools. William took Spanish from third grade and Cheryl was in the music program. We had two cars – a station wagon – and a dog and a very nice house. I worked at city hall. Willie earned good money as a trucker. My husband was a good provider, but we did not want the same thing. And then there was the beer.

After we moved, I got pregnant again, with twins, but I got sick. Cancer. I had to have radiation and a hysterectomy, and I had to have an abortion because the babies could not survive the radiation. And after that Willie was more and more angry and abusive, mentally and physically.   I didn't want to tell my family because I didn't want to hear "I told you so." I didn't want to hear that, so they were in the dark for the longest time. Then our house went into foreclosure. I went to see the man at the V.A. every day to find out what we needed to do, and the V.A. agreed to adjust the loan. When I told my husband, I said, "We are going to split this in half, but I am not going to ask my family."

It was about five thousand dollars. Probably they would have given it to me if I asked, but it was important to me that my husband step up to the plate. I felt like a fool. My parents had paid for a nice wedding and now it was all messed up.

I had a big, big issue with divorce. Plus I was scared. What am I going to do with these two kids? I can't afford to keep them in the lifestyle they are accustomed to. Where am I going to go? How am I going to do this? I'm going to be the first person in my family to get a divorce! My family is going to look at me like what did you do? All this crazy stuff went through my head.

I was faking it all the way. I didn't want people to know what was going on. Not to me, *Bessie*. She has it under control. On the outside we looked like the perfect little family, but if they only knew what was going on at home. And I felt that I owed it to my kids – especially William needed to have a father. I kept asking myself how did I fall so far on the Richter Scale? What happened to me? Then one night it all fell apart, and I had to run, grabbed those two kids and fled to my parents' house.

At my parents' house we were on the third floor. It was very stressful for William and Cheryl. They did not want to be back in the neighborhood in East Orange, which had begun to decline. William and I were sharing a room. I kept them in the Irvington Schools by driving them there every day. But being at home, I saw what was happening with my younger sister Karen. Later, after we moved back to Irvington, they gave me custody of her so she could go to a better school. Because of my illness, the cancer, I had to resign from working at city hall. I had temp work and then I got a job at Chubb and Sons making a pretty decent salary, but we didn't have the money to live like we used to.

So after my parents' house, we went to an extended stay, the Irvington Motor Lodge, and then I got an apartment on Linden

Avenue. It was just the three of us and Peppy, the dog, but William kept asking me to give his father one more chance. Willie would come around and we would fight. One night he kicked the dog out. Peppy was an indoor dog. At night he would check each door and then he would jump up on William's bed. When Willie kicked Pep out, the kids put on their coats and ran out and followed his paw prints. It was so sad. And that was it for them. That's the same night that Willie broke my nose.

The money was a mess. I tried to protect the kids. Cheryl was in high school, so she kept to her friends and her activities, but I see now that William didn't understand. Cheryl graduated and went to Fairleigh Dickinson. My cousin married my best friend and he became William's godfather, but when my father died there was really no man close by in William's life. I tried to provide a good support system. He had to be in the house by eight o'clock because I had a real job and had to get to sleep myself. But there were too many things I couldn't check on.

I didn't have a church or that kind of support group, but I did have happy hour at the Savoy. It's a lounge right across from city hall, and my friends said, "Oh, Bessie, you should join us." So I started going on Wednesdays. Most of these young women were in the same position I was – single, separated. But we never really talked about it. Nobody is talking about the elephant in the room. I do remember one of my girlfriends, maybe eight or nine years older than me, saying, "Girl, stay and make him pay!" We were angry. Women with two or three or five kids, and now we have to support them. And we have to think about starting to date again! So there we sat. Bougie, bougie, sipping our drinks. Harvey's Bristol Creme with a twist, smoking a cigarette. We shared our stories and laughed about it, only crying inside. One girl, her husband came and kidnapped her daughter. He was in the navy, and she couldn't fight the navy to get her daughter back. So we would all cry in our beer.

William got a paper route. I remember we had this big, round table and we would have a powwow there, a meeting. One day William called Cheryl and me into the dinning room, and he took his pay and he threw it on the table. He said, "Now I'm the man of the house." It was only twenty-nine dollars, but to him it represented being the man of the house. And he was so serious! He was just thirteen. I didn't want to take his money. What are we going to do with twenty-nine dollars? I told him, "You can be the man of the house, but you get to keep the money from your first paycheck."

Looking back on that I think that was very important for him, to take that role, to be the decision maker. He would tell me, "Now Mom, you aren't going to bring no men home to the house." I didn't date for a long time – not because of him, but because I wasn't sure what I wanted. I know I didn't want to meet anybody like this ex. But for William, he was supposedly making the decisions and he and Cheryl would clash a lot. Because they always thought they each knew what was best. It was like they were my parents. Sometimes I let them do it, and sometimes I wouldn't, because that's not how I planned it. I wanted them to have the best, to be engaged in all the best things out there. School activities. Music. Cheryl played music, tennis, track. I let them get away with a lot because I felt I had failed them in a way.

I was raised by strong parents, but with the divorce I see I really had to be a fighter. I learned lessons I didn't know I was going to need, but over the last twenty-five years they have been used plenty. I remember I was going after child support. I didn't want anything for myself. I wanted that child support because Willie and I had gotten Cheryl and William used to living a certain way, and I couldn't afford to keep that level. I went after him for child support, but you have to be so many months behind before they do anything. Anyway, long story made short, they told me, "Mrs. Elmore blah blah blah. The money goes to the court and then they cut you a check." And then they said, "This money is not for you. It's for Cheryl and William."

I know this! I understand. But we need the money. So I take Cheryl and William down to the director's office and say, "You told me the money is for William and Cheryl's food and clothing and shelter. Well, here they are, and they have no food, clothing or shelter." And she said, "No, *no*, you can't do this!" And I said, "That's what you told me, and you guys are dragging your feet. What do you want me to do?"

Of course I didn't let William and Cheryl stay there; and they still didn't get me the money.

I decided to contact Senator Bill Bradley. I had met him at one of the balls I went to in my job at city hall. He asked, "Well, Mrs. Elmore, what would you have us do?" So I said, "I want to get me child support."

Finally, child support said that if Willie Elmore's company would give me the money, we could do it that way. By now they want to get rid of me. So I called the ladies at his company in payroll, and they set it up. He got paid on Wednesday, and I got my check on Thursday. And it was a lot of money then, a hundred fifty dollars.

But there was still something missing at home. I didn't know it then. William was bringing home good report cards, and he was always polite and respectful, and Cheryl was going to college, but I was very preoccupied. I was the oldest child in my family of ten children, and when my dad died, that left me as the head of the family. I had that and my job and my worrying. The kids said, "Mom, you are taking care of everybody, but not us."

And when I look back, they were right. I felt that they were strong enough to take care of themselves, and these other people in my family were so needy. And I was the rescuer. Being the oldest I was responsible for so many things.

I didn't think my mother could manage. I always felt she was the weakest person. She didn't work outside of the house, and I always said I'm never going to be like that. I'm going to have a job and I'm not going to have all those kids. When my dad died, I said, "You can have a life now. You can go back to school. Daddy's gone." And she looked at me and she said, "I'm not as strong as you."

I never looked at myself as strong. I looked at myself as I gotta do what I gotta do. I have these kids and the dog. We were the Three

Musketeers!

I was so surprised when Mom said that, because I was ashamed that my own marriage didn't work out. My mother was one of those women who didn't understand being separated or being divorced. She married the love of her life.

When my dad died, she didn't have much money left. I stayed with her until my brother got her an apartment where rent was based on income. She had lived in her own house forever. It was a big change for her. Shortly after that, she got sick. The doctor said she had cancer, but I think she died of a broken heart.

This is where my sister, Cora, comes into the story. She and my brother were doing drugs. I never did drugs. That's where William would say I'm like Mr. Magoo, too blind to see what's going on. I did my little drinking. I never smoked reefer because I was always weight conscious and it made you act silly. So I'm just a wine person. And this is when William started on the street. But I didn't know anything. William and my sister Cora were very close, and when he started with this drug thing, she blackmailed him. If you don't do this, we are going to tell your mother. I didn't find out until many years later. My sister was a master manipulator. Her husband worked as a cab driver and she was a dispatcher.

Now I start to get in some fights with William. We have a big fight because he says, "Mom, school is boring." I remember I wanted to get him into a program at Seton Hall and took him there to take the SAT. I remember sitting in the car waiting, and then he comes out early. "You're done?" And he says, "Yes." Now I know that while I was sitting there waiting and hoping, he was inside looking out the window at kids he sold drugs to – what he calls his "customers" – and thinking, "No way am I going to Seton Hall."

He scored in the top fifteen percent in the state of New Jersey on that SAT!

Eventually William stopped going to school. That's when I started to have those fights with him about getting his GED. And then I moved to Georgia. Cheryl was working, and William told me he was "working" and looking into classes for his GED. I wanted to get a new life, to get away from everybody and start over. I was tired. I moved down to Georgia to try to have a life of my own.

William would call me and say, "Mom I'm fine and I got this job." And I would say, "What about school?" And he said, "I'm going to sign up at Essex County Community College and take the GED." But he was lying to me. He would say he would go to please me but not do it.

It was 1989. I have family in Georgia, so I went down with a friend of mine, got a ride in his car. His family was moving there. I had worked for Chubb and Sons, and one of my clients had an office in Atlanta. That didn't work out, but I decided to move anyway. When I got to Georgia, at first I thought I was going to die. The transit system sucked. I messed up my shoes walkin' all over the place, walking five miles just to get to a bus. I cried a lot. I got a job at Atlanta Bank, but then I got fired. It's a right–to–work state so there was no appeal. Finally, I decided to start my own business of skip tracing. I did it on the phone and I did pretty good. I charged a fee; a hundred dollars if I don't find the person, more if I do. My family showed me around and took me to Stone Mountain. It was twenty-five years ago and there were still farms and cows, I got an apartment and from my deck I could see that mountain. It was gorgeous. I said, "This is it. This is where I am going to live."

But here I am again like Mr. Magoo! I had to come up to Jersey for something and William was supposed to pick me up at Penn Station, but I get there and no William. I call Cheryl. She says, "I'm coming to pick you up. I'll tell you when I pick you up." So I'm saying, "What's going on?" And she says, "Mom, you *really* don't know what's going on?" And then she tells me he's been picked up for selling drugs. And I say, "Selling drugs?"

We go to meet his girlfriend Keisha, her family, and they are going to bond him out. And William says, "Mom you really don't know what's going on, do you?" And he starts to tell me, and he can tell by the way my eyes open wide that I don't know. He says, "Mom, I got bills, I got this and that..."

I was so upset. If his father had just done his job, maybe this wouldn't have happened. I thought maybe this man that William got himself involved with was – the guy was my age – maybe he was molesting William? But he wasn't. This man was a predator of another kind. We were arguing about this and my being so blind, and William said, "But dad got stopped by the police for having marijuana in the car and said it was mine."

I didn't know about these things. Keisha's family put their house up. It took me a long time to get their house released. I knew people who worked in downtown Newark, but it took me a long time.

And then William came down to North Carolina, and first there was an arrest in New Jersey and a bench warrant and then the incident happened in Raleigh and he was on the run. I had moved to Georgia and I thought I had begun a new life. But I got his call, and then I drove to North Carolina to get him because I didn't know what the hell was going on. I had yelled at him when he called, "You only call me on and off on a Sunday. You really must be bored to be calling me." He said, "Ma, come get me!"

I go, 'cause I don't know what else to do. I pick him up in Greensboro, and he is very quiet. We drive up to New Jersey and all the way he doesn't say anything. He's sleeping. I say, "Everything okay?" And he says, "Yeah, Mom, I just want to go home and get in my bed." None of it make sense, but I know something is wrong!

That's how it began – William on the run. One day we are at Cheryl's and the FBI come and search the house – 'cause William was living there with Cheryl. Cheryl tells me to just sit still. I don't know where William is. I'm smoking like a chimney. The FBI guys, a white guy and a Black guy, they know all about me; where I live, about my work, the skip tracing. And they say, "Mrs. Elmore, we are in the same business. You can turn him in and collect a reward and use the money for a good lawyer."

They didn't find him. He was hiding where they didn't look. So after they left, we got William out of there and he went on the run.

Later on, because now he's wanted, these agents did bring us down to the Gateway Building in Newark. I could see Cheryl was getting tired of this. She was trying to get her clearance at work and the agents told her they would destroy her life. They tried to play good cop, bad cop. Telling me if they find him in Georgia those good ol' boys are going to shoot him. And I'm walking around the room. I just couldn't sit. And I'm looking at all the people on the wanted posters, and one of those pictures was Joanne Chesimard, Assata Shakur. And I said, "You didn't catch her. She's in Cuba!"

They were going to put William on *America's Most Wanted*. Have you seen that horrible picture? He looks like a murderer. I was like, "Oh, no! Now my baby is going to be..."

I decide that I need to hire a private investigator and get an attorney in North Carolina and get to the bottom of this situation. But I don't have the money. So a friend of mine, Watani Tahimba, he tells me what to do. He's going to get William a new identity because it is taking me so long to get the money for an investigation and a lawyer. While we are waiting, I follow his instructions and I get an apartment on a cul–de–sac. There's a cobblestone bridge, and I can hear every car that comes and goes. He says, "Make sure you pay attention to any new activity. Does anybody new move into the neighborhood? Any activity change?"

So now, I feel like a spy. I can hear every car that comes in on the cobblestone bridge. I can't sleep now. I'm up all night playing solitaire. My thumbs were sore! And in my bedroom, I had a chaise lounge. So we even devise a plan. I told William to take out the bottom and see what's there. It has a base with three bars and a metal bar shaped like a U. It's long enough for a person to fit. That day my two brothers are there and my sister and one of William's friends. So we do a rehearsal to see how quickly we can get him into that and put the chaise lounge down. We do that and it worked perfect. I can't believe we did that. It's amazing what the mind can do!

But it never happened that way.

The day they caught William, he came to my apartment in Georgia to walk Brandy and Sherry, my two cocker spaniels. I had a friend who had told me that if the FBI is watching you, a person should never come in and out the same way. William would call me at seven before he came to walk the dogs and I would say, "Remember you gotta go out a different way!" And he would say, "Oh, yes."

But on this particular morning he says, "Oh, I forgot something," and he goes back in the same way he came. The FBI apprehended him that day.

They did bring William to see me after they arrested him. They were so nice to me, stayed with me until I calmed down. They told me that what North Carolina made my son out to be, they did not find him to be. I had to go down to the Russell Building, but they didn't charge me. They federal agents couldn't believe that North Carolina had made this case about William being a drug lord. They said they could tell that this guy was no big time drug dealer. They dropped the federal charges for unlawful flight, and they didn't charge me for harboring a wanted felon.

I went one time to see William in Atlanta, but I couldn't stand it. I was kind of glad that they brought him back to North Carolina. I had a friend in a big firm in Georgia who was going to come up to North Carolina and do an investigation, but North Carolina wouldn't give them a permit. Then we wanted to do the bail, and another friend was going to put their house up, but they set bail at a quarter of a million dollars!

We still thought, "We can win this case." Everybody was saying, "Don't worry. This case is a bunch of crap."

So that's how I moved to North Carolina. I still remember arriving with a rental truck with my stuff and parking at that Dunkin' Donuts in Raleigh. I was angry, and I was sure that after this was over, I would never set foot in North Carolina again. I didn't know how wrong I was. I didn't know I would be staying here for a very long time. I didn't know how many people would help me. I could only see the darkness, but it turned out to be much more complicated than that.

Chapter 3: Mecca Growing Up in Jersey, Way Back When

I was born in Orange Memorial Hospital in New Jersey on August 11, 1970. My family was living in East Orange. My mother is Bessie Johnson Elmore and my father is Willie Green Elmore. They were both born in Alabama. My mom moved to New Jersey when she was three. My dad moved to New Jersey when he married my mom. I have one sister, Cheryl, who is four years older than me. Maybe Mom told you about our family, but I want to set it down here how I know it, for the record. Lot of how I feel about myself as a man comes from that history, good and bad.

I used to go to Alabama in the summer, but I don't remember much. It was hot. It was shacks. It was the country. It was cows. And that's what Alabama was to me. I was a city kid on day one.

From what I know, my mom's father's father, my great grandfather, was Cherokee Indian. He was very well respected. He wasn't ever a slave. His name was Raspberry Johnson. I don't remember him much. They say I look a lot like him. He didn't have any facial hair like me. He was tall and he was lean and muscular. When I knew him, he was eighty. I would have never guessed that. I would have thought maybe fifty, because he was vibrant. And he was lucid. He wasn't mean but he was serious, and he adored me and my sister.

We were the first great grand-kids. He had a lot of land and he had a lot of juice and a lot of respect. When he talked, people listened.

My grandfather, Roosevelt, worked hard on his father's farm and on the weekends he would get drunk, and he didn't take no junk from any white man about calling him "Boy" or anything more demeaning than that, and he went to jail a lot for standing his ground. And because his father was so well respected, the sheriff would come to the house and say, "We got your boy again. And we not gonna hold him. You can come get him or we'll bring him to you. I don't know how much more we gonna take it. If it wasn't for you, things would be different."

My grandfather had a Cadillac, and that was like a thumb in the face of a white man at that time. He got pulled over a lot. "Boy, what you doing in this big old Cadillac?" And he wouldn't answer because the man called him "Boy." He would say, "Who you talking to?" My mother says she would be in the back seat and her mother would be cringing over there in the passenger seat. My mother's mother was very light, and my grandfather was my complexion, dark. They would always chide him about having these Cadillacs. "You sure you ain't stole this?"

My great grandfather, he could afford a Cadillac. But my grandfather, he wouldn't answer no questions. He wouldn't give no explanations, so they would sometimes just take him to jail. To be mean spirited. And that happened so much the sheriff finally told my great grandfather, "If you don't do something with your son, you might not see him anymore." So my great grandfather and grandfather had the talk, and he said, "Look, you got to leave town 'cause I don't want to find you dead somewhere."

I don't know why they picked New Jersey, but they moved to Newark. My mother was three at the time. In New Jersey they had more kids. My grandmother, Rosa Della Johnson, she was a homemaker. My mother has three sisters and three brothers, and she's the oldest. That's gonna be a factor in my story.

My grandfather, Roosevelt Johnson, was a truck driver. He was short; I would say my height, but very wide and broad, which made him look shorter. And strong, aggressive, and serious. Like his father. And I was his only grandson, so once again, they just adored me. And I adored them. And my grandmother was cool. I gotta repeat that. You don't think of a grandmother being cool, but my grandmother Rosa was cool.

I don't know how much school they had, but the way they spoke... they were well spoken and articulate. They still had that Southern sliver to them, sayings and things like that, but they were smart. I wasn't ashamed. If they came to my school to pick me up, I would tell everybody, "These are my grandparents!" I thought I had the coolest grandparents that you could have. And nothing about them made me feel otherwise.

When I came along, they had their own home and we were living there. It was a three–family home. We lived downstairs on the first floor, my mother, my father, me and my sister, and my dog, Peppy. My grandparents and their children, my mom's younger sisters and brothers, lived on the second and the third floor. So the whole house was like one big family. Doors were always open because it was family coming in and out. And the generations overlap this way. My mother is the oldest, so my sister is the age of my youngest aunts. Me and my sister were the only grand–kids. And I'm the only grandson, so you already know how they held me!

My father came from Alabama. He was like a Black redneck – country, wore plaid shirts, didn't know how to dress. Didn't care how to dress. He was also a truck driver. He wasn't social. And my mother was the total opposite. She was educated and she was outgoing. She knew all about New York and all about night life. My father... just put a tool in his hand and let him go to work. That was his way of life, just work. Give him some boots, a pair of jeans, and a lumber jacket and leave him alone. He's happy.

He is a tall man. I'm five eleven, he's six two. My mother told me that he had a rough childhood. I think he was adopted or given away, and he was raised by some friends of his family, so he never had a connection with his mother. That was something he never really reconciled himself with. She says that he never really felt loved or attached to anything. That includes me. Hadn't heard from him since before I went to prison. In prison not one phone call. Not one letter.

Maybe that's just because of how he is. Seemed like he didn't care much for people, unless it was the guys he worked with. When he would be with them, all they talked about was work. I couldn't figure that. And sports maybe. He played softball and he bowled. I think those are things my mother got him into. It was hard to tell if my dad was really enjoying anything. That's something that stood out to me. I could never really tell.

He would go to work early Monday morning. Maybe one or two in the morning. He drove across the country, so he would be gone all week, and when he came home from work it would be late Friday night. The only time I would see my father is when he would park his truck where he worked in New Jersey and my mom would go pick him up and I would go with her. It's late; I'm in the car sleeping, the door opens, I wake up, he gets in the car and talks about what work was like. That's it. I go back to sleep. If he stayed around the house long enough, I might see him. He'd take a shower, get a bath. He'd get something to eat, drink him a few beers and go work on his car or go out with his friends, guys he worked with. He'd go to their house and talk about work until they went to work.

My mom always worked. To my memory she's always working. I stayed home with my grandmother or with one of my aunts. I did go to preschool and kindergarten, but I hated it because I was leaving my grandmother. My neighborhood was all Black, but we drove a little ways to my school, and it was mixed. I would say my neighborhood was lower class. My mother said that before I was born, when they moved there, it was a really nice neighborhood, middle class, but it all collapsed. We had one white lady, older lady my grandmother's age, who lived to the left of us. And that was the only white person I saw in my neighborhood. But preschool was mixed Black and white.

All the time growing up, my mother was great at exposure. She exposed us to everything she could. "We're gonna get pizza. I'm gonna take you guys to get the best pizza in the world in this place in New York. We going to Symphony Hall. I'm gonna cultivate you guys!" That kind of put my sister and me ahead of our peers in our thinking. Museums. Bronx Zoo. You not gonna get a better zoo than that. My dad could care less, he'd rather stay at home. Give him a beer and a tool. Man, I'm good.

And that was probably a problem. He would make her feel guilty for wanting to be something other than what he thought she should be. He made little jabs at her, little digs at her about that. She couldn't understand why he didn't want more. I'm thinking that had to do a lot with his stuff about not being connected to anybody. Not having relationships. And maybe race, too. I've never seen – wow! – I have *never* seen my dad interact with a white person. I never have. My mother, she could interact with anybody. So could my grandfather and my grandmother.

We left that neighborhood and bought a home in a place called Irvington in New Jersey. And for me that was like paradise. We had big wide streets that were newly paved. I could ride my skateboard. I could leave my skateboard down on the street and then ride my bike, lay my bike down on the street and nobody would touch it. And my dog could run behind me. My sister could be on her bike way ahead of me or way behind me. People left their garage doors open. It was like *The Brady Bunch*. And that house that we moved to was about half a mile from the school, a good school. This was a total extreme from where we had started off. Back in the old place there were police sirens all the time. It was ghetto. So we upgraded.

My dad made good money for that time driving a truck, but my mother says that he said, "What you want a house for? Why that house? Why it gotta be that big? This neighborhood?" My mother had a plan, and he just couldn't see it. She said she was very gentle and patient with trying to explain to him that the decisions that she wanted to make had everything to do with the future for my sister and me. I think that my mother's personality highlighted my father's insecurities. I really do. If my mother and father walked into a room, he would feel like he just disappeared, and he would see her just being right at home no matter what the crowd was – and that became a real issue. Yeah.

I don't recall them arguing until our lifestyle upgraded. I can't recall them ever having an argument when he was sober, but in that house, he was always drunk. My father was an alcoholic. He would try to make me an alcoholic. He would get off work Friday night at two o'clock in the morning. I'm asleep, and he'd come in and wake me up and we'd go to the dining room. He'd have him a beer and he'd slide me a one. I was maybe eight. I wouldn't drink it because he was a different person when he started drinking, and I identified that even then. Whatever was in that can of beer, I don't like it, 'cause it's making you not like you. That's how my brain associated it.

To this day I've never had a drink. Never smoked a joint. A cigarette. No. I don't have anything against people who do drink, but I never had a desire, never thought, "Wonder what's that like?" Marijuana, when I would ask my friends who smoked it religiously, "What's the point?" they would say, "Man, you don't know what your missing. You get the munchies and you just eat and you laugh." I feel that way without that. So I never felt a reason. I've sold drugs of different types, and I've never seen anyone use any drug without using it in excess. And I'm glad that my mind interpreted it that way, because no matter what quantity of drugs I may have had on my table, packaging to distribute, whether it was that much or a tablespoon, I never thought about using drugs.

When it comes to my father, my sister is, in my estimation – and I tell her all the time – she's a lot harder. She's got less room. Second chances? Woe is you. Cheryl, she is tough. If she did interact with him, it would more be from a place of pity. It's her father, but she has limits. With me, I would want to nurse him back to health, would say, "You need to really get some help. I'll call somebody for you. You gotta go get some help."

When he was sober, he'd put on some music, country music. Lionel Richie with the Commodores. Listen to that, he be fine. It seemed like my dad was always longing for something... like he missed his country life or something. He seemed out of place all the time.

He's a Vietnam vet, too. My mom said that was a big turning point for him, when he came home from Vietnam. She said she doesn't know what happened, but he was different. Post traumatic stress disorder. And he has health problems. Agent Orange. But know that no matter how violent he got – and he was very violent toward my mother – he was never violent toward me and my sister. Never. We always had this respect for dad. When he spoke, we listened.

My sister and I weren't perfect kids, but we always had been the type of people, we don't like you telling us what to do, so we made sure it was already done. You want this table cleaned when you get off work? I don't want to hear your mouth, so I'm gonna make sure that even if I'm not here when you get off work, you won't be telling me to have this table cleaned. And we were like that about everything.

But my dad, he was only there on the weekends, and on the weekends we're out. My sister's four years older than me, so she's out with her friends. And I had a group of friends that were where my grandmother was. Those were my funnest friends, because they were the most creative – because they had less. In our new neighborhood, we had to be less creative because we had things. I had two worlds. When I went back to my grandmother's neighborhood it was all Black.

But also, no matter which neighborhood, I was different because I always enjoyed school. Even if I hadn't moved to this better neighborhood, I was different. More peculiar than my friends. School was fun for me. I didn't complain about I gotta get up early and go to school. I was ready to go. They didn't have to wake me up. I got my backpack on. Let's go to school. My teachers identified that in me.

In preschool and kindergarten my grandmother was a lunch aid at the school. If I was acting up, she give me that look. I don't care what kind of peer pressure going on, I'm through with that! And it wasn't out of fear of any kind of retribution. It's because whatever I'm doin' is displeasing my grandmother, and I love her too much to displease her. I knew she knew what was best for me. That's the kind of relationship I had with my grandmother.

And after we moved to Irvington, I still had the things that you need to grow up in the street from living at my grandparents in Orange. To have street credibility, you need to be able to take care of yourself. If that means fightin', you have to have those skills to protect yourself. I had that. I was always my own thinker. I was the most influential amongst my peers, but I wasn't the guy that they thought, "Oh he's smart. He's a nerd. He doesn't know anything about the games that we play in the street." I kinda had all bases covered not even knowing it. I just did it.

My mom is that way. If she's in it, she's running it. Same with Cheryl. If she's involved in something, she's usually running it. Even when she went to college, to Fairleigh Dickinson University, if Cheryl is involved, it's just a matter of time before Cheryl is leading the pack. Same with me. Not that I want to be. I rather *not* be up front. But if people that I trust say, "Listen, you are the guy for that," I would do it on the strength of that.

My sister kind of kept me honest in that way. Here she is, four years older, so when I'm in the fourth grade, she's in the eighth grade. All my teachers were once her teachers. And as soon as the school years starts, "Oh, I taught your sister and she was this this and this." And I'm, "Oh boy, here we go again." And Cheryl would say, "You have Ms. Smith as your English teacher? I did really good in class with Ms. Smith." And I go, "Yeah, she told me all about it."

But all this kind of changed for me as my home life got more crazy. School itself was fun, totally, because school represented some stability that would save me from the craziness at home. Somewhere between the fourth and sixth grades, that's when I start noticing that. As much as I liked our house and our neighborhood, going home was not fun. It was one of the saddest times in my life. I couldn't understand why my father kept beating up my mother.

Here's a classic case. He's in the dining room by himself in the dark, drinking. He's drinking Vodka, stuff like that. He sees that top is off the hot sauce bottle. He'll wake the whole house up:

"Who left the top off the hot sauce bottle?"

"What are you talkin' about?"

"I asked a question. Who left the top off the hot sauce bottle?"

And by that time, my sister would segue back into bed and I would segue back into bed, and when we got out of the way, it was a fight. And it was a noisy fight. And it was a confusing thing for me because I had never seen that stuff living with my grandparents. If they did have their fights, I didn't know about it. It was the deepest – the pain that I had from that and the confusion. I had nobody to talk to about it. And seeing my mother that way, at the hands of my father, the aftermath, was just crazy to me.

They never really said anything to us. My sister and I still did great in school, I think that kind of kept Mom from being aware that it upset us. Even when I really got into selling drugs, I realized early on that if I got a good report card, none of my family would know what I was doing. And I kept my curfew. I'm always early to bed. Even now. New Year's Eve, I'm in bed at eight o'clock. So I don't have none of the telltale signs. Good report card, there's no way he could be doing anything other than what he should be.

But I'm going into my head trying to make sense of it. Everything's so cerebral. My teachers noticed. One teacher in particular, maybe tenth grade, my guidance counselor noticed my attendance dropping off. She calls me in the office and says, "You missing a lot of classes, but you still maintaining your grade point average. How you doing that? Something not right, because technically you missed enough classes where I'm not supposed to pass you. I talked to your teachers about it and they assured me that you are not cheating. I don't understand that." She would have my teachers give me these pop quizzes, and I would pass them.

Before that, in ninth grade, there was also a gym teacher who asked me to try out for the basketball team. He said, "You know, you a natural athlete. You need to try out for the basketball team. I'm sure you'll make it." And I said, "When are the trials?" I tried out and he asked me to be on the team. I said okay, but I knew already I was not gonna be on the team. I never showed up. When I go back to school, he asked what happened, and I said, "I'm not gonna play basketball." He said, "Why not? I can't believe it. What's going on with you?"

I was already into other things.

What he didn't know is my main reason for not playing on the team was because it required after school practices. After school, I got a corner to get on to make some money. Because of that, I stayed away from a lot of after school activities, because after school I had to punch the clock and go to work. And I cheated myself out of a lot of experiences because of that, but that's how that went.

Here's a true story. My mother begged me to go to Seton Hall. It was time to go into ninth grade. That summer she said, "I need you to do me a favor." I said, "What's that?" She said, "I want you to take a test."

I liked school. Don't mind taking tests. It's like recreation to me. So I say, "Okay, where at?"

"We're going to Seton Hall."

"Where's that?"

"It's a preparatory school. I want you to take this test. Just do it for me."

"When, Mom? Saturday? No, can't do that."

"Do it for me please."

"How long is the test?"

"About three hours."

"Three hours? Sitting there and taking a test. What kind of test is this?"

"Listen, this test is so important. You cannot take it twice. It's the SAT. I really need you to take this test for me."

"All right, Mom. You owe me one."

In the parking lot she gives me this pep talk. I'm not listening. I'm gonna take this test. There's probably four Blacks and the rest whites. There's this lady giving us orientation, telling us all of this stuff, and I wish she would stop talking. She finally handed the test out. About two hours in, I close it up and take it to her. She looks at the clock and says, "Are you done?" I say, "Absolutely." She says, "Are you sure?"

I see it in her eyes. She's pleading with me to go back and go over this test. I got a whole hour left. She says, "Look this is indelible. They can't change it." I gave her the test and I left.

My mother is in the car asleep; she sat in the parking lot the whole time. I knock on the window. She looks straight at her watch and says, "What are you doing back? Don't tell me you turned the test in?"

"Yeah, I turned it in."

"You didn't leave nothing blank?"

"No. I'm all done."

"You got a whole hour. Why did you do that? Why did you rush?"

"I didn't rush. It was boring. I was ready to go."

She was sad about that. We left. What she didn't know was that Seton Hall was right down the street from where I was conducting some of my business. When I'm taking the test, I was up high enough to look out the window and I could see the activity. I could see clients down in the street. It was like they were calling my name while I'm taking this test! I'm like, "Man, I gotta get out of here." I'm adding up how much money! I'm in here on a Saturday taking this stupid SAT test. What am I thinking?

About a week or two later, I come in from outside. She's on the telephone and says, "Here he is!" We are living in an apartment now. Dad is gone. Everything's changed. We downgraded. She's jumping up and down for joy and says, "Your aunt's on the phone. Your aunt wants to speak to you." Kind of chaotic. My aunt says, "Congratulations! I heard you took the SAT test." I'm like, "Yeah. Okay," and give the phone back to my mother and go in my bedroom.

She hangs up and runs into my bedroom and gives me this hug saying, "You did it. You did it."

"What did I do?"

"You scored fifteenth in the state of New Jersey on the test!"

"Okay, so what?"

"You don't get it, do you? You don't understand; that has so much to do with your future."

She's beside herself. I changed clothes and left. I didn't understand anything about that. When I came home for the evening, she's is saying things like, "We gotta get you a blazer. We get you some shoes."

"Hold on. Time out! What you talkin' about?"

"You gonna go to Seton Hall and usher you right into college."

"What's the matter? You not getting it? I don't want to go to Seton Hall."

"Are you serious?"

"Yeah. I want to go to my own school."

"What school do you want to go to?"

"I want to go to Vailsburg High School in Newark." All Black, that was the school I wanted to go to.

"Are you *kidding* me?"

But she actually let me make that decision. I didn't know then, but I know now that that was a very stupid decision that I made.

My mother had no idea what was going on down the street from Seton Hall. My mother is savvy, but when it comes to that life of the street, she doesn't know anything about that. Nothing. 'cause of my sentence, she's had to learn. I love school, so it wouldn't have been the academic challenge. But what was going on down the street, eventually I would have gotten caught and kicked out for sure.

Chapter 4: Out on the Street, Gambling, Drugs and Cash

Things were a mess in my house, so I would go to school, come home, change, and go out to the street. People trusted me too much with their things – even when I was thirteen or fourteen years old. Most of my peers were gettin' high and drinking. I didn't do none of that. The older people would ask me, "Why you hanging out with them?" They would try pull me away, get me to do things for them. They might say, "Hey, park my car."

I was probably thirteen when I learned to drive. It was a Buick Ninety–Eight. My father used to let me sit in his lap and drive. I'm just really steering. For these older guys on the street, I did the whole thing. "Hey, take my car to the car wash." Off I go and come back. Car's clean. I get paid a little something.

There was also gambling. I gambled in the street a lot, and I was pretty good at it. Older guys like to see my play. Thought it was cute to see a little kid, fourteen, who could do that. My father taught me all the moves, how to blow in the dice, things to say. So, now I would get invitations to these gambling houses. Going in there with the big boys. You need to get referenced to get in these places.

This particular guy, he has been like a mentor to me all my life. He's about twenty-five years older than me, Pops. He came to visit me in prison ten or twelve years ago. How we met is he used to see me on these corners, doing my bidding. I love arcade games, and when you take grace from the corner – which means the police are coming and you need to get missing – I would go by these places with video games and he would be in there playing. He said, "I play you. I pay for it." Okay, so he put the money in, we played and made small talk. He would notice my habits, say, "Hey, you gonna get some pizza?" and get some pizza for me.

He seems friendly. I don't have a car. I'm using public transportation. Come to be he lived a few blocks from where I was living, so he would give me a ride home. He and I had the same interests. He and I were doing the same things. I was already dealing drugs, and so was he. He would talk to me, we'd play arcade games, and he became like a father, the father I didn't have, the kind who talks to you and takes an interest in you.

So he introduced me to a lot of things. Atlantic City was one. Sometimes we would go to Atlantic City together. Then I went on my own. Go to forty-second street, get the fake ID where I could go in and out of the casinos. My business is growing, so I got more money. Got to where I could go down there with fifteen thousand, twenty thousand dollars. Played blackjack. That was my game of choice. Even when I gambled in the street, dice, sometimes I won thousands of dollars.

And I shot pool. I went to pool halls for money. I learned to play just watching. There was this pool hall in Elizabeth, New Jersey, and late at night, way past my bedtime, this same guy, who was very fond of me, took me into these circles where some real players were. Con men. Pool sharks. Slummers. Slummer is a guy who goes around and sells fake jewelry. Disguise it as real jewelry. They go to jewelry stores and they do this slight of hand. Say a man has one real gold bar and ten fake ones. He can go to these greedy jewelers and show them this real gold bar and he would test it out and negotiate a price. And then he says, "Well, how much would you give me for ten of them?" And the other ones are fake.

Same guy, he explains to me how you gotta vary your game, have a variety of hustles. I even met guys who sold fake deeds to houses. Somehow or other they present themselves as a Realtor. Dress the part. Speak the language. Put an article in a newspaper and find an unwitting couple that want to buy a house. You set it up so you can show somebody around it and you know some things about this house where you can describe it top to bottom, blah blah blah. You negotiate a finder's fee and get some kind of down payment from people, and it's all a scam!

I know people that would stick up tractor trailers that carry fur coats and then sell 'em to people. Go where the truck is parked and take the coats and sell them on the street. Sell them to other drug dealers who might say, "Get me five of those." Might be each coat would be worth twenty thousand dollars, and he might sell a coat for five thousand, so that's five thousand in his pocket. I never buy a fur coat from any of those guys. Not my style. But I know guys who did that.

I meet guys that did counterfeit money. A friend of mine had stacks and stacks of counterfeit money. He gave me some. He told me for every thousand in real money I gave him, he would give me ten thousand in counterfeit money. This can kind of go with drug dealing. When you go to the drug spots, under the guise of night, you camouflage the counterfeit money with your real money. You wouldn't go to your main drug spots, because if you were my main drug person, I'm coming back to you because I know the service I'm gonna get. But I could go down the street, old rundown place, house that I never been to before and never gonna go back to again. I would place an order, and they would bring it out, and I would have like two thousand in real money and eight thousand in counterfeit money. Real money on top. By the time he finds out that it's counterfeit money it's all shuffled in with whatever money he made that day.

People get caught doing stuff all the time, but it's like jumping double Dutch rope. You gotta know when to jump in there and when to get out of there. I've always been good at that. Managing my money. Choosing my timing.

Now people on the street, some of these older people, they would ask to meet my mother. That would be my escape signal. Hear that and I'm out. I don't want them to be seeing that my mother was not parenting me like she should, 'cause my mother is so bogged down with her own reality and we are not communicating. She is too invested in her problems and people like her baby sister Cora, Cora's husband, my uncle, all them and their lives. Truth is, I felt abandoned.

I felt, "You should be showing more concern. I just saw a guy get killed! I come home, I'm traumatized. No one to talk to." Now, she is working. My mom, she's not, never gonna be a vegetable. So, yeah, she's busy, but I thought that parents – especially mothers – were supposed to sense when something's wrong with their child. Sometimes I would call home and she would say, "What's wrong?" and I would celebrate that; but when I didn't get that, it was a disconnect. Didn't try to say nothing more to her. Now we talk about that, and she says she felt... says she just could not handle it.

That's why when I got to prison, I never anticipated what I have now. I figured she would say, "I've failed. I've lost him. There's nothing else I can do." I was at Central Prison, where there's no contact visits and no phone calls. The first thing I said when she and Cheryl came, I said, "I don't have no more time for this bull jive, this pretending like reality is not what it is. You guys can just go." I had this life sentence and I was trying to make sense of it. I wanted to die. I would hope I didn't wake up the next morning. I had no room for nothing but real food. Anything artificial, processed, would kill me.

My mom and Cheryl, they stepped up.

But we are talking about way before that. When I'm doing the gambling and dealing, my mom and me, we are in different worlds. Seems then like I'm invisible to her, so I be invisible.

Also we have these money problems at the house, so I'm looking for ways to address that. That's where it starts. I'm not using drugs, and I don't need that kind of money, but at home it's crazy. This friend of mine, Robin, street name is "Jabb," we were maybe thirteen when it starts. He's dead now. He died when I was thirty. He had started using when we were seventeen, started to smoke marijuana. Then he started to mix cocaine with marijuana, and that took him to another level.

When this is starting, we are both in school and both studying, so nobody is going to suspect nothing. We can be up in his room and nobody is going to check. Just kids doing kid things. We decide to get together some money, earn enough money to go on the PATH train and go to New York and get some marijuana to sell. I try the newspaper route, but that's not real money. And so next thing, Jabb and I went and raked some leaves that summer. I'm real good at saving money. And I'm patient. After the leaves are done, the winter came, we got on the bus with our shovels and we rode the bus to the suburbs where the white people live, Montclair. They have these big houses and they don't have nobody to shovel. There was so much work. When we got back, we had six hundred dollars. That's a lotta money to us. Cash money.

Jabb, had an older brother, and I got some information from the older guys on the street that there's this long street called Edgecombe Avenue in Harlem that sold every kind of marijuana you could imagine. As soon as you turn the corner on that street, there's a thousand of those Caribbean guys dressed up with the dreads and asking you what you want in heaviest accents with marijuana sticks hanging out of their mouths. I didn't smoke weed and, at this point, neither does Jabb. We had to just go on faith, on how it smelled and how it looked. We made a contact we felt good about. I liked the way he did business. He guaranteed his product. He said you can take it back. Okay, we try this guy. So we ended up buying a quarter of a pound of weed. Cost five hundred dollars. We used the rest for transportation to buy us tokens to get back, to get some pizza. I love pizza.

We got to Jabb's house. He lived on the third floor which was good because you couldn't sneak up on him. The stairs were real creaky. If his parents or someone came up, we had time to throw a blanket over what we were doing. His family knew me and that him and me were together. Both did good in school, so we didn't get no suspicion at all. We packaged it. Put it in nickel bags. That way we could triple our money, make fifteen hundred dollars. We had a scale, but you do that long enough that gets in the way. I'm really good at math and I'm really good at getting a visual on something. I can look and tell if it's not right. I won a lot of bets on that.

Once we packaged it up, there was this really grungy area where everybody got drunk and bought drugs, Orange Street. People don't send their kids through Orange Street. You want to go someplace, and you say that's the shortest way; your parents gonna say don't go through Orange Street. But it was real close to our house.

Only problem is going to be that I have this Aunt Cora and she runs on Orange Street. She lives in our house and she's a bully. She's about six feet two and she probably weighs about three hundred pounds and she's aggressive. She says she seen me on Orange Street, and there is no other reason for being on Orange street unless you are buying drugs or selling drugs. And if my mother found out my whole family would have found out and my grandmother. Just knowing how that disturbed her would have been worse than any kind of physical retribution. This is why you are gonna see how Cora got control of the situation.

Today, Cora, she's passed. My mom – when she moves to North Carolina, guess who shows up? "I'm gonna get my life together," Cora says. Here we go again. But Durham is full of heroin. Cora, she ended up dying of AIDS. So now, my mother is raising Cora's daughter, Keisha and her son, Jamar, who is deaf.

Back to doing business. Me and Jabb, we were pretty crafty. We gotta find customers. We're standing there on this corner on Orange Street. It's maybe six o'clock. Transportation goes to and fro. You got a barber shop and a deli shop. You got a corner store. What happens is we see customers getting off buses, out of taxi cabs, out of their cars, going to talk to people, going around the sandwich shop and coming out happy. We see that guy over there – he's getting a lot of business. Gotta find out his name. Herman. He's selling heroin.

Great for us, because we don't want to do heroin. So we say to him, "We send you heroin customers." Now we don't know no heroin people! "You send us the marijuana customers. We trade off like that." We never send him heroin customers, but he starts sending us marijuana customers, 'cause that's not what he sells. When he's done with them, we see him point to us. People come and they want, say three or four or five or even six nickel bags.

I'm a nobody on Orange Street, but this guy Herman he's somebody. Older guys, if you're young guys and you're willing to take a chance, they warm to you. Herman starts to let us in his circle. And eventually marijuana money is not enough, and the guy we buying from we start to pry about cocaine. He says, "You ready to go there? That's a different animal." We say yeah, we're serious, and we start buying and find the parts of the neighborhood that you go to sell cocaine.

Jabb and me, we work out our schedules. We are going to different schools, so we have to coordinate. We are using that for our cover. You bring home a good report card, everybody is happy. His father had passed away. My parents are going crazy. Creates a space. And the dealing, figuring out the street, that takes a lot of critical thinking. For me that was the fun part about it. Like, how can I figure out how to be there and not be there? And we look like students – because we are students. I'm going straight to there from school. No hoodie. That's never been my style. I got my book bag. I got my Walkman, big cassette thing. After I pick up, I look like I'm just going back to New Jersey, 'cause you do have students going back from New York. Never did look like somebody that was peddling some drugs. Could be a policeman, they hold the door on the train, and the whole time I got a knapsack full of cocaine.

I was selling what they call natural powder. Crack cocaine came on the scene in eighty-four, later. I got into that, but that was evil. People who smoked crack, they was all fidgety and nervous. They transformed, and that was scary to see as a kid. Also, by now this lifestyle is having an effect on my mentality. I am losing respect for people.

The ultimate was when I saw a woman give up her baby for crack. I stumbled into that. I had a pager by then and I got paged by this usual lady. She said, "Can you come to my house?" When I show up, there are some strange faces there. I figure she's going to introduce me to new customers. Then she pulls me in the back room and says, "Don't think I'm crazy, but I need some stuff." She tells me these people are looking for something else, a kid. A kid? I thought that was some kind of slang for a drug. She goes, "Their looking for a kid. You know a baby." She's making her buy and she smoked some already. She's all geeked up. I say. "You so high. Say what you mean." She says, "A baby, you know a baby that comes out of a woman's stomach. You'll see."

There's a knock at the door, and there's this lady with a baby and that was enough for me. These other people that were there, they were dressed up. They weren't drug users. They weren't none of that. They weren't social service. They come to buy this baby. I left. I was so distraught I just left. I had heard about that but to see it... I journal that to this day. I relive it by journal. That's when my conscience went somewhere else. I've seen a lot of things. I've seen people get hurt, get brains knocked out, I seen people... that's something else. That baby was less than two years old and I hate that I ever saw that.

You must be thinking I should quit. But I had developed a lifestyle, a level of responsibility that I felt like I had to continue to uphold. I was the cash cow. Somebody had a need, they call me. I had elderly people in my family, church going people, and they would have their sons call me for money. That did something with me and religion. Not with God, but with religion. These were the same people who told me I shouldn't stop going to church, had me really thinking about my soul going to Hell. But then these people found a way to contact me for money that they know I didn't work for. It made me see the world different. Everybody had a price. Everybody had a jihad. Everybody had a place of struggle that they would compromise for this money. It made me feel like what I was doing wasn't so bad. Just part of everything.

And now there are some close calls with my mom. There are people that when I was on Orange Street they'd be on public transportation. And they would call my mother. "I could have sworn I saw your son on Orange street. What color hat did he wear?" And she would say, "Your great aunt says she was on the bus and she saw you on Orange street." And I would say, "Lotta kids got that hat. A lotta kids look like me." But it probably was me.

How am I spending all this money? After I'm done taking care of things at home, helping my mom pay her bills and dealing with these mooching family members? Still plenty left over. I buy some jewelry. I went to Canal Street in New York City and I bought my first gold chain. We were so excited. That says something. That says we have arrived. I bought a medallion. It was a solid plate with a scorpion on it.

I got a name ring. Yeah, it go across. Four–finger ring or two–finger ring. And you get the name and you get diamonds on the letters. You get what you can afford to get. Ring would say, "Swill," my street name, or Will or just a big old W. Now I'm getting jewelry made 'cause the older guys see that stuff from Canal Street, they finally say to me, "Why you keep buying that bubble gum jewelry? How much does it weigh?" And I say, "Man I just paid two or three thousand dollars for this chain!" And they say, "Take the chain off. Let me see it." And it's hollow, like a Christmas ornament or something.

But I never wore that stuff in the house. Never. I put it on after I left the house, or I tuck it under my shirt and make sure my shirt covered it from the back so you couldn't see it. If I'm near my mom or adults I respect, I kept all my rings in my pocket. And I'm giving this money to my aunt Cora, who is giving it to my mother as if it is hers so bills can get paid. So I am taking care of business first. This other money is extra after that.

People set up businesses based on guys like me. Car lots. Jewelry stores. Clothing stores. You come in there with wads of cash money, right, and say there's five or six of you. I tell a story of when I went to buy my motorcycle, my first motorcycle.

There was a store in Belleville, New Jersey, called Motorcycle Mall. I was fifteen or sixteen and it was a summer night. The store closed at nine. Now we all had been there at different times window shopping. This particular night we all decided to go to Motorcycle Mall to purchase motorcycles, right? And there's eleven of us. Eleven bikes. The average price of each bike I would say seven thousand. Right. So eleven guys have at least that much in their pocket.

We are all Black, young, full of money, jewelry and everybody sold drugs, so we had cash money on us. When we get there it's eight forty-five. The store closes at nine. Store's empty. You got the owner of the store and you got the guy who works in the service department. So while we are there looking around the owner comes out and says, "Guys, we closing in about fifteen minutes." And we go, "Okay."

Figures we are there to window shop. So one of us finally breaks the silence and says, "I want to buy this bike right here." The owner, he has this pompous attitude. "You sure you want to buy that bike? Probably be like eighty-two hundred." Friend's like, "I want it. Would you throw me in say two helmets if I bought this bike as it is?" Owner is like, "If you bought that bike right now, I have my guy service it, oil it up, get it running, I will give you two helmets."

And everybody else starts saying, "Well, I want this one," "I want that one." And he asks, "How you guys paying for that?" When we say, "We paying cash for 'em," just like that, his whole demeanor changed. He put the "closed" sign on the door. He's getting ready to make close to a hundred grand. Right now.

We didn't leave the store until about eleven o'clock because his guy had to service every bike. Had to do all that paperwork. None of us have a driver's license. He does not care! I didn't even know how to ride a motorcycle, he taught me right there in front of the store. I bought a Kawasaki five hundred. Blend down and four. Black with red stripes.

We bought cars the same way. My first car was the Audi Five Thousand Turbo, ice blue. I bought it at a used car lot. The car said seventeen thousand five hundred, but I came with fifteen thousand cash, and he sold it to me. He don't care how old I was. And I have a jalopy. Jalopy is what I do my transporting drugs around in, what I drive to do my business. Chevy Celebrity. A K–car. Reliant K–car. You go buy little cars like that for three or four hundred dollars. You get somebody that you know that does drugs but is a master mechanic. You give him a little bit of drugs. He overhauls the car and the car will burn forever. You got a jalopy, something that you can get rid of at any time and get another one the same day.

This goes on 'cause it feels like you can get away with it forever. When you're a kid, you feel like you can do anything forever – anything short of dying, you could do forever times two. You see so much around you and you're still alive the next day, you develop this mindset of invincibility. Also, from what I'm seeing on the street and from the adults that are taking this money from me, I start to be like I don't trust anybody. Everybody's trying a game. Now I'm deeper into myself and what I'm doing than ever before, because at this point, I feel totally disconnected from my family. I'm on my own totally.

The one light is that I have a girlfriend. My first love, Keisha. I kept this photo with me all the time in prison, prom picture of me and her. I met her in a diner after a rap concert in East Orange. She was sitting across from me at another table with this guy. He can't see me, but she just kept looking at me. I don't mess with other people's property, but I can't help but notice how beautiful she is. We just can't stop looking.

Next part of it is crazy too. My friend is driving and I'm on the passenger side and we are driving by this shopping center and they cross the street, Keisha and this other girl. We make eye contact, and they stop right in front of the car. Cars behind are blowing their horns. My friend says, "Do you know her?" And I say, "That's the girl from the diner!"

We circle the block and there she is waiting on the corner as if she knew we would come back. We make small talk, and she gives me her address and this street was in proximity to where I used to live. I said, "I used to live on Park Place!" And I was in love with that in and of itself, because of what I felt about that place we used to live. And one thing led to another and we dated for four years.

Now, she never saw me sell drugs, but one thing she did know is I didn't work, and I had money and things that said I had money. She doesn't like the drug dealing, but she likes the perks. So she knows but she doesn't know. And if I happen to be riding out with her in my Audi in the area where I work and somebody tries to stop me or flag me down, I ignore them. And if I see them later, I tell 'em, "How dare you try to stop me and talk to me. You don't see me in my car with my girlfriend? She doesn't know what I do." 'cause not everybody does it like that. But I have my family and Keisha, and that part of my life is clean.

And her parents loved me. We got serious, and she said you gotta get a job or it's not happening. That was two years into the relationship. Her father said one day he didn't know where I got my money, but, "Son, you keep buying my daughter these things that I can't afford. And I make really good money. You spoiling her, and you making it hard for me because around birthday and Christmas time, she's giving me this list of things that she wants, and I'm like, where in the world you even heard of this stuff? Saks Fifth Avenue. Gucci Shop. Fendi Shop. Shouldn't be buying her these things. She's just a teenager."

Now, he drove a truck, and he heard things from the truck driver's network. One day he leaves word for his wife to tell me to be there when he got home. His wife tells Keisha, and she tells me, "I don't know what's going on, but he says to be here."

"But he don't come back 'til midnight."

"You better be here."

I'm frightened. He could tell me don't never come back to this house no more. She brings me a pillow and a blanket and leaves me in the den saying she has to go to bed.

Her father comes home and calls me in the kitchen and says, "I got some questions and you better answer them right, 'cause I got some concerns. My daughter is crazy about you. And I'm kind of liking you. My daughter's my baby, my only daughter. I don't play no games." And then he says, exact words, "I got an old rusty Colt pistol upstairs in my coat pocket, and I will bust the cap on you if I find you are not being honest. I have to have answers, because I'll give my life for my daughter. You don't work. I'm a country boy from Georgia but I'm no dummy. If you can't tell me, don't come back. What do you do?"

I lowered my head and I poured it out to him. After I finished talking, he said, "I need a drink. Look in that closet and get me a bottle of Canadian Club." That's what he drank. Then he said, "Man, I wasn't ready for that. I'm sad for you. You're just a kid, but I can't give you my blessing for my daughter. I can't tell you what to do for your family, but you're just a kid and they're adults. You shouldn't feel responsible for them. I make great money, but I couldn't handle your responsibilities on my salary. No wonder you act older than your age. You can't transition to a job. That won't help you. You gotta make some tough decisions. Wow, I got a whole different view of you."

We became so tight after that. We went to Atlantic City. We would go as couples, but he wouldn't let us stay in the same hotel room. He said, "Don't get any ideas you and her getting a hotel room. You and me get a hotel room and her and her mother and we meet for breakfast! That ain't happening if that's what you thinking." To the chagrin of his son, he and I became real tight. That became another jihad.

He died of cancer. My mother and Keisha's mom, they still talk. Keisha and I occasionally have contact. She's an ad executive for a newspaper. She's still in New Jersey. But back then, I never let him meet my family.

None of this is right, and I'm hiding all this from my mom. She doesn't know anything about my life except what I choose for her to see. Even today, she is not aware of how deep I was involved with the drugs. I've never displayed my lifestyle where my mom could see it. She never even saw my cars or any of the stuff I bought. I paid a pretty penny for this deception. I dealt with Cora. To see the pain in my mother's eyes – no way I was going to let her know. I guess she will know if she reads this, but I don't mind if she never does.

Chapter 5: From Cheryl's Side of the Table

I don't remember when Willie was born, but my earliest memory of him is that when he was a baby, his sleeping pattern was not normal. I remember driving around with my parents with him in the car to get him to go to sleep. He would be up all night! Which is hard to believe now, because he is never awake at night. I also remember going to drive–in movies. We would have on our P.J.s and our parents would be in the front seat. We were very close growing up.

I think it was when William was two that he ate a lot of aspirin. I was probably five or six. I know I couldn't have been home alone with him – at the time we lived on the first floor and our grandparents lived on the second floor – but we were together, and I was watching him. I didn't know that he had gotten hold of the aspirin, but I knew he was sick. Then my parents came, and he was rushed to the hospital. He was in a coma in critical condition for a while. It was very scary, because I was responsible for him and didn't know he had gotten into the aspirin.

I always reminded him that I was his older sister and I was responsible for him. So he would have to do these certain things if I told him to, because I was older. He had to adhere to that. I didn't tell him to do anything bad, but I did boss him around a little bit. And he would always question my authority over him and say,

"You're always going to be older than I am?"

"Yes, I'm always going to be older."

"Even when we are a hundred? Hundred and four?"

In his little mind I guess he was just trying to figure out a way that he could somehow gain some type of equalization between the two of us. One day he came to me and said, "Okay, I know you are always going to be older, but I can be smarter than you." And I said, "You're right; you can."

I was in the seventh grade when we moved from Orange to Irvington and that was a bad time for me. The school in Orange was mostly African American; I knew all the kids. So, once I got to Irvington, it was leaving what I was familiar with and going to some place different. It wasn't just being in a predominantly white neighborhood, it was also my grandparents, my mom's parents that I would miss. It was leaving them; and that was so hard, because that's what I knew all my life. It was safe. They were spiritual and they were safe. All of our aunts and uncles were there. Because my mom was the oldest there was a span, so some of my aunts and uncles were only ten or five years older than me. And my grandparents were in love. When my grandfather died, my grandmother lived as long as she could without him. I think she went as far as she could go and then she died. My parents were very active, going out bowling and different things, so my grandparents looked after us.

In Irvington, we had a big house. We always had our own room in Orange, so that wasn't different, but this was a house and we had responsibilities. It was on a corner lot and we had two addresses 89–93 Park Place. This corner property had English ivy all over and a big garage. There was an expectation without anyone saying it. We just knew: you have this house, so you have to do something, take care of it. It not like my stepfather said, "You have to mow the grass," but we figured it out. There was an allowance attached to it. We were just little kids, but my stepfather was a truck driver, so he was gone all week and we had our responsibilities.

Willie Elmore was not my father. He was my stepfather. He treated me like his daughter, but he was not my father, and when things got bad that mattered to me.

My birth father was named Jeffrey. He lived in the neighborhood, in Orange. He and my mother grew up together, went to high school together. I had to do a lot of work and research to get to the whole situation figured out. They were teenagers. They fell in love, planned to run away and get married. Then she pops up pregnant. Now they're definitely going to run away. But his mother, she had three sons and her husband was killed in the Second World War, so she was very protective of her sons – no woman would have been good enough, and she was not happy with my mother at all. My father had a brother, David, who did get married, but his other brother, Lloyd, never married. He was always with his mother, and when his mother died, he died a few months after.

But my father was always in the neighborhood. He would come around, because in the circle that my mom was in, he was like a relative. He knew my uncles, knew all of our family. If we had a cookout, he was there. When I was ten years old, I found out that my father's mother lived not far from me, and I decided I was going to meet her.

I don't know how I found out where she lived, but somehow I did. I went to her apartment; they lived, I think, on Burnett Street. Lloyd lived there too. Uncle Lloyd. I rang the doorbell, and she came to the door and asked who was it.

"It's Cheryl Elmore, and I'm here to meet you."

"Who?"

"Cheryl Elmore."

"No."

And then I wouldn't leave. The door closed. She waited and I waited, and nothing happened. So I knocked on the door. No answer. Knocked on the door again. I waited and I waited, and then I heard my uncle Lloyd talking to her saying, "What's going on? Somebody at the door?" And she didn't say anything, so he opens the door and says, "What are you doin' here?"

"I'm here to meet her. I'm here to meet you, too." I maybe saw them, but I had never spoken to them before. And he said, "I know who you are!" Then we talked. He was so ashamed of his mother for doing that, and finally she came out and she met me. I can't think of her name now, but I remember she was Ms. Johnson because they had the same last name as my mom's parents. That was ironic.

Lloyd got out their photo album and started showing me pictures. Then my grandmother showed me a picture of my grandfather, who she talked about, but you could tell it was still very painful for her, losing him. She's a very stern woman who had a difficult time raising her sons as a widow. She never remarried. And, in the end, it turned out fine. She wasn't this horrible monster, she was okay; but I never saw her again.

I remember telling my mom's mother what I did, and she was just like, "I can't believe you would do that." But I just had to know. I had to find out who she was. I remember my grandmother asking me, "Well, what do you think?" And I said, "Well she isn't going to be my grandmother, because you're my grandmother!"

I just wanted to let her know that I existed and tell her that you can't just discard me or act like I don't exist. And I got a chance to meet my uncle Lloyd, and we kind of stayed in contact before I left, before I moved to North Carolina.

I'm not sure what Willie thinks about all this. We talked about it maybe once or twice after he was in prison. I told him on a visit, "Look, we don't have the same father." He asked, "Is he alive?" And I said, "I don't know, but Jeffrey is my father."

We knew that this is our mother and we're brother and sister and nothing changes that. It's a matter of fact kind of thing. We don't have the same father, but it's really not a problem. There's no change. With my mother there was a bone of contention growing up, because my father was always around. I would see him at a cookout or at the bowling alley or somewhere in the neighborhood. He never approached me, so evidently it was spoken or unspoken that he was not to talk to me. She'd moved on.

After Willie got arrested and sent to prison, I did stay in touch with his father, Willie Elmore, because my brother asked me to do that. I was the bridge, so to speak, to get in touch with him. Somehow my aunt Karen knew where he was, and I got in contact with his sister and did contact him. He was in the Vietnam War. He was exposed to agent orange and was fighting prostate cancer and has other illnesses from that exposure, so he spent a lot of time with the V.A. doing different studies so that he can be compensated. He was in a bad relationship at the time I contacted him, and he had broken his ankle because he started having blackouts. The situation was really sad.

My mom warned me, "You gotta be careful with him. I know he is kind, but remember he is very manipulative, and he'll pull you in." I was on a mission and I did my mission for my brother. I tried to stay in touch, and then he just kind of dropped off.

Now before this, I did actually see him one time. It was funny, odd. I got a speeding ticket on one of our many trips north. I show up for court in Oxford, North Carolina, and I'm getting ready to go into the court room when he gets off the elevator. Willie Elmore! I'm looking at him and he's looking at me and I'm looking at him very fiercely – I can kill you kind of look. And he looks at me kind of sheepish, like "It's me."

I didn't even know he was in North Carolina. I said, "What are you doing here? I can't believe you," and I walked away. I had been dealing with this speeding ticket, so I started to focus on that and get out of there. He's in North Carolina, and I'm disgusted and angry. I was looking at him and I could have sworn he had tears in his eyes, but I didn't even care. I went and did what I needed to do, and I left. I haven't seen him again. That was in ninety-five, ninety-six.

He had been saying for years that he was going to come to North Carolina, to visit William, but he never did come. I told him that I've been this bridge, but there are certain things you need to do to complete this agreement. You're going to come to North Carolina. You can stay at my house. He even sent me a copy of his license, which you need to submit to be on the visitor's list, but he never came. Excuses. Excuses. And I'm saying, "What is your problem? Why are you not coming here to see your son?"

He's still alive. I have a picture of him on my phone, sent to me by one of my aunts. Last year he called me out of the blue and asked, "How you doing?" And I was, "How've you been? I haven't heard from you for months or years!" He starts telling me about his situation and what's going on and I just cut him short. Then he asks if I'm going to be coming to Mark's wedding. That's his sister's son. I'm not cool with Mark like that. I don't really know him that well.

He says he's going, and I say, "You are? Well I hope you have a good time, because I've been waiting for you to visit your son in North Carolina, and you still haven't done that. I have been in contact with you because Willie asked me to, otherwise I wouldn't be talking to you at all. So just understand this is a bridge." And he was like crying and everything. I'm just doing this for my brother. I hung up on him.

He's textbook addictive behavior. Drinking. Erratic. Depression. When I think about it now, it was easier for him to be alone than to be home with us. It was easier for him to reconcile to himself that he has to drive this truck to this place and do this thing. But coming home and interacting with us – that was probably very difficult for him.

And he was a gambler. Didn't matter what it was, he would bet on it. They bowled in the league, but that was over by eight or nine o'clock, and they would stay on and there would be betting. My mom was a better bowler than he was, so, from what I understand, she would win back the money.

That marriage was a big part of our problems. After the marriage was over, we're in an apartment and we are *poor*. My mom had always worked, but we knew that this was different. I had my own room, but my brother, who was maybe nine, he had to sleep in my mom's room. Things were getting worse. That's when William decided to have his paper route. I helped him arrange it. I can see him thinking, "I'm not bringing anything to the table."

I'm in high school and I'm busy – tennis, track, school government – keeping busy because I know that's probably the best thing for me. By the time I graduated, I had clear, defined goals: I was going on to college, gettin' out of here and doing what I have to do. I told William that he better do the same thing. Those were my words to him: "You better do the same thing."

There was no doubt where I was going, but I didn't really notice what was happening with him. We talked, but I didn't understand. I didn't really find out until after my freshman year in college and we had a situation. I can't remember how it went down, but I do remember a conversation where I asked, "What are you doing?" And he told me that I left him and went to school, and he did what he had to do. I said, "What are you talking about?" And after he told me, I said, "You're smart and I know how smart you are. This is not a game that you can win. So if you think you can win that game. you go right ahead, but that's not something that you're going to win."

He's on a fast track, and he has this mentor who completely has his ear. I remember asking him, "Who is this guy? What is going on here?" And him pretty much telling me he knows what he is doing. But this mentor led him onto this path, and guys like him, they're not looking for the vulnerable ones; they are looking for people that are smart, people they can use.

I realized then that this was escalating. And I realize now that it was *way* more than I thought it was. Willie shielded me, too, so I would not know everything. I remember they used to have summer league basketball in Elmwood Park in East Orange and there was a young woman... Queen Latifa? Queen Latifa is a friend of my brother. So I'm going to this league and I meet her. We're talkin' and somehow his street name comes up, "Swill." She says something, and I say, "You know my brother?" And she's like, "That's your brother? He never told me he had a sister." So of course, after that conversation, I immediately got in contact with him. I said, "Queen Latifa said this and that, and so what's up? On the street you don't have a sister?" And he says, "For certain situations." And I go, "Oh my God!"

It wasn't like he was ashamed of me, because by this time I'm out of school and I'm working at Merrill Lynch and I'm bonded and everything. He doesn't tell anybody about me, so that I wouldn't be affected by what he is doing.

By this time, he's already taken the test at Seton Hall and this is where he's going to be going. So I tell him, "You think you're a smart ass, but you're not going to be able to have these two identities. You want to hit the streets, you have to accept what goes along with it."

About that SAT, I see that my mom wasn't in tune to what he really wanted to do. Maybe she didn't want to know. That irritated me. My mom, she rescued a lot of people. When we were growing up her brothers and her sisters were so pivotal and so prevalent in our lives that sometimes we really didn't want to have anything to do with them. They were our idols and our mentors, but then, for some reason, it seemed like they couldn't manage their lives. There was some kind of neediness. Every time we turned around, they needed this or they needed that or they wanted her to do this or that.

So I knew where I was going. But even though a lot of drama was going on, I was focused – but I wasn't focused enough. I was still affected by it. There is a cost to being as fiercely independent as I am. When I look back now, I see it drove me to do a lot of things – relationships, stuff like that. And just fierceness. My mom said to me just the other day that I need to work on being compassionate, more empathetic. Maybe we need to meet in the middle. She has a level of patience that I'll never have.

Before North Carolina, Willie only got in one situation in New Jersey. He and this guy got into a fight or whatever, and the guy tried to get him for assault. Which, to me, was bad, because Willie never really experienced the ramifications of that, and it probably just fueled him even more because he didn't get caught. He thought he could be the person who could figure it all out, and I always told him that was not going to be true forever.

Now Willie's probably forgotten about this, but before he got in trouble in North Carolina, my mom and I, we had this hint. My college roommate had family in North Carolina, and back then you could just hop a flight, fifty bucks on Piedmont Airlines. We were back and forth all the time. So I was in Raleigh at a restaurant. Was it Sizzler? And I could have sworn I heard his voice. This is before I knew he was coming down South. And I was, "It fucking can't be!"

I waited, then I said, "What are you doin' here?"

"What are *you* doing here?"

"*No.* It doesn't matter what I'm doing here. What are *you* doin' here? I work. I have a job. I can buy a plane ticket. What are you doing here?"

"I have a friend down here."

"Whatever you are doing, you need to get out of here."

Then I left and called my mom in Georgia and said, "Willie's in North Carolina." And she's like, "What? If he's in North Carolina now, he's been there before." So we had this hint.

Willie, he had weaknesses in his own group, guys he was hanging out with that eventually were the downfall for him. One in particular... My brother would always pick up the underdog, and when you befriend someone like that and bring them close to you, eventually they want to have your life. Jealousies come up. They are grateful to you, but in the middle of the night, they're thinkin' they wish they were in your position. Willie failed to recognize that. And in the game, if you don't recognize that, it's bad. It was like that movie, *New Jack City*.

I met Keisha. She was a very sweet girl, and he loved her and her family. Her family was like our family used to be. They have a mom and dad. They have a house. That was his alternate family. But he already had this thing now, on the street, so he couldn't assimilate completely. He wasn't going to Seton Hall. The life that he was trying to assimilate into again with them; that was gone. I knew when I met Keisha's mom and dad, the sister and brother, it was an exact mirror of our family. Except the brother was older and he had problems, was on drugs, not doing well. His parents had problems with him, and my brother became their son.

My brother, he never drank, never smoked, no drugs. But he had an addictive personality. One addiction was people, and he gambled, then, eventually, not drugs but the adrenaline that he would get from selling drugs, from being out on the street, from being in the know like that.

I can't remember exactly how I heard when he finally got in trouble for the shooting. I do know that when he went on the run, the other guys got arrested on federal charges and were singing like canaries and planning to testify against him.

I remember one thing especially that happened when he was on the run and living in my place in Roselle, New Jersey. But he's been in North Carolina, so I haven't seen him for a month. It's murky, but my mom calls and tells me what's going on, and she comes to the house and then he comes to the house. We're talking about the situation in Raleigh, and Willie says, "Look that isn't how it happened. I didn't do it. I was with these guys but..." He knows that his shots killed someone, but he doesn't feel that he's responsible.

I'm at Merrill Lynch. I've been there for six years. I don't know what to do and I gotta go to work the next day. I can't deal with this situation. He is living in my house, but I say, "You have to leave. You can't be here." Then the FBI, they come to the house late that night. I thought I might lose it. What is going on? I say I'm not opening up, and I whisper to Willie, "You have *got* to get out of here." But we don't have any time. He's in my bedroom in the back and there's a closet there with sliding doors. They are knocking on the door, so I put him in the closet and went to the front door, but I left the one side of the closet doors open.

I let them in and ask them what this is about, and they start telling me they are looking for me. They have a warrant to search my place looking for Willie and take me through the whole process of showing me this warrant. My mom comes out and we are both reading it. I say it's not my property, 'cause I don't own the house, but they say they are going to search it, so I have to say it's okay.

We sit down in the living room and they start going through the house. We are not angry at Willie, because we believe what he said, that he did not kill this man. We don't know what we are going to do, but we're going to deal with it. We can get a lawyer, figure it out, but before we got a chance, the FBI are here searching the house. My mom is a wreck. They go through the whole house and the two–car garage. Then they go back to the bedroom and they come out. I guess because the closet was open on one side, they never even looked. They looked under the bed, but they never looked in the closet.

When they left, my mom is all distraught and asks where he is, and I tell her. I'm angry but can't show how angry because now we have to figure out what we're gonna do. By this time it's almost six o'clock in the morning. I can't do what they are planning, go to Georgia where my mom is living. I have to stay and go to work. So I sit an' listen while they make these plans about whether they are gonna leave the country or whatever.

At dawn we look out and the FBI are gone. Then I got angry. I said someone has to stay and be responsible. I felt that that was my job at the time. We put Willie in the trunk of my mom's car, and they drive out and I have to go to work.

It's important to understand that our family had these problems, but we are very close. I am very protective of my little brother even when I was so angry about these charges. Let me tell one more story. I wrote this for a retreat for story–telling that we did at work. It's on my phone.

One early Sunday morning my little brother and I are walking our dog Peppy on Nesbitt Terrace. The sun is up, and it feels real good outside. We like Nesbitt Terrace because the lawns are flat, unlike our hilly former property. We're talking about the things we have to do and are sharing ideas about how we will accomplish our projects.

All of a sudden, a pick–up truck drives up with music loud enough to hear. Several boys are shouting from inside the truck. We keep walking. The truck gets closer and the boys continue to shout at us belligerently to get the H— out of their neighborhood. We don't belong there they say.

They scare my little brother. And he almost lets the leash drop. I get angry.

They keep driving and shouting. And I shout back with a loud voice, "We Live Here. This Is Our Neighborhood."

They speed away still shouting. I don't try to explain to my little brother what I think we just experienced. He's only eight years old. I'm just angry that it took me a minute to recognize it. I'm twelve years old.

That was our first experience with racism. And it's important, because I always felt I had to be responsible for my little brother. Always – when we were kids, when he's in prison, when he gets out. I'm still older.

Part Two: Doing Time

Chapter 6: From Nash to Texas and Back

I have assumed the role of silent scribe while giving Mecca and Bessie and Cheryl the floor to tell their side of the story, but when moving into the world of incarceration, the number of voices becomes overwhelming, and requires me to switch from scribe to guide. Now that Mecca is imprisoned, and instead of contracting the story expands. I begin in his first stop after Caledonia, Nash Correctional, which is where Mecca moves from neophyte to prisoner, from street kid to young adult.

Friendship is an important element in Mecca's survival. He likes to call himself a "lone wolf," conjuring the image of an independent and secretive shadow persona moving stealthily through the prison system. In truth, Mecca is fiercely attracted to other people. He's discerning and slow to give away personal information, but once he's vetted a person, he opens his heart and, over time, becomes a fiercely loyal friend.

So Mecca is a lone wolf who collects people. I see this as an essential factor in his ability to survive in prison. It's a fine–tuned combination of discretion, independence, and a capacity for what must be called love. He's like a magnet. When the poles are lined up right, there's fierce attraction. If not, there can be suspicion and animosity. In prison this can cause problems with "administration" – officers, superintendents, people with power who are used to using that power to intimidate. At Nash Correctional, Mecca does not get along with the superintendent, will call Mecca into his office to announce, "I've been to college, I've studied psychology, and I can't figure you out." Eventually this is going to get Mecca shipped again, but not for almost seven years. During that time, Mecca is moving from street kid to adult and taking his love of other people with him on that journey.

Early in his time at Nash, Mecca meets Edward Scott, "Scott-so." Their friendship is one of the strongest bonds in Mecca's prison life, and after release, Mecca continues to support Scott-so. He makes time for them to get together every time Scott-so gets a pass, and they talk on the phone several times a week as Scott-so goes through his own struggle to earn a MAPP. Full disclosure. I get swept into this net, and sit beside Bessie for two parole hearings before Scott-so is finally granted a MAPP in 2019.

The story of Mecca and Scott-so begins in 1996, about four years into Mecca's sentence, when he and Scott-so are pulled out of separate prisons and placed in the same transport to Texas. The North Carolina prisons were seriously over–crowded and as a temporary, make–shift solution, plane loads and bus loads of shackled prisoners were moved to other states. There was supposed to be an upside: job skills training, education, better housing than in North Carolina. In fact, all of the men I have talked to about the shipments say that the displacement made family visits impossible and resulted in isolation and boredom. The benefits were policies on paper, not hard currency.

Soon after Mecca was released, Scott-so came to my house on a CV Pass, a privilege that can be earned by those who have earned honor grade. Mecca stopped by and we recorded the story of their friendship while sitting on my porch on a fine spring day. Their friendship has been like a badge, a special anointment that other men in prison noticed. They've been bursting to talk about it and to carry on their effort to educate me about prison life.

"Where did you first get to know each other?"

"It was 1996," Scott-so begins. He eyes Mecca for confirmation. "I was told I was going to Texas. I had been in prison exactly five years and I was housed at Odum. Guys from Odum were going to different states, but first we all went to CP [Central Prison]. They put a bunch of inmates inside this gym and then they started shipping us out in groups, going to Texas, Oklahoma, Rhode Island, Tennessee. At the time I didn't know Mecca at all, but he was in the same block at CP waiting for shipping."

"Did you go up to him and start talking? How did you get to know each other?"

Both men eye me with amusement.

"You don't do that in prison," Scott-so explains. "You don't try to make friends. You go up to guys shaking hands or something, that's open season. But I had spotted him at CP and, as the time went on, after we got to Texas, I kept noticing that glow that Mec' had. I was tired of doing the things I was doing. I was into a little bit of everything, Ms. Simone. I was dealing drugs, marijuana, gambling. Whatever I could trick the officer to do. Whatever I could do to make money. I was thirty years old. People done give me a life sentence. I said to myself, 'I'm gonna do my time like I want to do my time.'

"But I was miserable." Scott-so's eyes get wide the way they do and both men laugh. "I was trying to find a way out of being miserable. I see this glow this young man had, and I said maybe that might be my way out. I think, 'You know I'm gonna try to embrace this a little bit. See what happens. I've done everything else!' Why was he so happy all the time? Here we are heading to Texas, going to be thousands of miles from home and he be looking like that."

"Which is strange to me," Mecca jumps in, "because going to Texas was a very traumatic thing for me. I finally get out of Caledonia to Nash and I'm working in the clothes house and I have my own cell and my rhythm and then, out of the blue one day I hear the officer at the desk call me in. She says, 'Mr. Elmore. They want you in the sergeant's office.'

"So I get there, and he says, 'You need to go and make a phone call to your folks.' I said, 'Do I?' And he said, 'Yeah, man, you are going to Texas.'

"I called my mom and I'm all over her and she's saying she's going to make calls. I'm calling her to help stop this from happening; but next minute I'm in shackles and I'm on that plane, and no matter what Scott-so be seeing, I can't figure any way out."

"Yeah. Wearing all them shackles." Scott-so crosses his wrists. "They told us on the tarmac, 'If you gotta go to the bathroom do that now 'cause you are not going to be allowed to move once we are on the plane.' We lined up like slaves on a slave ship, even if it was an airplane."

"It was traumatic for me, it still is," Mecca says. "Going to Texas, that was when it really hit me. I was in a situation where I had no control at all. That was probably the most traumatic experience of my time in prison. I realized they could do anything they wanted to me."

"I see you man," Scott-so says. "But from here today, I'm looking back at this situation with Texas, and where I'm coming from, going to Texas was bad, but it was also good, because it was a sign to me that I got to be changing, doing something different. The way I was doing my time – for life? In Texas, I finally say, 'This is not going to work.' And here's this young man – well, few years seem a lot younger when you thirty – and he seems to have something to teach me. So after we got to Texas, I started talking to Mec', and, Mec', one of the first things you start talkin' about is books you read."

"You weren't doing a lot of reading yet?" I ask. I first met Scott-so when he came to OCC in maybe 2012, and I've been watching him struggle to build his vocabulary, work on grammar– so I will wager he was not much for the written word back then. When I first asked Scott-so about school, he told me, "I went to the street, Ms. Simone." He described the projects and the streets in Brooklyn near the Pratt Institute, where at about that time I was teaching and working on a photography MFA. I could have walked right past him, tightened my grip on my bag, and kept going.

"So I said okay," Scott-so continues. "I could start doing these things. Maybe I start reading some books or something like that. Maybe I could start to *write* somewhere down the line. I remember the first book he gave me was *Malcolm X, The Autobiography of Malcolm X.*"

"And the Mohammad Ali book too," Mecca adds.

"Right. And both of them be Muslims. And that's when my journey began. We talked – man, we talked for the whole time we were together in Texas. He left before me. I was in Texas for seven months and the first three were with Mec' and it started me on my change."

"Weren't you supposed to work? And go to some education programs?"

"Nothing happening out there," Mecca says. "You could get something if you really wanted to – work for the kitchen area, which is something I hate. But no real jobs or anything. You could go to the yard, workout. You could go to the library, but there were no work assignments."

"Yeah," Scott-so confirms. "We just waiting our turn to come back to North Carolina. We didn't do nothing in Texas. We played football. Played basketball. That's all we did. All day to talk. Hang out. But we did go to school. We went to computer class. Remember?"

"Man that wasn't school. We just going 'cause we didn't have anything else to do," Mecca scowls. "You went in there and taught yourself. Just jump on the computer. You wouldn't believe it. Texas was just the weirdest. Whole place was like a ghost town with rooms, computers, clothes house, nobody doing nothing. Kinda self–serve."

"Mec', we had a teacher. Remember. She was nice but she passed everybody. Just for showing up. And the food. The food was different. The pancakes was the size of a quarter or fifty cent piece. Small."

I have to laugh. "They're called silver dollar pancakes! They're supposed to be special in Texas."

"Also no pork," Scott-so adds. "I wasn't a Muslim yet. Not sure why, but they didn't have no pork, and that was strange to us coming from North Carolina."

"So tell me more about your change. How did it go?"

"I was into a lot of stuff. Smoking reefer. I had one bag left. And after talking to Mecca, I told him, 'This is it. I'm not doing this no more.' And after that I never touched a cigarette or marijuana or buck – it's like homemade wine – I never touched none of that again. I didn't do no program or AA or NA or nothing. I made up my mind. Saying this is it.

"And that right there put me on the path for knowing that I don't have to do those things that were not healthy for me. And by my leaving that stuff alone, my mind begin to open up to bigger and better things. Having conversations with Mec', building my own thinking so that this is the way I am today. I thank God every day that I met him. I'm not putting Mec' on a pedestal, a high pedestal, but he's a good friend. That's what God do, Ms. Simone, that's what the universe do. They put people together and you can appreciate, or you can destroy. It's up to you. Ever since then, we've been like brothers."

"What did you talk about?" I ask.

Mecca has a list. "Family. Girls. Guys. Music. Drugs. The streets. Girls again! (laughter) More girls and relationships. All of that stuff. We knew some of the same people on the street in Raleigh. We were there at the same time, doing business in the same circles, even though we never met each other. We just started sharing about our life and what we were thinking. Not much going on out there so we have all day for this."

"What's the rest of the camp like? What are other people doing?" I'm trying to picture the place, and it is looking more and more like *Shawshank Redemption*. I try not to fall into clichés, but Texas is inviting me in that direction. Mecca's description only reinforces my stereotype.

"The dorms were set out so that the guys from the West, they were all together, and the other dorms were guys from North Carolina. When there's time for movement, there's one alley where everybody merged before they went left or right coming in and out of the yard. You could get fenced in there. It's like a corral and you can't get out."

"Somebody could kill you?" I ask.

"Easy," Mecca assures me, with that gleam he uses when he is half trying to scare me and half remembering something real. "Kill you easy. Nobody would know. They didn't have guard towers, none of that."

"And," Scott-so adds, "the guards out there were gang members too."

"That's how everything was approached," Mecca affirms. "If there's a problem started by a guy from North Carolina, you could try to say, 'I'm not even from North Carolina. I'm just in prison there.' But they don't do time like that in Texas. They really are a brotherhood. In North Carolina you can say, 'You know I'm gonna be alone. I'm gonna be a lone wolf and just do my time.' You could not do that in Texas. You gotta be affiliated. So a few of us had to really talk to the guys from North Carolina that had the knives, shanks and stuff. If they did something violent, that was going to affect us all."

"You could just see it," Scott-so says, almost standing up from his chair. He's got built out arms, and when he flexes them, it's intimidating. "How they moved, in gangs. Even the Muslims – 'cause that's where I began to be reading the Koran – all hung out together. All the MS13s hung out together. The Crips and the Bloods.

"Real story about Texas, how crazy it was." Scott-so leans in and signals Mecca with his eyes. "My youngest daughter's uncle was there with us, her mom's brother. He was a real knucklehead. Every morning they bring your food and they bring you coffee or juice or whatever you supposed to have for the breakfast meal."

"Bring it to the dorm on a little cart, like on an airplane or in the hospital." Mecca mimes pushing the cart. "Medications on them buggies. That's how they push it by."

"And the coffee was cold this particular day," Scott-so continues, "and he, my daughter's uncle, ended up cussing one of the guys out about the coffee... a dangerous guy, the kind who might have knives this long."

Scott-so spreads his hands a foot or two apart. He and Mecca are clearly enjoying this.

"This is out West." Mecca says. "They serious about it. No shanks."

"*No*," Scott-so confirms, "they got swords. My daughter's uncle. He did that yelling about the coffee. Then it was time for us to go to the yard. They on one side, the regular West guys, and we on the other side. But to get to the yard everybody going to have to walk through that alley before they can go to their separate sides.

"So we went to go outside to the yard and these Texas guys were standing out there waiting for us. So now we stop and back in and close the door back up. You could lock the door from the inside. If the C.O. came it could be real trouble, but we lock the door. Now the crazy thing was that the C.O.s were gang members too. The guy serving the coffee, he was Hispanic. Hispanic gang member."

"It was like this guy complaining about the coffee was on a death wish or something," Mecca says. "That's how he was moving. And he knew that if he got into something it was going to be taken out on everybody, because the guys from Texas thought that we were all a unified front. We weren't. but they thought we were, because they were."

"Finally we sit down and have a meeting with these guys and talk to them," Scott-so finishes up. He looks out at the trees in front of my house, sounding relieved even though the event is long over. "Let them know it wasn't between gangs or personal. It was a misunderstanding. Won't happen again. We killed that beef, but it was just bad."

"So in Texas," I ask, "what was the population?"

"I didn't see any white," Mecca says. "Did you?"

"After you left there were some. They came from Missouri."

"How did you figure out the affiliations? Tattoos?"

"You could tell by the flag they might be wearing or the bandanas they might have on their heads," Scott-so says. "Even some female officers were MS13. And even some of the guys in our dorm. They were very open with that. After Mecca left, one day I actually saw someone open the gate and guys went inside to where the Oklahoma guys were. Went in and stabbed a guy and came right back out. The officer opened the gate for him again. Never found out what it was about, but I saw it happen. That's how it is out West. The officers stick together with the inmates and all of them are in these gangs or affiliations."

"How does Islam fit into this? Mecca, you weren't interested in Islam, were you?"

"No, but I knew a lot about it. New Jersey is like a Muslim state. Almost everybody – all my peers anyway were into Islam. I been around it so much, that's how he and I got talking about it. I don't think he ever met somebody that practiced Christianity that knew as much about Islam. And the Muslims were the other way around. Christianity? Man, you better get out of here with this stuff. But we dialogued about both. Scott-so told me when we were in Texas he was going to convert. See, in Texas I used to get up at three o'clock every morning; and I used to journal and study all the time and work out. Work out, study, write in my journal. Then Scott-so started getting up doing the same thing. And he experienced for himself how different the day was, the mindset, dealing with prison. You get up early and nobody is doing anything. They all in the bunks sleeping. So we both got up in the morning and he was studying the Koran and telling me he wanted to convert."

"When Mec' gave me books and I was reading about Malcolm X, I was reading a letter that Malcolm wrote back to his wife when he went to Mecca, and that moved me to embrace Islam. That trip that Malcolm took to the Haj. It really touched me, and it made me want to research more and learn more about what I really wanted to do.

"When I was coming up, my block, being in New York, it was half Christian, half Muslim. So I been doing it, lookin' into Islam, since I was fifteen. It just wasn't my time then for me to become Muslim. So when I read *Malcolm X*, I said, 'You know, I'm going to take this to heart.' I've been striving ever since.

"To me I think it made our friendship stronger because we respect each other's religion. I respect what he believes in and he respects what I believe in. We don't look at our relationship as religious. We are way beyond that."

"After Texas, North Carolina wasn't so bad," Mecca reflects. "It's easy to forget when you have a life sentence and you feel frustrated, but nothing was so hard for me as that time in Texas. I would call my mom and tell her, 'I have to get out of here.' And she would say, 'I'm working on it.' Seemed like it would be forever, and I had no power to change it. Like a kind of slavery life. I was there three months and then they shipped me back."

"After Mecca left what did you do?"

"I just did my time, played basketball. I missed him, 'cause I missed the conversations that we were having. I was just starting off changing what I was doing, how I was thinking, and I was missing that.

"Mec' left his information, and I knew about his mother, Ms.

Elmore. When I got back, I was at Lumberton and Mec' was in Nash. My grandmother and grandfather were living at the time, and they talked to Ms. Elmore and she helped them get me to Nash so Mec' and I could be in the same place. At Nash, during visits they could meet my grandparents and I could meet Cheryl. By now, Ms. Elmore, I'm calling her 'Mom' and she be calling me 'Son'."

"What kind of friendships did you have before you met Mecca? Before Texas?"

"There were some guys that I knew, but it wasn't really intimate like I was with Mecca. I'd been knowing them for a while, but I never really trust them that much. Where I come from you don't put your trust in a lot of people. I didn't give them my life story, talk about my family or my children or the women I was with. But it was just something about Mecca. It was easy for me to open up to him.

"Now, we didn't agree on everything. Say for example, if I would say something about a girl, Mec' would be like, 'Man, what's wrong with you? The girl like you.' And we go back and forth. 'I don't know, man, 'cause she might try to hurt me.' And Mec' would say, 'Dang, you gonna never get hurt for the rest of your life? Take a chance.' Stuff like that."

"Was that about the mothers of your kids? Who were these women?"

"They were some women I was meeting. Should I tell her?"

"It's your oral history! You wanna tell her?"

Before Scott-so gets into this, it's important to explain that in prison there are two ways incarcerated men get to be around women: visits and staff. It's also helpful to understand the law on this matter. In 2003 the federal government passed the Prison Rape Elimination Act or PREA. This legislation opened the door for more detailed research into prison rape and instituted a zero tolerance policy for staff and volunteers in which the onus is always on them, not the prisoner, if there is any level of sexual activity from harassment to rape, from friendship to romance.

There is also a violation called "undue familiarity," a catch all that can be used to take away the privileges of just about any person coming in from the outside, staff or volunteer. Undue familiarity includes many of the ordinary elements of trust and friendship. It's meant to keep the incarcerated from pressuring staff or volunteers for favors. On the downside, "undue familiarity" precludes many connections that might otherwise be considered a therapeutic element of the work that staff and volunteers do. On the upside, it limits the power of staff or volunteers to use intimacy to control the incarcerated.

In sum, in the nineties, prisoner interactions with staff posed a risky situation and the power was all on the officers' side. A prisoner might get visits or occasional contact with a volunteer, but day to day, female officers are the only women around, so the rewards of getting closer to them, even just for casual conversation, are tempting and officially not allowed. "It's not just sexual," Mecca tells me. "It's the energy that a woman has. In prison you be missing that."

"Baby mothers and them didn't come around," Scott-so goes on. "It was other females. Female officers that liked me. And it's not just the power of the female officer that's risky. I'd be telling Mec', I'm not gonna go over there and talk to this female too much because you got guys that they be jealous. They were jealous because females... they liked me and him. Liked to talk to us."

"Were you a lady's man? I'm not asking were you someone who played women and dumped them, but were you someone that women found comfortable?" I ask this because Scott-so has several children (now all adults) with a couple of different women.

"You know what? In my case, Simone," Scott-so says, with an ironically soft and flirtatious look, "I'm a very shy individual. I don't talk too much, so a lot of women are attracted to that because they feel, 'He ain't gonna tell our business. He ain't gonna say too much about what's going on.' So then they get to ask you a question; a female officer, she might say, 'I see you don't talk to many people. All you talk to is Mecca.' And that's how it starts. And then they start asking personal questions and you start asking them personal questions and there you go. You sitting at the desk. You talking a lot. You got other guys looking, and they get jealous because they saying, 'Every time she come on duty, she gonna talk to you.' It's not no sexual thing going on. She just like the conversation. She's got nothin' else to do. You not really supposed to be doing it, but to be truthful, it happens all the time.

"Let me tell you about this one time, Ms. Simone. Him and me, we have argued about this. There was a guy that met a female at Eastern Correctional. She was an intern. And me and this guy was kind of cool. We weren't as tight as me and Mecca, but we was kinda cool. He got out, and they start seeing each other out in the street, him and this intern. Then he started getting high, smoking crack. Stealing.

"Both of them used to come visit me. But when he started getting high, she just come alone. And she be like, 'What should I do? Should I try to do this? Try to do that?' And I try to give her the best advice I could in a situation like that, because I've been in a household like that. My mother used drugs. So for some reason, she started liking me. And I shared that with Mecca. I said, 'I can't do this right here.'

"And he was like, 'Man talk to her. Talk to her.' Mecca was just telling me to just be there for her. But I didn't feel comfortable, because it's this man's girlfriend. 'cause I'm trying not to be the same person I was no more. I'm trying to be living right, but I still didn't trust me enough for her to come and visit me. Because if we start that, I'm gonna be looking for things from her. Not money or stuff like that, but I'm gonna want her to come see me each week. I'm gonna look for that, 'cause that's what you do in prison!"

"Yeah. I told him go for it," Mecca admits. "But, honestly, you ask me now and I say it's slippery. It's easy for it to go the wrong way. You take a guy that's doing time, and if he just halfway takes care of himself, he's gonna stand out. 'cause most of the guys don't even take care of themselves. So he keeps himself groomed and he exercises. And he's not a busy body. He's just kind of to himself. That's attractive to women. And this intern, she's needing to feel some of that energy, a man to give her some advice or something.

"Same thing with the female officers. Prison is boring. Especially if she works the night shift. She wanna keep from falling asleep. Say the guy can have a stimulating conversation. And the guy may know that she is not directly interested in him, but he's practicing how to interact with a female. He may even say it, 'You just don't want to go asleep on your shift, and you just want to talk until I can't no more and I gotta get back to my cell.' And they might laugh about it. The cards are up front."

Scott-so adds, "Now you have PREA, but back then you could do that, and she won't be charged."

"Won't go to court." Mecca says. "She might lose her job or resign before she lost it, but no legal charges. So everybody's safe. For her, when she come to work, she can talk to you or interact however she wants to. For the guy, whenever she comes to work, he can go in his imagination and pretend like he has a girlfriend. And everybody's happy with that."

"But Scott-so," I have to ask, "the intern who was seeing you, technically she has a real boyfriend, but he is going downhill. Does he have any recourse if he gets angry at you?"

"He doesn't know. She doesn't tell him nothing. And he's busy. He's got the thing going with the drugs. So Mecca was telling me, just let her know that it's no romantic relationship but you can be there for her. I told her that, but that's not what she wanted."

"She wanted to be more intimate?"

"Right."

Mecca leans in. "I got a story about that too. I know I was telling Scott-so then to go for it, but maybe I wasn't giving the best advice. Perry Haynie. Scott-so, you remember him? Doc. This was with his daughter, in Salisbury. Name's Annette. I had been in prison more than ten years, and probably a dozen times a guy thought enough of me to want to introduce me to somebody. Sometimes, like this time, I didn't think enough of the guy to trust his judgment, so I didn't want anything to do with it. But this guy was persistent. We slept beside each other and I saw him all the time. But his lifestyle – the way Doc did his time – was totally antithetical to my ethics. He was the quintessential inmate. He lived his life according to the code of the penitentiary."

"So how did he get to you?" I'm remembering Mecca's story about his crime and the friend card. When Mecca gets himself in a situation he can't control, it's usually going to be because of some combination of the downside of his loyalty and his charm.

"He just kept on it. 'Man, my daughter's always looking around the visitation room and asking, "What he in prison for? He don't look like he should be in prison." And, man, she's a good girl too. I think she'd like to have a friend like you.'"

"You're vulnerable? If it's Salisbury, we're getting into the early 2000's. You've been in prison a long time and you are still looking at natural life."

"No, not really vulnerable. I had so much going on at Salisbury. I had a job. I'm talking to my mom and my sister, writing in my journal, playing some basketball and doing weights. I had so many outlets. I didn't give myself time. I'm not thinking along those lines. Maybe in a blip here or there, but really just minding my own business. I have a long stretch and I'm learning how to do that kind of time. You need to understand how obsessing or thinking too hard on something, like women, that's detrimental to you mentally when you are doing time. If you don't keep your desires in check, if you don't have the discipline, you leave yourself open to things like relationships with female correctional officers – and like Scott-so is saying, that can get complicated real fast. Yeah. You gonna see how that worked out here.

"Doc was older than me and out of respect to my elders, when he spoke, I answered. He's a savvy prisoner. He knows the system inside out. So this time he's in the hole, and he got word to me to call his daughter and tell her he is in lock–up."

"So you call her. Just to tell her that, not anything more?" I raise my eyebrows. I like to push sometimes, because there's usually something coming when Mecca starts a story with too much talk about self control.

"I say, 'Look. Your father asked me to call you and relay to you that they are going to transfer him. He's not sure where. He doesn't know his restrictions. He's probably still gonna be on lockdown. Probably not gonna be able to call. He got some serious charges. I know you seen this before.'

"Her father's in and out of these situations. And as soon as I finished telling her what her father said, she went right into, 'Has my father not been telling you what I had been saying?'

"And I said, 'Yeah, he's been telling me.'

"And she said, 'Well, I'm glad you called. Thank goodness you called. And how are you? What's going on with you?' And she directed the conversation to me. The phone cuts off every fifteen minutes, so when the fifteen minutes was up, she goes, 'Are you gonna call back?' And when I said I doubted it, she said, 'Thank you for doing that for my father and take care. Keep the number if you want to call back, that would be fine.' And I think I also got a thank you card in the mail. And I wrote back thanking her for the card. And she wrote back, and slowly but surely we start corresponding."

Scott-so and I are both smiling. We love a good story where Mecca's rules for Mecca fail. Of course we are also waiting for the part where Mecca transcends his own folly.

"It's okay. I like to write and I'm in control when I'm writing. I'm patient. In real life I'm patient about relationships, so prison hasn't made me want to be speedy about them. I'm thinking that any day she'll snap out of this. Besides, her father is gone, so she won't see me in visits no more. So I'm like, hey, this will play itself out.

"Lo and behold eventually she said, 'Well look, I was so accustomed to coming there to see my father, put me on your visitor list.' I told her that's probably not going to work 'cause my mother and sister, they come every weekend. My visits are pretty much already allotted, and we don't like to share them. And she said, 'That's OK, but one day they might want to take a day off and then I'll come.' I figure that's it, but I sent her the visitor form anyway.

"And something happened – my sister and my mom both went to New Jersey. And Annette came. And she asked, 'Well, when can I come again?' She wanted to visit same time as them, but I tell her that won't work. Eventually she started coming once a month.

"One time, she overlaps with Cheryl, and afterwards Cheryl asks, 'Who is this chick?' And I was like, 'Calm down. Settle down. It's just a friend, potential friend.' And she was, 'All right but I'm gonna meet her one day. I'm gonna come up here one day that she's here.'

"Annette, she met both of them once," Mecca says, and I can tell having to hold Bessie and Cheryl at bay was not a comfortable move for him. "They try to be neutral, but Annette, she left early. I wasn't surprised, because my sister has the tendency to run people away. She's too direct. But it was awkward for me."

Scott-so and I are laughing. Cheryl is very straightforward, protective of her younger brother, and not interested in chit chat. Bessie sees her family as the Three Musketeers: no room for a fourth.

"I'm trying to be fair, divide my attention up. But my sister visits to talk about what's going on in her life. She's newly married. She's having a house built and all that kind of stuff going on – which is how we do our visits."

"And she's not going to talk in front of a stranger the way you talk together?"

"But she did! She just went right into it. Like nobody was there." Mecca lowers his eyes and shifts around as if this is all happening again right here. "Like I said, Annette left early. For me this was a headache, because it had been a long time since I had to divide my mind between family and a stranger. I learned that no matter how common you think an experience is, if you haven't had it for a while, it will drain you."

"So is this moving to romance? With Annette?"

Mecca dodges the question. He does not like it when I lean into his weak spots.

"After maybe a year and a half, I am coming up for honor grade, minimum custody."

For a person with a life sentence under old law, honor grade is the holy grail. Until the MAPP program, it was the only relief you could hope for. And at this point, Mecca has never heard of a MAPP. As far as he's concerned the goal is to make this life sentence as bearable as possible. Bessie and Cheryl were working a bunch of legal angles, but it seemed like all were dead ends.

"Here's what happens," Mecca continues. "Doc stays gone for a year. Then he comes back, 'cause he has respiratory issues and Salisbury has an infirmary there. When he comes back, she's on my list so she can't be on his list. So he starts to say something about that. I'm trying to influence her to get off my list and get on her dad's list. I don't need any trouble. And she is saying, 'No way. I'm not doing it.'

"So now he wants me to funnel notes and messages telling her this and that. And remember, I'm thinking about honor grade. I'm not looking to mess that up. Next visit I said, 'I'm not comfortable with this and I don't have the same lifestyle as your father. I'm not into *anything* he's into. *Anything.*"

"And she said, 'I already knew that about you.'

"I said, 'Well now you know because I said it.'

"So we went from visiting once a month to visiting twice a month, and she told me if I ever got my minimum custody, to come – you know – live with her. 'I got my house. I got my two kids.' They were pre-teens, eleven and thirteen. She goes on and on... 'I told my kids about you. I tell people in my church about you. And you know, it'd be great. You need a place to get on your feet, get yourself together.'

"When this started, I said, 'Wait a minute! In a perfect situation, that is the last thing I would ever do.' She was offended by that and asked why.

"I tell her, 'Because the kind of guy that I am, I think a guy that would do that would be a bum. Because any day you could come home and have a bad day and tell me to get my little few things and get ou'cha house. And I'm gonna have to get out'cha house. I'm not gonna allow that to be my situation with you or nobody. So it's not personal. It's just a principle I live by."

Honor grade does not mean release, but clearly, Annette had a vision that included freedom. Mecca asks me why women get attracted this way to men in prison, and I remind him of what he just told Scott-so. A man who is cleaned up and will listen to you? I have seen it myself in the visiting room. Man who is talking just about himself, looking all around? No. Man who is leaning in and listening? Yes.

And in prison there are men who fall in love and get married to women who wait years, even decades for them to earn their release. It's a dream but not always a fantasy. Just not a dream that works for Mecca. In his cell he keeps a prom picture of himself and his pre-prison love, Keisha. For now that is the safe zone.

"So," Mecca moves in for the finale, "she's still talking, being real supportive, and says, 'You know you come up in six months again. Look, I'm still serious about you. When you get out... I think it would be a great fit.' That's when I went to the sergeant in visitation; got a pen from him, got a paper towel and wrote down all of the hours. Twice a month, two hours each visit. It came to like three and half days.

"And I said to her, 'That's how much time we spent together. And you want to invite someone you spent three and a half days with into your home. Not just with you but with your children. What kind of logic is that?'

"She pushed back from the table. Tears ran down from her eyes. Visit was almost over, but she didn't waste no time. It was like she was trying to duck the strip search. She was outta there. Then I didn't hear nothin' from her. Maybe nine months went by and I got a letter from her that said to me how that felt. She felt embarrassed. Insulted. Inadequate. And she said she never thought in her life someone in prison would — that she would experience rejection from someone in prison."

"I wrote back, and I said, 'I really wish you would look at it as a presentation of respect. I respect you too much to play that game. You are not a convenience for me.'

"Then she even sent me money one time. I sent it right back."

"It's hard to break it all down," Scott-so says. "This intern, same thing. She used to come every week. What finally made me say something to her was when she said, 'When I first saw you, even then I was wishing it was you instead of him.'

"I said, 'Listen, Right now you just emotional. You just going through something right now 'cause you going through something with him, so now you want to look at me. I can't do that. I just can't do that.'

"I knew he was no good for her, and I could have used that to my advantage but I didn't. I been knowing this guy for five or six years. Morally, it just wouldn't be right. So I told her that. And she's just like, 'Okay.' Visits stopped. Nothing more.

"Same with me and Doc's daughter," Mecca is visibly struggling with this. "That's the ultimate rejection for a woman. 'You are in prison and you are not going to allow me to make my advances?' But it's about your values. Yes, it's nice to talk to a woman, to have that female energy, but when it moves to the point where you are not aligning it with your values, it's not good for anyone."

"I couldn't do it," Scott-so says. "Now if it was ten years before that, I might have come at it totally different. I could have stepped in there and got something for myself. But now – after Texas – after deciding to make my living different, I couldn't do it."

Mecca and Scott-so can go on forever with these stories, but I'm interested in going on with what happens after Nash, when after a few years, they are shipped to different facilities. So I ask, "How do you keep this friendship going when you are not in the same camp?"

"Now in this story of me and Mec', after Nash we were apart maybe thirteen years, maybe more, but I carried him with me," Scott-so explains. "I left Nash in ninety-eight and went to Pamlico Correctional. But we kept doing letters. Mom would send his letters to me. Or I would send a letter to my grandmother and she sent it to Mec'. We're not allowed to write to a prisoner in another facility, but we fix it this way.

"So we were in touch, but when he got honor grade and got his MAPP and he was shipped to OCC, Mom didn't write to tell me. He surprised me. I was at OCC and I was in the mowing job – mowing all the lawn outside the gate. When I get off work that day, I go back in the gate and I'm coming around the corner to the dorm and *bam,* Mecca come from behind somebody. Whoa! I didn't know he got his MAPP or none of that stuff. I was the happiest guy in the world when I saw that guy. I kept saying, 'Man, that's great!' And that started it all over again. Talking and giving advice, and it's been that way right to today."

Scott-so's original release date according to his MAPP contract was to be June 21, 2021. However, on June 2, 2020, he was awarded an early release due to the COVID-19 pandemic. Scott-so went to live at the Straight Talk Transition House in Durham and teamed up with Mecca to start a business, Community Landscaping. As Mecca explains it, "We were friends on the inside and now we are learning how to be friends out here. It's real and it's surreal."

Chapter 7: Northerners in the South

During the Great Migration, many African American families moved north. Today there is a slow reversal or return going on and professionals from New York and New Jersey are finding better jobs and more affordable housing in cities like Atlanta and Raleigh. Older people are retiring and returning home to cities and small towns all across the South. In an odd way, Mecca and his family are part of this movement. Cheryl and Bessie moved to North Carolina to deal with the trial and found themselves settling there after Mecca got his sentence. Cheryl married a man in the construction industry, and they built a house in Bahama, just north of Durham. Cheryl now works for the city of Durham. Bessie worked in a series of women's shelters and led educational programs for various outreach groups. When William got his MAPP, the pressure was off, so she decided to put her experience with "the system" to good use, first founding the Straight Talk Support Group in 2013, bringing together friends and families of people who are incarcerated to have frank conversations and share resources. In 2018, Bessie took over a former youth facility, the Troy House in Durham, and opened the Straight Talk Transition House. The transition house offers a place to stay and programs for men coming out of prison and jail. The Elmores are not outliers, but part of a north–south diaspora.

That diaspora also touches the prison system. In state prisons most of the people are from the state in which they are incarcerated. However, in North Carolina, neatly situated as it is on sections of both Interstate 95 and Interstate 85, there are a growing number of opportunities to "get in a situation." The men who testified against Mecca at his trial are in federal prison because they were charged with interstate drug trafficking. Mecca is in state prison because he did not get caught moving drugs; he got caught on a murder charge in North Carolina.

Scott-so, too, is a man with his feet in two cultures. He has family in North Carolina and spent time with his grandparents, who moved back South from Brooklyn to family land in Franklin County. When Mecca met Scott-so, they found they have the Raleigh street scene in common, but they also share New York area origins. Shortly after meeting Scott-so, Mecca connected with another New Jersey native, Frank Walls. Frank was serving a set term and had a release date, but he was just as unsettled as Mecca about doing his time in the South, and, unlike Mecca, he's a bit hot headed. Not a good idea in the North Carolina state prison diaspora.

I met Frank for the first time when he was going through volunteer training at OCC so that he could take Mecca out on passes. At Orange Correctional, once a person has been out for a year, they can take volunteer training at a state facility. In order to qualify for his volunteer card, Frank had to attend three activities at the prison. He did not want to go to NA or AA, so he asked to visit the workshop I lead. I was a little bit shocked, as I didn't know that former prisoners could qualify as a community volunteer, but I learned that it's not unusual. In fact, after he has been out for a couple of years, Mecca will get his own volunteer card and attend the workshop as part of his training.

Frank is not a man to show all of his cards until the game is clear.

The day he takes Mecca out on pass and they show up at my house for an oral history session is probably the first time we have an extended conversation. At the workshop, Frank was guarded and quiet. He's a careful man, but he's also passionate about his friend Mecca and agrees to talk. I turn on the recorder and cue the beginning of the session.

"So, who wants to begin the story?"

I'm not sure what will happen, but Frank immediately leans in toward the recorder as if he has been waiting to tell the story.

"I remember the first time I saw Mecca," he says. "This is… for me… when you meet someone – I don't know if it goes like this for everyone, but I can go back to the actual moment that I first seen him. If I was home, in front of my wife, Bridgett, this would be a little hard for me to say, but I really remember it like the first time that you meet a girl that you end up in love with. I remember I was in the cafeteria at Nash Correctional. The camp is broken down into units, so based on where you work is where you live. Mecca was actually living in another part of the camp, but they fed us at the same time.

"I was already eating, and his dormitory was coming in. I could tell that they were doing some type of activity because he was sweatin' and he was like dirty – maybe from softball or something. But I remember he looked different than everybody else. I understand it now that we've been brothers for years, but I didn't then. Just something attracted me to him.

"It's also a thing about being from the North and being incarcerated in the South. A lot of us stick out. Say I'm with some guys and they know I'm not a local, and they say, 'Oh, there's another guy; he's not a local. You guys need to…'

"But this time nobody said anything. We didn't speak or anything like that. We might of met eyes or something and do like guys do, kind of nod at each other. But that was about it. It's funny how exactly I can remember it – even the sneaker he had on, because that's the only thing that you have on other than the prison garb. We were in brown clothes because that's medium security. They have rules about that. Minimum, OCC, is green. They also make you wear state–issue shoes, but Mec' he had on a Jordan shoe and it was blue and white. It's crazy how I remember!"

"How did you end up at Nash?" I want to know more about Frank's background, but I'm also aware of the protocol. Frank operates on strong privacy signals, and we are just getting to know each other.

"I had processed at Central Prison," he begins carefully. "It was weird because according to my sentence I was supposed to go to one of the farms, Caledonia or Odum. Nash had just been built and just opened, so it would not be the place you go right after your sentencing. I was waiting a long time in the processing unit in Central Prison, and it was horrible because it's a medical unit. Guys have HIV, all sorts of stuff. So I'm asking myself, 'When am I going to leave?' I have not been in prison before, and I have never been living in the South. But I'm also hearing stories about "the farm," so, yeah, I don't want to be here, but don't rush me down to Caledonia either! Then I was shipped to Nash. It was this new camp. And it was clean!

"Was Mecca already there?"

"Mecca got to Nash maybe six months before me. So what happens is they put me in Unit Three. That's called "unassigned." Means you don't have a job or anything. With the sentence that I had, I needed to get a job to gain time. If you have a job, you can start working to drop time from your sentence. So somebody maybe I knew got me in the kitchen. And the kitchen workers just happened to be in the same building where Mecca was at, and we share a recreation yard.

"It's crazy that I can remember the first time I saw him, but I can't remember the first time we really spoke or how we got close. It happened like a whirlwind. We went from not knowing each other to spending every available moment getting to know each other. He was on one side of the dorm building and I was on the other side, so the only time we can see each other is if we can go to the chow hall together. Maybe when the yard opens we can talk together. And library call. If there's inclement weather, the yards are not open, so we would go in the library just to talk."

"What did you talk about?"

"Same as what we talk about now. Life. Talking about our lives from before we ended up there."

"Did you talk about your crimes, your trials?"

"No. It was a long time before we talked about how we ended up there and that Mecca had a life sentence. No. To understand you need to know something about being from the North that I want to talk about. In the South, they will ask you about your sentence, but in northern prisons, people don't go there. I don't know if I had seen enough movies or I talked to someone who was in prison before, but certain things I just knew: you don't ask anybody what thing you in for and how long you have. So Mec' and I, we never did that.

"Now in the South, they ask you anything... personally, felt to me like they are innately nosey. Northerners, we get this reputation for being aloof or not social and not polite. I feel like we get a bad rap and they get an unwarranted complement for being polite or, in my view, nosey. They don't say hello to be polite. They say hello to be nosey."

Mecca is eager to take up this line of thought, which surprises me a little, since he is usually reluctant to get into a blanket criticism. But he pitches in like they are basketball players making a clean pass. "I had that same feeling. We socialize differently. In the South they were always asking things like, 'What's your mother's name?' 'Where you from?' I had never been to prison before either, but having so many of my friends that's been in and out of prison, I kind of learned how *not* to ask anybody those questions, sometimes even stuff about where they come from. You could tell a person stuff, but you didn't ask. You give me the information when you want me to have it.

"I had to learn that they don't mean any harm here in the South. That's just the way they socialize. And for me, at that time, it was different because of my sentence. I knew that if I didn't learn how to adapt enough, to blend in, I would constantly be bumping into these walls and get into a lot of trouble. I do this, but in my mind, I don't know anybody here, and I'm not going to get to know anybody. The few guys that I did allow myself to connect with were all from where I was from, up North, like Scott-so. We had a connection. They see your movements. They might never speak, but if they see you in a sticky situation, they do come your aid. That's just unsaid."

"So did somebody connect you to Frank? Sort of pair you up?"

"No. I don't remember noticing Frank until he moved to the kitchen job and we were on the yard together. It has something to do with basketball. People ask me now, 'How did you get to know Frank?' And I say, 'It's like I been knowing him all my life.' Even when I just met him at Nash. My mother identified it immediately. At visits – we were in the same building, so we had visit at the same time – she and my sister picked up on it. It was like I was saying to him when he got to Nash, 'What took you so long to get here?' I really feel like spiritually, it was really, really the way it was supposed to be."

"Did that cause problems?" I want to know because even in minimum custody, in the calm of the workshop, I see men pay attention and tag this. "B.K." is from Brooklyn. A guy might be from rural Michigan, but in North Carolina he's "Detroit." An older guy who got out recently went back to New York, to Queens. The men were a bit awed when they told me.

"Yes, people noticed," Mecca says, both descriptive and proud. "Absolutely. Everybody else who I had been housed with became aware. They would say, 'Your man finally came!' – as if I was waiting on him. 'cause they saw how every moment, library, or store we would be talkin'. The store – it's called the canteen call – they would call over the loudspeakers for my side of the building. When my side is finished, they call for his side. But there's this small window of time. If they call my side first and I get in the back of the line, if I linger a little bit, they'll call his side for the canteen, and then he can come out and he'll be the first behind me. He and I keep letting everybody else get in front of us until the sergeant finally says, "You still out here? We called canteen is over. What's taking you all so long?'

"We would squeeze out every moment we could to the point that the administration knew – these two guys, they are inseparable. Which means there is going to be a flip side to that coin. Administration is thinking, we gotta watch these two guys. We're under suspicion because everywhere the officer goes, he sees us. He goes in the library... they're there. On the yard... they're there. I don't work in the kitchen, but I might ease over there to the back door just to get a word in with him."

"Yeah," Frank confirms. "What is this? If it's not a sexual relationship, then what is it? You guys are related or you guys are up to something."

This is a state prison so there are a lot of relatives passing through the same camp. This can be good or it can be bad. To cover their bases, administration has a slew of rules dedicated to limiting communications between prisoners, breaking up bonds, discouraging commitments that might inspire people to band together to move contraband, or even to plan an escape.

"What we have can look the same as some other guys who come from the same hometown or the same family, but it's not the same. So people tried to test it, to get under it. Frank worked in the kitchen. I worked in the clothes house. People would come to me with a certain issue with him. 'You know I was working with your man, Frank, and he forgot to take the trash out. What's up with that?' And I would say, 'Man, I don't know. You should go talk to him about it.' Because with us, there was no divide and conquer. When people saw that they couldn't penetrate what we had, they began to back up a little and respect it and then admire it. And even kind of envy it.

"Which is how our friendship became a real issue. In prison, from the inmate to the administration, they don't want to encourage genuine relationships. If it had been homosexual, leave them guys alone. They can go behind the building to get it on. We don't care because we know what they are doing. But when it's not, if it's a genuine friend, that's a problem, because in prison the idea is that people don't have real connections. It doesn't happen in prison."

Over and over again I have heard men say that staying away from other people is the best survival strategy. You never know who you can trust. This is a conscious part of the incarceration strategy, and it can be very destructive. A person becomes isolated in prison, that seeps out into their behavior with friends and family. Some men will even deny themselves visits and phone calls. A bizarre, monastic diet of unrelieved prison time and suspicion is going to cause big problems when they get out – and ninety-five percent of these people are eventually going to get out. This atmosphere makes closeness stand out.

"Guys would notice," Mecca continues. "Guys I had been knowing for a while, see that Frank is a lot further in my life than they were, and they would come and ask me about that and question me. 'Why are you closer with him?' In my mind, high school stuff. You used to sit here and eat lunch with me all the time, and now you go to the table where he is. But I can also be empathetic about it, because this is prison, and closeness is a more serious factor. We talk about it all of the time because it's a recurring thing. Somebody as dear to me as Scott-so, I love him with all my heart. But that was the issue for him, and he would say to me he couldn't understand how I can have time and love and respect and rapport with him and also with Frank. Like you couldn't be loyal to two people at once?"

"And honestly, I struggled with that too," Frank admits. "Like I said about that time I first saw him in the mess hall. Mecca, he has an attraction, and it's not physical per se. I refer to it as *the light.* I've never really met anybody that didn't like him or wasn't attracted to him. Or they might not like him, but they are still attracted to him. It's kind of like that cover that goes over the light. It's a shade, but bugs are still gonna go to the light, be pulled to it.

"So what I struggled with when we became close was how was it for me to be this guy that was taking up the space where everybody else wanted to be. I struggled with that because he and I were so close that I had no – what you call – no insecurities. He could still talk to as many guys as he wanted to, but other guys came and treated me like I was in the way.

"At the same time for me it was different than it was for Mec'. You would think we were two peas on a pod, but we were very different. Back then I didn't know what he was in for. I didn't know some of the internal decisions he had made about having a life sentence. I didn't have a life sentence; I had a long sentence, but one day I was goin' home. Mecca didn't know if he was ever going home. So our mentalities, internally, were different. I was much more suspicious.

"Example: in visit when he put me next to his mom and his sister, that was crazy to me. I didn't understand that. I would never do that. I don't trust anyone in this place. I don't care how nice he seems. I don't care if he's from North or South. None of these guys are worthy of what's between me and my mother. He might not have known it, but that was how Mecca put me to the test. When he called me over and he said, 'Hey, this is my mom. This is my sister.' Whoa! I know that I'm no harm to them or him. But to be knowing he even trusts me with that...

"And from that, introducing me to Mom and Cheryl, I got a feeling of who he is. I know he's not making light of it – like 'Anybody can meet my mother.' And I knew that now I had to be worthy in that. So that kind of accelerated what I would do back for him. That's when I learned to trust. Hey, this guy may be somebody that I could really, really trust."

Trust is a loaded word – everywhere, but especially in prison. Sometimes we will be having a discussion in the workshop and someone will turn to the others and say, "I don't say this to just anyone, but we are here, and I trust you guys." And maybe they will say something about their family or their crime or their emotions. Vulnerability is not something they feign, it's something they hide. For Mecca and Frank, the friendship is like a giant release valve, a form of freedom.

"Hey, but before I go on," Frank says, "There's a crazy thing I want to put in about how close we got to be back in Nash. There's a problem, and I got shipped to Caledonia. I am having a visit with my girlfriend at the time, and I have my head down on the table. I'm down, down inside, so down I can't keep my head up. Then somebody comes up to me and I hear voices behind me. It's Ms. Elmore, Mom, and Cheryl, coming all the way to Caledonia to see me. Seriously! They came and they continued to look after me, and I was not having an easy time.

"You gotta see Caledonia, you have to picture it. I will never forget when the bus took me to that place. The bus goes inside the gate, like *Shawshank Redemption*. The gate closes around the bus and the driver says, 'Last stop.' I'll never forget the sound of those words.

"When we got off the bus, I had to carry all my stuff. I had a good support system, so I had a lot of sneakers and personal property from Nash that you're not supposed to have in other camps or guys just can't afford. So other guys were looking at me and my bags of stuff and I knew it was not going to be easy. Caledonia meant doing some serious time, but Ms. Elmore and Cheryl looked after me."

Mecca raises the ante and asks, "Maybe we should also tell her about the time in seg? About how this came about?"

"Thinking about it now, we didn't have that much time together," Frank says. He's a strong looking man, but he has a perpetual wisp of a smile. Mecca complains that when Frank takes him out on pass, there are too many things going on. Radio. Cell phone. GPS. But when I am with them, we are just sitting and talking. The phone is quiet. Frank seems to have all the time in the world for Mecca. He exudes affection.

"We met," Frank continues. "We cultivated our relationship to where we knew we were close, and then I got in trouble. I got an institutional violence infraction. I got into an altercation with a guy that was just like me, not a fighter, but inside, things can get to you. When this fight happens nobody can believe it. These are two guys that you have to melt them down and pour them on somebody before they explode. It was a crazy, a crazy day.

"Things just came apart. It wasn't an incident – like planned or anything. We were both young. We were having fun and me and two other guys were laughing at something, and this person – I guess he was having a bad day, which is typical in prison. You could've got a letter the day before. You could have lost somebody in your family. You never know what these thousand men are dealing with. You never know. He took our laughing that we were laughing at him. And then he said something, and I took his comment as directed at me, but it wasn't. He was talking to the guy over my shoulder. Before I know it, we were fighting. Yes, fists. Definitely. And it gets worse.

"He hit me, got a really good shot on me, and I tried to retaliate. I missed him and hit an officer! Nash was so new that the officers at the time didn't even carry any type of mace or anything. This officer wasn't even security staff. He was a gym guy, a rec officer. He wasn't trained to break up a fight. He didn't know what to do or how to get out of the way. Instead of standing back, he moved in. The guy I was fighting with, he hit me really good. My eye swelled. There's water in my eye. I can't really even see. I kept throwing punches, and I thought I was fighting with the inmate. I remember I heard this vicious scream when I made contact. Then they grabbed me, and I was shipped to Central Prison for my nose because it was broken. They took me out of there so fast I still didn't know what happened. When I got back from medical, I found out that I had hit the officer. I'm going to lock–up."

Mecca says, "I was in disbelief, but I also knew that if he had gotten in a fight, Frank didn't provoke it. Whether you in prison or not – things happen. So it wasn't a big deal that he got into a fight. I was more wantin' to know what happened. Was he okay? When he goes to CP, everybody wanted to run up on me to be nosey. They think I would know what happened because of our relationship. Even staff that might have been off or shift changed, they come and ask, 'What happened to your boyfriend? He got into a fight.' I tell 'em I don't know, but I will know, and I'll decide how much information I want to share."

"After I got fixed up at CP, they shipped me back to Nash and I was in seg for six months!" Frank says, his voice tight with indignity, then shifting to pride. Mecca and Frank are not at all arrogant, but they are clear that they are not going to bow down under the weight of some southern prison protocol.

"There's four units at Nash," Frank tutors me. "The segregation unit is right behind the unit where we are housed. This is excellent for me. Seg is twenty-three/one: twenty-three hours in your cell and one hour for recreation, and that hour also has to include time for a shower if you want that. And everything I need that I can't get to because of losing my canteen privileges, now I have to find some way to get that stuff. There's this guy, the inmate that works everywhere, the trustee. He's housed down with Mecca and we connect through him. So all the time, six months, Mecca got stuff for me, and he could give it to that guy who would carry it to me in seg."

"This really forces the strength of our relationship, because one way or another we are living like the mob. We have to do this under cover," Mecca boasts. "We are covering our bases, but that raises more suspicions and more eyes on us because officers are expecting something. We have to work with that. But, listen, we got it worked out to a point where when Frank gets one hour for recreation, I could be at work...

"Whoa! We laughing now, but..."

I'm not sure if it's telling this to me or remembering it like old war heroes that cracks them up. Prison is odd that way. It's like a cross between a battlefield and high school. Petty risks laced with serious danger. Serious friendships growing in fields of long, empty, meaningless days.

"Now guess what!", Mecca challenges me, knowing I have no idea what is what. "I figure out that I could leave work and come stand on the yard right when Frank's on his rec time. The only thing separating us is the fence. A lieutenant or a captain could even come up to me at work and say, 'Your boy is out there right now. You want to go up there?' They might put it more indirect. Or they say it this way: 'Hey, take these paper towels to so and so.' I'm in the clothes house and all the supplies come from there, so part of my job can be running supplies all over the camp. When the officer says that, it's my cue to know that Frank is outside recreating. As crazy this might sound, it was to a point where I could even ask some high ranking official, 'Can you give Frank these batteries?' and he would do it. Because of the transparency. If they *see* what you are doing and how you are doing it, that's transparency. No problems goin' to arise from the situation."

"And when I am out in the yard," Frank explains, "I get my visit. I only come down for half an hour, because half an hour is for the shower, but I been up there, and they know Frank Walls a good guy. So some officers might leave me out longer. Of course, on the flip side, you can get an officer who'll say, 'When I take Walls out today, I gonna take him to the other side of the yard where he can't talk to his friend.' I have to yell around the building to a guy that's at the fence that could see Mecca and tell him I'm there. It's crazy stuff, but we did it all and we got through it. We adjusted to the situation."

"What did you do for the other twenty-three hours?"

I've heard the answer to this question a lot of different ways. In her book *Shakespeare Saved My Life*, Laura Bates is reading *Richard III* with men in solitary. One of the men, Newton, says, "Old boy Richard was right." Bates asks, "About what?" "Pacing. We all do it. Man! Wheee! Does Shakespeare get this insight?" Newton goes on to explain that if you cage an animal it might sit still for a while but when it realizes it's trapped, it starts to pace the cage. Newton explains, "When tigers start to pace, it's taken the wild out of them. The psychological shift is happening. We do the same thing."[7]

When I had asked Scott-so what it was like in solitary, he said, "You might try to read. You can't, 'cause the walls are closing in on you. You hearing things." I asked, "Did you do the pacing thing?" and he says, "Yeah. You sleep so much that you just can't sleep no more. I tried to stay up all night so I can sleep all day. And pacing. Yup. That's what you do. You get up. You lay down for a second. You jump back up. You go to the door. You look out the window. You don't see nothing, but you look out the window. All the other cells. You talk to the other guys. You can talk through the vent. You get back up. Say to yourself, 'Nothing going on.' You get back on the bed. Put the radio on. Cut the radio off. Get back up. Bed. Chow call. You eat the food. You try to save a little bit, 'cause it's a long night. Canteen... nothing like that. It was rough, but you learn so much when you in there. I learned how to boil my coffee. I learned how to 'fish.' You just learn so much in the Hole, 'cause you gotta survive."

Frank laughs when I recite Scott-so's monologue on the Hole. He has his own version, but he also adds that what saved him from boredom was journaling. "I wrote journals. I got that from Mecca."

Frank looks at Mecca. He'd rather forget solitary, forget prison. It's Mecca who is important right now, and Frank's mind moves from the fight to the man sitting next to him. He's free, Mecca is almost there and it's a beautiful warm day. Frank says, "I can honestly tell you that he really became a part of me. It's like us being the same person. Mecca, he's a few months older than me, that's all. And now how's this: Mecca gets out on December nineteenth and my birthday is the twentieth. Have to be his rebirth and my birth party."

He puts a hand on Mecca's shoulder and says, "What I want to say about Mecca in prison, for the record, is that he was in a place –

---

[7]   Bates, Laura, *Shakespeare Saved My Life* (Naperville, IL: Sourcebooks Inc., 2013), 37.

maybe it was because of his sentence or maybe just because of who he's been all his life – but he had it together more so than me. He taught me how to move, how to relate to the natives if you will. He might say, 'Look man you just can't...'But there was really nothing he sat me down and said; it was more that he showed me. There's always a greater level of respect for somebody who moves a certain way and teaches you that way. I'm walking side by side with him, so I'm learning the way a puppy does with its mom – that type of thing. How do they say it? Preventive maintenance? I'm seeing he does a lot of that so things don't come his way like they come in my way.

"For instance, I'm really frustrated. I'm working in the kitchen with all these fools – or I consider them to be fools – and I don't understand why I can't duck altercations with them. There is nothing that is becoming physical, but it's getting on my nerves. Mecca, he showed me that maybe it's about who I am, how I am acting and reacting. That's why I'm having the trouble. He shaped me up by being this kind of witnesses and asking, 'Why this? Why not that?' He's saying that even in prison, even in the kitchen, you have choices.

"So I start to look at my friendship with Mecca as having a level of responsibility. He kind of represents me when he does what he does. And I meet his mom. She has put her faith in me, she trusts me and she is someone who is making herself known to the administration. So I kind of represent her, and I couldn't have her come up there and I was in some mess. I learned she and Cheryl were going to support me regardless, but I was also responsible to them and that whipped me into shape.

"That's when we really became like brothers, and after he left, I became that guy, the person that guys needed to come to. I was the confidant. I had picked up this wisdom. And guys would ask, 'Man, how do you do this? How do you do the time?' And I was learning a lot of spiritual things. I have to credit Mecca with that. Him and his mom and his sister. If it wasn't for them, I don't know what would have happened to me."

This is the just what Scott-so also told me. I am learning that the expectations of people on the outside can be an inspiration, a reminder that you are visible. Isolation, pitting the men against one another in competition for limited resources and limited attention is a strategy. Divide and control. Food, medical care, space are limited resources. Rehabilitation might be the public face of incarceration, but inside it's all about control. In this scenario, families can be a critical counterbalance. They can help an incarcerated person remember he is somebody who has people rooting for him and looking to him to do his part.

Frank is struggling to figure out who he is, and Mecca has the advice he needs.

"Ms. Simone", Frank says, "the lesson is always, you have to keep it cool. It's contradictory. In prison they try to indoctrinate you to think that what you do is of ultra importance. Mopping floors. Important. At the same time, you are in prison where, supposedly, you are nothing. Too many people buy into that. I understand, because if you maintain a sense of your own personality, you mark yourself. Then you have another problem, because that stands out with staff and inmates. They'll be saying, 'Who do you think you are?', because you seem to be a thinking individual and that doesn't go over well. That makes them think, now we have to find ways to remind you and break you so you can be like sheep and just do what you are told. Go too far one way or the other and it's bad news."

"And that's part of the problem I was having trouble seeing," Frank says, straightening up a bit in his chair. "It's not just that I'm from the North. I've been places. My family is well traveled. As a young guy in the drug trade, I had seen money and what money could do and what money could not do.

"So in prison, I'm thinking, those guys working here – in a prison kitchen – you can't tell me nothing. Get out of my face. That was my attitude. My mom raised me to be well mannered, but that was my attitude and it resonated so that I had to be humbled. Mecca taught me that. They don't have to know what you think, Frank.

Every time we are in their presence, they don't have to feel like they are in competition!

"And sports! This is the part, like high school. Mecca doesn't watch sports. With Mecca, they could never say, 'Ah, your team lost.' But they could give that to me. All I do is say, 'the Nicks, the Nicks,' and they could get to me."

Coming from the outside, I thought prison would be a classless society. After all, everyone in there is at the bottom of the social pile. But I am learning that there is a subtle and complicated differentiation going on. Some men have education, some have no formal education but have gotten their GED and a college degree in prison. Some men are proud of families that hold themselves together penny by penny, some have no family or a string of baby mothers who are bitter or kids who think their dad's off at some mysterious job somewhere. They might even be proud of families that have to move on and see to themselves. Men like Frank and Mecca walk a fine line with their good education and steady canteen accounts, regular visits, and healthy collection of non–government issue athletic shoes. There are a lot of hours in a prison day, plenty of time to carve out differences.

"Another thing too," Mecca adds, grabbing onto this idea of social distinction. "This is a very key element. It's something he and I discussed. When I sold drugs, I sold drugs on the street corner hand to hand. I interacted with people. That taught me how to handle people. Frank didn't sell drugs that way."

"Right, right. Mecca is right. I'm selling a larger quantity to one person. I'm not dealing with the mother holding her baby and the young guy on the street. Mecca's dealing with everybody, on the streets, hand to hand. I went to colleges. Bought drugs in New York and then charged more for them other places. When I came to prison, I had no information on how to relate to the guys I was living with.

"I wasn't even on the ground in North Carolina. I was dealing interstate when I got caught coming through North Carolina from

South Carolina. I don't think I was angry in prison so much as I felt really marginalized. I felt like, for my age, I had seen a lot. I thought that everybody around me didn't know anything or hadn't seen anything. Y'all are hicks. Like that. I'm a respectful guy, but I learned that I exuded that.

"So in this friendship, I saw that he was having an easier time moving about. And I saw that, maybe they resented us the same because we were from the North, but based on the way Mecca was carrying himself, they couldn't make that an issue. With me, they could. Trusting too much in my intelligence to see anything about the other people around me. I was thinking, 'I don't have a problem with them, why do they have a problem with me?' Like I say, there was never any speech, he didn't even talk to me about it if I'm honest, he just proceeded in a way and because we were so close, I began to see that, wow, that works."

"And I would say that is something that I've done with everything I've done, not just prison." Mecca adds. "I sold drugs, but I never took on the whole persona of a drug dealer. So I can say that I kept my own way of doing things, across the border, my whole life. I went to prison. I had a natural life sentence, but I didn't get into none of the things that came along with that."

"Example," Frank says. "True story. It just came back to me, this specific instance when we were playing Scrabble, he and I. Early morning we played Scrabble and we talked like we are now, maybe all day long. We were playing and some huge fight broke out and everybody – I mean *everybody* – is going to this fight. I don't know who's fighting or what it's about, but prison is so boring that if something is happening, you get pulled to it. Everybody is gravitating to this fight, and I looked at Mecca to see if we were going to stop the game and move that way, and he just walked away!

"I said, 'Where are you going?' And he said, 'I don't want to see that.' That was one of the biggest impressions. Who's not going to the fight? You understand what I'm saying? It's like a bug to the light! What bug is going to the darkness?

"So Mecca was showing me... saying with his movements, 'This doesn't mean you any good. Do you understand that that's a choice? Forget what everybody else is doing. Forget what everybody else is saying. Why are *you* going to that fight?' And when I couldn't answer the question in my head – this is not a conversation we had; I'm just telling you that was the conversation right here in my head. Mecca went back to his cell, and you think I went to the fight? No. I would have felt dumb at that point. I went to my cell. And that's when I begin to ask, 'Why you fucking doing what you're doing? Why are you doing it?' Because at the end of the day, you don't have to answer to all of those people. Why is it a joy for you to say, 'Oh yeah, I saw it,' because they all saw it? I could take more pride in saying I didn't see it. Didn't want to see it because it didn't mean me no good.

"And I began to live in that. People could say, 'You're Black. You're young. You're handsome. You're in good shape. You have to like this.' But Mecca, I see that if he does something, he has a reason for it. That was a big lesson. I'm forty-six years old. I probably was twenty-three when that happened, but I remember that like it just happened! I remember we were inside the dorm and the fight was happening in the hallway. So you would have to go to the window to kind of look through it. And everybody's going to that hall. The officers are running. Everybody's going. Everybody. This is a time when you could do anything. Like they say, rob a bank when the Super Bowl is on – go in everybody's cells and take their personal effects. Everybody's tuned in. But we weren't. Mecca just walked to his cell. He wasn't going to be into the fight or these other opportunities.

"And once I learned that, I feel like it just changed everything that I was encountering. There were still ups and downs, but I finally got it and I never again had any problems dealing with the population or the staff."

"There's one more thing I want to tell you about," Mecca leans over and touches Frank. "It's about Bridgett."

Frank takes the bait. "Which is also how I ended up staying in North Carolina after my sentence. Crazy how things work. I thought I hated the South. Bridgett is my wife now. We dated in high school, and she graduated and went down here to UNC Chapel Hill, 'cause she has family down here. I stayed up North. When I got my sentence, it was maybe six or seven years since I had connected to her. Mec' and me, we always talked about our lives prior to coming into prison, so I used to tell him about this girl all the time. I used to tell him about a lot of girls, all types of girls, just like he did with me. But this girl I was so crazy about. I would be telling him about Susie or Janet, and he would say, 'No, tell me more about Bridgett.'"

"I sensed there was something special there," Mecca warms to another story in which his instincts are right on. "I sensed that. And when we were in a conversation, it was also more interesting to hear him talk to me about Bridgett, because it resonated with me. To me, Bridgett, that was the most wholesome relationship he had, and it reminded me of Keisha, my high school girlfriend who I'm thinking about in prison. In prison these kind of things keep you alive inside, talking about not just women but feelings for women."

Frank is right on the thread. "I'm talking to Mecca and having these cathartic sessions, and he convinced me that I had this girl and she had been crazy about me and I did bad. I let her down, 'cause I lied to her about myself. So he convinced me to write a letter. But I just assumed... She was smart. She was pretty. I just assumed she was married. Our friends are married, having kids, families. I knew she went to Chapel Hill, but I just assumed she was married with a family back in Jersey. So the only intention I had in my letter was to apologize, to say I had matured and was working on getting my life together and wish you the best. That was the *only* thing I wanted to do in the letter."

Mecca clarifies his own motives, "To make amends. I wanted him to make amends with this girl."

"So I write the letter and then a letter comes back saying, 'I was just on the computer looking for you,' and 'I'm not married.' What!!! She had graduated college, moved back up to Jersey and was working as an executive for Singular Wireless. She was an executive!"

These two men are not superstitious, but I can see that in prison they are as open as everyone else to omens, portents or strands of hope. Mecca showed me a prom picture of himself and Keisha. He's in a tux and she wears a very nice dress. She is like a moment missed, a close call with another outcome. Mecca has held onto her photo, but they don't stay in touch and, truth be told, he's pretty sure Keisha has moved on.

"When we would talk, Frank would keep me up past my bedtime – remember prison, the street, now, I'm in bed by eight o'clock – and my endorphins would go up. When he told me that he heard back from her and she wasn't married and all that, to me it was like, that's how it's supposed to be! We gonna move from this point. I was the happiest joker in the world, because I believe in that kind of stuff. True love. It's real.

"I thought it was awesome, because to me it reflected how things could go for me. I used to tell him that all the time. I said the only thing in the way of that in my situation is what's left of my time. I don't know how that's gonna go, but I'm hopeful. And I'm a hopeless romantic. I believe in love. I told Frank, you need to go for it. How can you not try to make amends? Initially, that was the only thing that I encouraged him to do. If you love somebody, you do that, and you let them go. But then it turned out even better.

"You want to hear something else real weird?" Mecca goes on. "When Bridgett did come to see Frank at Nash, several other people were coming in through the gate. I went down toward the visitation area to pick up trash. In prison that's a green light to go to anywhere. You get a broom and a trash bag, and they don't bother you. The area I was in was off limits unless you were actually doing some kind of work detail. So I'm in that area picking up trash, and I'm seeing the visitors in the line and I saw her. I had never seen her before, but I felt that that was Bridgett. When Frank comes back from visit, I describe to him what she had on. He said, 'Yeah, that's her.' I was just a guy with a trash bag, but I recognized her."

"And I asked her to marry me on the first visit! It was like almost fate," Frank pitches full force into Mecca's magical thinking. "After all this time, all that happened to me, all the years that have gone by for her to still be available and still feel that way about me! But there was a difference in her. She had grown up a lot. When I asked her to marry me, she didn't say yes, but she didn't say no. She said that she would answer me at a later time. She would consider it."

"And," Mecca places his stamp on the whole thing, "for that I had the ultimate respect for her. That said a lot to me about her."

"I had seven years more. I was at the mid–way point," Frank wraps it up. "Bridgett stayed with me for seven years. So while we are celebrating our ninth wedding anniversary next month, I look at it like we've been together sixteen years. Since we started, she didn't date anymore. It was just all about me. She moved down here at the end of my sentence. We decided to build a life here. And what's also crazy is that Mecca never met her. Soon after this a situation came up and he got shipped. So he never even met her at visit. He won't meet Bridgett until he's released."

"How does this end, your time together?" I ask. I'm always a bit mystified by these intense friendships. I can't shake the idea that everyone in prison is riding in a solo chariot, but then reality surprises me. It was not easy for Frank to go back into the prison to get his volunteer certification, and it's never easy for him to pull up to the gate and see Mecca walk back inside, but he has made a commitment.

"Way it ended at Nash, I'll never forget. One day Mecca doesn't come from his work assignment at the time he's supposed to. I creep down there. I've figured out how to move around. I say to my supervisor, the lady that did the mail, 'Listen I gotta go somewhere.'

They open the door. I walk down there, and I peek in the door and see Mec' being interrogated by the superintendent. I don't know what's going on, but he's in trouble. He goes to seg, and I can feel it... he's not coming back.

"Before he was shipped, before they even put him on the transport, I was writing to him in seg. I said, 'Man don't worry about it. Hold your head. They can't stop us. They'll never stop us.' That's what I said in that letter. We are in different facilities for more than seven years before I got to my date. But we wrote all of the time up until the day I got out of prison. As soon as I could, I go visit him. He had this life sentence, but I kept knowing he would get out! I knew inside me that he was going to get a MAPP. I told Mom and I told Cheryl he would receive a MAPP!

"One more thing I got to say about him and me to bring it full circle. I use the word preventive maintenance and we talk about chess. Mecca's always been way ahead. I pride myself on *playing* chess, but he is *living* chess."

"Say that again!" Mecca leans over to embrace Frank and then looks me dead in the eye. "That's the most painful, piercing aspect of my crime. That's the one time I took a day off. Like you say in sports, I took that play off. Man, it cost me. That's all it takes. That one time I took the play off and it cost me twenty-four years of my life. That's huge."

I watch them get back in Frank's car. I can see Mecca is already on Frank because Frank has his phone out and his GPS going, and the radio lifts up and fills the air with music. I'm not sure if Frank just does this or he does it to challenge Mecca. I see them laughing and arguing and Mecca reaching for the volume. I know they can't wait until this has a better ending, without the prison drop at the end of the day.

Chapter 8: The James Leone Experience

After being shipped from Nash, Mecca lands in Piedmont Correctional, referred to by its location, Salisbury. He has been in prison for twelve years. As far as he knows these are twelve years of a natural life sentence. He has figured out the things he needs to know to stay comfortable. What he can't figure out is what to do about the power of the state to move him around like a chess piece. Some men stay in the same camp for decades, but a forward–footed guy who gets too comfortable is going to find himself shipped. Get too friendly with the staff, with other prisoners, get too settled in the routine... it's time to move that man to another facility.

There's something else at play for Mecca. In addition to not liking any kind of constraints on his style of doing things, he is in a back and forth with himself about his father, Willie Elmore, who disappeared in 1983. Cheryl saw him fleetingly in that courthouse elevator on her way to pay a traffic ticket on the Virginia/North Carolina border, but none of his promises to be in touch have ever been followed up. No letter. Silence. Mecca admits he's been looking for a father figure for a long, long time; someone with high expectations and a personal code of discipline. He is up front about this, which is why, in October 2016, he says he wants me to meet

James Leone. Cheryl would say that search is a big part of what got Mecca tied up with the older men who drew him into dealing and gambling. Mecca would call these men "mentors." That's a difference the two of them have still not ironed out.

All I know about Leone at this point is that he was the officer in charge of the main clothes house at Salisbury and he is a former Marine. Mecca is visibly excited. He tells me Leone is the person who bumped him from being a solo flyer to a man who knew how to work for somebody else. He taught Mecca about holding down a job, setting an example for others, and taking on responsibility. He taught by authority and by example.

An important part of Mecca's story is the fact that he is aging out of his youth and becoming an adult while inside a prison. While time can seem to stand still, people do age and mature. It's easy to miss that transition, to think of people as caught in an ageless limbo. For someone who is imprisoned, the place invites a passive mode of living that reinforces this kind of protracted adolescence. Even people who are mature when the are convicted can respond to prison like petulant children. Every day is the same. Schedules never change. Staff come and go at regular intervals. Meals are served at a regular time. Men move in the yard in regular patterns. There's no scenery. There's no place to go to shake up the routine. As Frank said, fights are entertainment, something that's happening. Jobs are more like the chores your mom gives you to earn pocket change. It's not about working; it's about getting by.

This is fine if you spend your life in prison, but it is not very useful outside. That's why Leone is such an important person for Mecca. He treats his workers like adults, and he expects them to reciprocate. He treats them as if they are human beings who just might have a regular life some day.

Before we get to Salisbury, Mecca sets it up for me.

"While I was in Texas, my mom was calling everyone she knew to get me back," he begins. "Prisons do not appreciate this kind of concern; they call it interference. But finally I got my old job back and my old cell at Nash. What I didn't know was that Sergeant Hardy, an officer who had heard just a bit too much from my mom, had gotten a promotion. Now he's Superintendent Hardy, and he's in a good position to push me around.

"This isn't an instant kind of thing, but he's watching me. I saw it right from the beginning, and it just got worse. He goes by where I'm working buffing the floor. He backs up and looks at me and makes a beeline in my direction. He says, 'When did you get back?' And I say I got back Friday night. 'Really?' And he takes off back to his office like something had gone wrong.

"This same guy, when I was gonna get shipped to Texas, he was just the opposite. When my mom called Hardy, he came over to where I'm working and he said, 'I talked to your mother and she asked me what can she do to keep you from going to Texas. You got a great mother. I told her, out of my hands, ain't nothing I can do. I know you up here every week. I know you love your son. I would if I could, but I can't do anything, Ma'am, so you make sure you tell him that.'

"Listen to this. This is how these people are. Their word is nothing. I didn't leave for Texas as soon as they thought. The weekend came. My mom came to visit, and I asked her did she call Hardy.

And she said, "I didn't know what to do. I called Raleigh, I called everybody. Yeah, I called Hardy and he was real rude, like he got some kind of a kick out of me calling him, asking for his help. But I don't care. I want what I want and that is for you to not go to Texas. I got to a point where I asked him, did he know the story of Moses? And he said, 'Yes I do Ma'am, I go to church all the time.' And I said, 'My son will be back.'"

"He's one person to me, one person to my mom. You can't tell what these people really feel. It's all how they choose to use their power. This going on the whole time I'm in Nash. After Texas, Hardy is the superintendent and he doesn't like me, and he never likes how I got back. He doesn't like anything. He doesn't like the way I carry myself. Not good, but I got used to it, because that's how prison is:

somebody like Hardy having it over you for years, waiting for their opportunity.

"Finally, one day he calls me into his office. He has his handcuffs on his desk. This is unusual. I know the first thing when they know you going to lock–up is they are going to cuff you, because typically the guy's going to balk. He's going to get violent. But Hardy doesn't do that. He just leans back and says, 'Man, you know I studied psychology in college, and I can see something I don't understand here, so I'm telling you that you are goin' to lock–up. You need to call your mother and let her know that you gonna be in seg and let her know how visiting goes with seg.' That's non-contact visits by appointment only.

"He goes on, 'I see you every day. And I've done my homework on you. You've got this long sentence. You ain't never supposed to get out of prison. But nothing about you says that. I can't put my finger on you and that bothers me.' Hardy's a Black guy so it's not about race. He says, 'I've asked officers that I know are racist, that don't get along with nobody that's not their color, but when I asked them about you, they tell me good things. That's a problem for me. Sounds like you are manipulating my officers. I don't know what you doin', but I'm gonna find out and you going to the hole until I do.' Some white officer treats me fair, there must be something in it for that officer.

"Hardy puts me in lockup, and he figures it out. He will solve his problem by getting rid of the problem. He can do this. Doesn't need no justifiable reason. Then Hurricane Floyd happens, September 1999, and the whole camp is evacuated, and I ship to Odum. Hardy does not want me back. They move me to Salisbury. For Hardy, that's great. I am no longer his problem. For the next eleven years I am Salisbury's problem, and for the last six of those years, I am James Leone's problem. Which turns out to be one of the best things that happened to me in prison.

It's Halloween night 2016 when we pull up to Leone's house. As we get out of the car, Mecca drops his ambling style and assumes a brisk walk. This is the first time Mecca and Leone have seen each other since Mecca was transferred out of Salisbury. As soon as we walk in the door, Mecca brightens. He lights up in Leone's presence and stands up tall. I'll see this happen a couple of years later when Leone comes to the opening celebration at the Straight Talk Transition House that Bessie opens in Durham. It's a crowded event, but when Leone sees Mecca across the room, he taps the top of his head. Mecca immediately pulls off his trademark baseball cap.

Leone's of medium height with something direct and imposing about his presence. His face shows he's moved to see Mecca "free." There's a reciprocity between them – father and son and teacher and friend all running simultaneously, and clearly he holds Mecca in high regard. Right away I can see that Leone carries himself with authority that's set on a foundation of compassion.

The house is spacious and orderly and we settle on stools at the kitchen table. Leone begins in a very formal tone that makes me think this might not go as well as Mecca hoped.

"My name's James Leone. I started working at Piedmont Correctional in August of 1995 on second shift, progressed to the canteen, the inmate stores. I was there until 2003, when I was out on military duty. When I came back, I started working in the clothes house. That's where Elmore came to work for me."

"I was already in Salisbury before that," Mecca explains, "but I was working in the gym for a long time. I was in charge of the sports equipment and being scorekeeper for games. After a game, I was responsible for cleaning up. It was a good job. Met a lot of guys, but I could keep to myself when I wanted to. Had my own routine and my own cell. Then they had a problem and the kitchen was short of help. They have to feed everybody, so if they are short handed, they can pull help from other jobs on the camp. The programmer calls me into the office and says, 'Look, you gotta go in the kitchen.' Technically speaking, you have the right to refuse a job. Wanna sit in your cell. Fine. But there's a twist on that. Programmer says, 'You are coming up for minimum custody review and you don't go in the kitchen, we gonna say you refused a direct order. That's not gonna look good.'

"Getting reviewed means I get a chance to ask to be given honor grade, minimum custody. So I said I'd rather transfer. And they said, 'If we do transfer you, we still gonna put in there that you refused a direct order. So rule's rules: you gonna go in the kitchen. It's just temporary. As soon as we get some guys into the camp to run the kitchen, we pull you back out.' So I went in the kitchen against my will. And if you want to know what I didn't like about the kitchen, the answer is *everything*. The main thing I don't like about the kitchen is you work every day. You don't get a day off except on your birthday. And then everything else after that: the atmosphere, the food, the dirty pots, the scraps."

Mecca scrunches up his face in disgust, like the insult is washing in all over again. I can see why officials like Hardy did not like this in someone in their custody. There is a right to refuse work, but the men are not supposed to exercise that right. When there is pressure to keep services going, turning down a work assignment is not an option. Add in that no work assignment means no single cell, and no single cell means the prisoner loses that precious modicum of control over his or her life. Mecca is not in a position to choose.

"Where I work in the kitchen," Mecca explains, shaping a small map on the tabletop, "Leone comes through there all the time to get to where he's going. He runs the main clothes house. He knows me from working in the gym, and now I'm not in the gym. He said, 'What you doing in here? You working in the kitchen now?' I told him the story and said, 'Man, I gotta get out of here, and I know you probably be the only one to get me out of this kitchen.'

"Which is true, 'cause Leone's reputation was all over the camp. Leone said, 'I'll see what I can do. Right now, it's tough to get you out of the kitchen, but trust me, I'm gonna get you out of here.' And I know he's a man of his word. He's a Marine. He keeps his word.

"Shortly after that I get moved to a clothes house, but not his clothes house – the same prison, but a different part. Less stressful than the kitchen, but it wasn't for me. Leone saw me there and told me, 'Just be patient. I'm gonna get you to my clothes house. Trust me.' And soon after that I went in his clothes house."

Leone shifts in his chair and his face softens. He's serious, but it's mixed with the kind of nostalgia people have for a good war story. He says, "I have pull, but not enough pull to add a guy to my clothes house if there's no opening. When there is one, I don't just let them assign guys to me. I pick my workers. I ask the guys who already work for me. I take that to heart. I'm not easy to work for and they know that. I knew William, and I had seen how he carried himself. So with that and the word of the other guys, I put him in the next opening. And it worked out. After he started working for me, it soon became William's decision. I did the paperwork, but I let him say who I brought in to work in the clothes house."

"Now you gonna hear I call him William. I don't mess with prison names. It's part of my policy. I'm respectful, but I am not easy. In the clothes house dealing with me was ninety percent of the job. I'm demanding."

"*Demanding!*" Mecca rolls his eyes and jumps off the stool to stand at attention. "He's a *Marine*. I had to learn what that meant. A Marine – so it's: you do this, you do that, you wear a uniform? No, there was a lot more than that to it. He had these rules, standards, like we were doing something important. *Strict* is a good word too. Always saying it's not good enough. I wasn't used to that. I was used to deciding for myself what was good enough."

It's important to remember that on the street Mecca ran his own show. He did not have a crew and he was not part of a crew. In prison, he avoided any kind of "affiliation" – as he called it in Texas. He was willing to take risks for a man he trusted, but he kept his options open. This was good for his survival and peace of mind, but, at thirty-eight, he was still avoiding anything that forced him to cooperate, work in concert, weigh his own impulses or ego against the requirements of the job.

"Nothing was ever good enough working for me," Leone stands up with a puff of pride and casts his eyes around the kitchen and the living room. All is straight and orderly. He sits back down and straightens his back. "My name was known – probably throughout the state but mainly at Piedmont Correctional. Everybody knew who I was. And some people wouldn't come work for me because it was me."

"Whole time I worked for him," Mecca confirms, "people would say, 'I don't know how in the world you work for that blankety–blank. I would never work for that blankety–blank.'"

I suspect that Mecca's interest in the job was not hurt by the idea of doing something other men found harsh and too challenging.

Leone jumps in, "It wasn't just that I was demanding. It was everything. Everything! I followed the rules. I enforced the rules to the point – and I had to use this – to the point where I would embarrass somebody to make them follow the rules. You need to understand, I was in the Marine Corps Infantry. I really had no other facet of life. We were only trained to follow orders and to kill people. I hate to say it like that, but that's how it is.

"That's how I ended up in corrections. People asked, 'Why are you doing this?' And I said, 'Why not?' My only goal was to support my wife and son. That was it. I didn't care about anything else in the world, and if it meant taking a prison job, then it meant taking a prison job. And whatever job I take – 'cause I am a Marine – I do that job perfect."

Leone did finally leave Piedmont in 2016. He learned coding and software and works for Tata Consultancy Services. It's a good fit. It requires precision, and he's good at it.

I watch the two men volley. Mecca presents as very easy going. His eyes flash and he's never the first to speak. but inside he has a similar resolve. Not taking a plea. Not pleading guilty. These come from a similar place. I can see why surviving Leone holds a certain cachet.

"Yeah, if you worked for Leone," Mecca jumps back in, "they would be thinking, 'What's wrong with you to even want to deal with that?' Before I got in the clothes house, even though I never worked with Leone, if I didn't see him, I heard him. He was over there talking junk to somebody. He couldn't walk from here to there without running his mouth about something. Yelling across the yard. Just doing what he wanted to do. But me, I never had no problem with Leone. Every time him and me did talk, it would be brief. I say, 'What's up?' and he says, 'What's up with you?' or more often, 'You need to get off the yard' or 'You need to tuck your t-shirt in.' He was always telling people, 'Keep it moving.' Leone was just being himself. And even though I was an inmate, I was just being me. That's where we connected. We saw each other as just people. You work here. I live here. We kept it moving like that."

"I knew he had a good work ethic from the gym," Leone continues. "I knew the people that he worked for and I asked them how he was. I didn't ask the people in the kitchen, because I knew he was hateful about being in the kitchen. But people did tell me he's slick mouthed, which I already knew. You don't think you are slick mouthed?"

"I can be," Mecca admits. I feel more of that pride of shared defiance. These two men haven't seen each other for six years but they are immediately in synch.

"He was slick mouthed. I didn't have a problem with that. He ran his mouth, 'cause... you want me to be honest now?"

"Yeah, all the way." Mecca says.

"One, to make himself sound smarter, and, two, to get him out of whatever he was getting himself into."

"Some people say it's slick mouthed. I call it intelligent," Mecca interjects. "I didn't get in any trouble 'cause of what I said."

"No, he did not get in trouble for his mouth, ever. Not that I know of. But he wouldn't ever stay quiet."

This conversation is fascinating to me. When Mecca arrived in the workshop at OCC, he took a week or two to survey the scene, but once he saw some value in what was going on, he was going to say what he wanted to say. He was respectful of the other men but never pretended to go along if he had a different idea about things. In prison this is quite a balancing act. At first, I thought the other men would resent it, but Mecca showed an underlying respect and concern for other people that wiped out any leaning toward resentment. When Mecca was released, I expected there would be a gap, a hole in the conversation, but the group filled in. He took up space, but he didn't push anyone out.

"Yeah, I would give my opinion," Mecca picks up. "If somebody asked me what I thought about this and that and if it was different from everybody else, I said it, but in a way where it kept me from getting in the cross–hairs. But people – whether you get in the cross hairs or not – people don't like opinionated people, period."

"They don't. But I have to say that William was never detrimental to the purpose *ever.*" Leone puts his hand firmly on the table. "Yeah, he tried to resist. The eye rolling. He would try to walk away. I told him, you don't walk away from me, not if I'm your boss. I told him what I told all the men: you can have a thousand 'atta boys', but one 'oh shit' ruins it all. I learned that in the Marine Corps and it's true. True to life."

"I tried it all. I told him that I never had a boss," Mecca says – almost falling into eye rolling on the spot. "Never had nobody in my face yelling at me about what I did wrong when I didn't in fact do it wrong. So when he got in my face, I said, 'I'm outta here, man. It's my last day. I don't want to deal with that.' But I stayed for six years.

"I'm not lazy, but Leone had to teach me about work ethic. About responsibility. A lot of things I didn't really want to deal with – Leone forced me to deal with them. Washing those clothes means you are responsible for everybody's clothes. The guys you work with and all of the people in the prison. Doing inventory means you're responsible, and if the inventory's not right, he would say, 'That's your head, Mr. Elmore, because it falls back on me.'

"I didn't understand. I would say, 'I don't want the responsibility. I wanna just wash these clothes and leave.' And he would say, 'No, that's what you gotta do.' I resented that for a long time. Every week there was something else he would have me to do. And when something wasn't right because of somebody else – because real soon he put me in charge – I suffered for it. That was not right to me, weird, and I was not used to that. Now, in my jobs outside, I see how this works. And I see how other guys might not understand this. I tell someone to do something at my landscaping job and he be only half doing the job. I got to explain to him – and a lot of these guys I work with are also just out of prison – it's not about you. It's about doing the job."

Mecca laughs at himself and Leone cocks his head in pride.

"Leone told me, 'What you gonna have to realize is that in a leadership position, you're responsible for everybody else.' I didn't like that. I want to just be responsible for me. I got a sentence to do. I wanted a simple assignment, and I wanted it to be mine. Nobody else's. And he made me realize a lot of life is not like that, no matter how much you want it to be like that. That's one of the things that I learned.

"The second thing I learned was he helped me to be a better leader. We talked about Scott-so and Frank. I could see the attraction, but I did not see that as *leadership*. And now, in this clothes house, I don't want to see myself connected to the people there. But Leone broke that down and got me to see it differently. He said, 'A lot of these guys look up to you.'

"I'm resisting. I'm thinking, I don't want to lead these men. I don't even want to talk to 'em. But people did look at me and at how they saw me deal with humility with what Leone was telling me. That kind of helped them think about themselves, that's another thing I use at my jobs out here: if you have a boss, they get to be the first to decide how it's going to be done."

I can sense something more personal underpinning this conversation. Mecca is not usually quick to parade this kind of respect. He's looking right at Leone now. I'm hardly there.

"That first year, you would ask me questions like 'How was your visit?' or 'How's Mom?' and I would think, what did he just ask? Staff in prison don't show concern, don't treat you like some person they know. There's talk, but it's all on the surface. So I think maybe he cares a little bit. And that's when I began to receive his instructions differently. I see the human being he is, and he started to see the human being I was. That kind of changed the shape of it. I began to learn things from him, life skills, tools I had to use everyday. And it made my time easier. Before Leone, I didn't want to do anything for anybody, and I resented everything about the situation. Since I had to work to have a single cell, that was a problem.

"I remember it be time for work on Monday and I think, 'Dang, I gotta go to work. What kind of mood is Leone gonna be in?' 'cause it could be like coming into your house, and you see your couch is flipped over, all your dishes thrown on the floor. And you like, 'What happened? Somebody broke in?' No. Leone said that the pillow wasn't right and you gotta GI the whole house from top to bottom. That's what going to work was like when it wasn't right. And it was my job to fix it.

"And one more thing I have to tell you that he told me. We were walking to the hi–rise clothes house and he just stopped. Leone walks real fast, and we were behind, so we almost be bumping into him. He turned around and he said, 'What's taking you all so long? What's wrong y'all?' Then he looked directly at me and said, '*What are you doing in prison?*'

"That was an epiphany for me because, as many times as I had asked myself that question, the way he asked it to me that day made me think about it in a different way than ever before. *You're right. What am I doing in here?*

"That changed the shape of what I thought about myself being in prison. I never felt like I was supposed to be in prison so much as I kind of walked around the prison like I wasn't there. But when he asked me that, a light went on. *What am I doing here?*

"Mom says the time to prepare for leaving prison is the day you go in, but up 'til then I was not preparing for anything but the next minute in prison. And for Leone to say that... the way he said it let me know he cared about me."

"And I gotta say," Leone picks up, "I didn't know why he was in prison in the first place. I don't know to this day. But I could see he was smart, too smart to be wasting his life this way. Now, there's a reason I don't ask guys about what they've done. Back when I first started in the clothes house a guy asked me to look up something because he was coming up for honor grade or something. I happened to see what he was in prison for, and it made me change my opinion of who that man was. After that, I said to myself, I will never look at the record of another person who works for me, because I don't want my opinion of them to be swayed by what they did in life before I knew them.

"So I don't care about the details, but I do care about him, Mr. Elmore, as a person. *What are you doing with your life?*"

"He would call me 'Mr. Elmore.' That was big."

I see a connection now that I have witnessed in other men. It's the point in a prisoner's life where they cross over, where they de–incarcerate themselves. In his book *Solitary*, Albert Woodfox calls that chapter "Maturity." Woodfox served forty years in solitary for a murder he did not commit and for his activism as a Black Panther in Angola Prison. In this chapter Woodfox is just about the same age Mecca is when he meets Leone:

I believe life is in constant motion. Even in the prison cell with the numbing repetition of the same day over and over... By the time I was forty I saw how I had transformed my cell... I used that place to educate myself, I used that space to build strong moral character, I used that space to develop principles and a code of conduct. I used that space for everything other than what my captors intended it to be.[8]

Listening to Leone I see something similar happening to Mecca at Salisbury. He is outgrowing his street self and becoming a man in a new way, a way that is going to be very useful whether he is paroled or serves his full sentence. For Scott-so, in Texas, Mecca was the right teacher at the right moment. For Mecca, Leone is that teacher at that moment. He brings a standard, a level of expectation to the table. He is not a parent who looks the other way because the grades are good. He's not a father who promises to visit and never does. And, most important, he is not a person who is going to gloss over the ethics of what is going on. In the clothes house, Mecca's charm is an asset, but Leone requires real work to back it up.

"What was it that made me like certain guys?" Leone asks himself out loud. "They were more – I don't want to say cleaned up – but yeah, they were more cleaned up. You can be in prison and be just a dirt bag. But they carried themselves a different way. And I respected that, knowing where they were, how hard it can be to respect yourself. I was tough, but I didn't try to go in to work to make their sentence harder or longer. I went in there to do a job to put food on my son's table. Any problem I had with the job, that was my problem. I wasn't gonna make them pay for it. But I also wasn't going to go in there and bring them drugs or cigarettes or let them be sloppy in their work. I expected them to be perfect, and they knew that.

"I expect perfection. My wife will tell you that right now. That comes from the Marine Corps. There were times that William did not understand the meticulousness I wanted, the value of it. Say the button wouldn't be buttoned on a pair of pants. It would just get thrown on the floor."

"Yeah!" Mecca jumps in. "No lie. We have shelves of pants because we have hundreds of people that we provide pants for. Each person gets at least four pair of pants. So there's four hundred people there.

---

[8]   Albert Woodfox, *Solitary*, (Grove Atlantic, 2019) 206.

Four hundred times four is sixteen hundred pairs of pants! For some reason Leone might go look through the pants. See if they folded right. Label up so you could know what size they are. You come to work Monday morning and all those pants are knocked down on the floor."

"On the floor," Leone confirms.

"All of them."

"Because there wasn't a button on one of them," Leone says.

Mecca raises his eyes to Leone. "Let me get this off my chest while we here. I don't sew, so I'm not responsible to put buttons on the pants."

"You are still responsible," Leone affirms.

"Guess what? I am responsible to make sure that the other guy put the button on the pants, but to do that I have to deal with that guy, the other inmate. Now I used to tell Leone, 'When you go home Friday night after work, I'm stuck here with these guys all weekend.'

"And he said, 'I don't care. You deal with it. You figure out how to deal with it.'

"So how do I approach a man about this button? How can I think of a way to get you – this inmate – to do your job and not seem like I'm an officer? How do I get that out of you without you thinking I'm your boss? I'm not your boss, but I need you to do this, 'cause I gotta hear Leone's mouth if I don't.

"Same as now. I'm a manager at my job, and I gotta hear my boss Wendy's mouth when guys are doing this landscaping and it's not right. I don't cut your check; I'm a middleman. So I learned through the clothes house by trial and error how to get you to do something that you're supposed to do for everybody's good.

"It came at the right time, the clothes house, at the right time in my life. The work ethics that I learned from him were transferred to what I had to do at other camps, in work release, in my job after prison. I didn't know anything about the work I was going to do when I got my work release or any other job – how to cut up a hog or how to care for a yard – but the way I did my work, my work ethic, spoke for itself. People were willing to teach me what I needed to know."

"And there were rewards," Leone adds. "The guys knew – even though they heard the things like, 'Oh, you working for that guy' – there were perks in working for me. A thousand rewards. The biggest reward was they weren't going to be messed with *ever* by another inmate or by staff members. I'm not gonna say they were untouchable, but a staff member would have to deal with me if something happened to them."

"Yeah. We're clothes house," Mecca claims this badge of honor. "It was like 'Okay, you one of Leone's boys,' and light–heartedly they would just leave us alone. I guess because they felt like Leone ran his operation in such a way that we were in check and we were in step, in line with what we were supposed to be doing. And when we weren't and somebody found out, the first thing they would say is, 'Leone know you doing these things?' Then you got to deal with Leone when he found out.

"And once staff knew I worked for Leone, if they did come aggressively to bother me, it would be dealt with that way: 'What you doing with this extra t–shirt?' 'I work in the clothes house.' 'Which one? Two–oh–eight, with Leone?' 'Yeah.' 'Leone know you got this extra t–shirt?' 'Yeah, he does know.' 'Okay' If there's a problem, staff's not gonna get involved, 'cause Leone's probably gonna be worse than them about it.

"But remember, it's an earned perk. There's some guys who worked along with me in that clothes house that were so reckless and ridiculous that Leone left them to swim in the ocean with the sharks on their own. 'I'm not gonna help you. You lied to me. You stole from me.'"

Leone leans in conspiratorially, "If you're using those t–shirts to sell around to other guys, you are going to pay for it."

"Here's the conversation I would have," Mecca says, looking sternly at me. "Listen. Leone will give you anything you want. Don't steal it. If you do steal anything and he finds out, you gonna be in worse trouble. If you can handle that, I will vouch for you to get the job.' And some people still stole, because it's prison and that's how guys are. The liberties of working with Leone – it's either gonna bring out the best or the worst in you, 'cause he's gonna sit back and he's gonna either let you hang yourself or allow you to step up and be a better person."

Leone sounds tough, but I can see that he's also introducing an alternative for his men. This is unusual in prison. It's also very valuable. How can a person function in the outside world if he can't make judgments about what is going on around him? That may sound like a crazy thing to say about prison hustles, but in the bigger picture these trivial choices are practice for making big choices.

"If they were doing something wrong, I already knew it was happening," Leone explains. "I'm not stupid. I know there isn't a job in the camp that doesn't have a side hustle. And theirs was selling clothes. But when I said the store was closed, that meant there wasn't nothing coming out of my clothes house and they knew that. And the guys that they 'owed' stuff to? It was over. The store is closed."

Mecca fills it in from his side. "The guy paid for these t–shirts, and since Leone closed the store and it's Friday and this customer has got a visitor Sunday, he's gonna ask, 'Where are my t–shirts?' And you are going to have to deal with that."

"Right," Leone concludes. "Everything was under my control. I made sure of that!"

"Which was another lesson for me," Mecca says. "It taught me that if you work for, befriend, live with, or have somebody that has your back, you should be transparent with that person. Because they can't help you if they don't know the Truth. If I was honest with Leone, he had my back. He taught me the value of that. That worked in my favor. When there was a time when I needed not to do anything – to stay clean, but maybe I didn't know it, he knew it 'cause he was staff. He'd say, 'Look, not now. Not today.' Then, as much as I might have wanted to do it, say provide some t–shirts, I trusted his word. I knew that if I did do it and something happened, he would not have my back. It taught me the value of your word."

Leone's son Jimmy passes through the kitchen on his way out. Mecca watches Leone talk to his son. When Jimmy's gone Mecca says, "Another thing Leone taught me about was from his relationship with Jimmy. I would say, 'What do you think makes your relationship with Jimmy so good?' 'cause the way my father was, I'm always wondering about this. And he said, 'I'm accessible to Jimmy. I always keep myself accessible. He knows that I'm there. He can reach me when he needs to.'

"I understood that because Leone was that way with me. Accessible. Not something I had experienced from my father growing up. If Leone was working at the camp but maybe not in the clothes house and I had a situation not even relevant to the job and needed somebody to handle it if he could, if he was on the compound anywhere, they would page him and say I wanted to talk to him . He could be going out the front door, he would U–turn and meet me in the back lobby and say, 'What is it?'

"This was something I had not experienced before. Maybe I got a visit coming up. They be here tomorrow for a visit and they're not on my list. And he would say, 'What's their name? On my way out, I get it done.' And I would get my visit. Stuff that he didn't have to do. He's putting his credibility on the line for *me*.

"And it's different from the street. At Piedmont Correctional, I don't have any control. In the streets, you can call some shots; you can use money to get something done. In there it was just your word and your character. Dealing in the street – if people don't like what I ask them to do, they do it anyway. 'How much you want me to pay you to get that done?' Money and it's done. But in prison, it's your word. That has got me out of several situations.

"Another example. Say I was talking to too many female officers. Leone would get on me and I would say, 'Are you serious?' 'Yes. You gotta slow down.' See, I would talk to them, male or female officers but especially the females, because they come to the clothes house to get their uniforms. When they come there, they hear it, the way Leone's talking, and it's like we are in the ballpark somewhere and I'm not an inmate and he's not an officer. When new officers see that, they kind of warm up to that. And when they start work and see me on the floor I live on, maybe some female officer... guess what you gonna do when you see me? You gonna be chatty. But then other officers see that, and they say, 'What's that all about? Why's she always chatting with him?' And it can be trouble."

"My opinion," Leone is standing up when he says this, "is there should *never* be a friendship between an inmate and a female officer, because it's gonna end up bad. It always will!"

"And this is related to another thing. I remember one day Leone called me into the office and he told me to close the door and sit down. This was about my ninth or tenth time coming up for honor grade. I had no infractions. I did my job, but I kept getting turned down. I still remember how you said it: 'Man, you look closer to getting it this time than you've ever been. I'm looking at your stuff and it looks real good. You might get it this time. You know what your problem is? This is the problem: *You're not in prison enough*.'"

Mecca flashes Leone a smile.

"And I said back, 'What you mean by that? You mean I don't break my back enough?' 'cause I would talk to staff, male or female as if I was talking to a human being. Respectfully. Cordially. But you can't do that in prison. You can't be talking as if you are equals. Looks like manipulation. Like you have some plan in mind. I did that when I talked to people, and it didn't go well for me – in more ways than I probably know. He knows better than I know."

"It did not go well for him. I didn't have a problem with you, but other people had a problem. *You are not in prison enough.* You don't carry yourself enough like you should."

"He would warn me, 'Sometimes you gotta tone it down a little bit.' And I would, and sometimes I would question that."

This makes sense to me. I have seen Mecca move around the prison camp like a shadow, but I have also witnessed the way his posture, his self assurance can look like superiority. This is especially true in the prison yard, where men tend to amble around as if hunching down a bit would make them invisible. You don't necessarily have to be doing something wrong to get a write–up; you just need to look like you might be doing something wrong.

"The way he carried himself," Leone continues, "it was asking people to say, 'Who does he think he is?' Remember, I'm not the only one making the decisions. My eyes are not the only ones that are on him."

"Leone, you helped me learn that it's not that it's *wrong* but sometimes it's not beneficial to carry myself like I do. Sometimes it's offensive to people, because you seem that you are not being humble and respectful. I don't like that, but I understand that it is real."

"He was extremely self–confident, and that doesn't always play well in prison."

"I haven't told you this, Leone, but I'm telling you now because it's a big part of who I am. You don't talk about this stuff in prison – your crime, your trial, but I'm telling you now. When I went to trial and I sat in that chair and I had to speak my Truth to a jury that was not my peers and I got sentenced, that changed the trajectory of how I felt about power. I knew if I could get on the stand when my life hung in the balance and speak my Truth, I was never not going to speak it. I don't care if it's a superintendent or lieutenant or captain or officer. From that day, in prison or out, I was gonna speak my Truth.

"But Leone, you showed me that I was going to have to also learn to be very wise about how I spoke. He would tell me, 'That's enough.' As a – I'm gonna use the word – as a *friend* he would tell me that, and I would grit my jaw and walk away. Because he knew things from a side I wasn't privy to.

"These people are working in the prison, but they don't know me. They come through a room with their bars on and they want everybody to stand and salute. Sometimes I would keep doing my job. Not being rude or anything, but you a man like me so I am going to treat you like just another person. In that environment, they don't want you to think like that.

"It's a fine line. I've been blessed to have people in my life like Leone who cared about me enough to say, 'Hey, if you do that one more time, you gonna cross the line and be stupid. You need to stop right there.' Say I had stayed in the kitchen or some job like that. Could have been trouble. I probably wouldn't have learned the lesson, because in prison nobody would have cared enough to try to teach me. Now, for some reason, Leone thought enough about me to teach me the things that I needed to learn for me to have my MAPP and be out of prison."

"And we had a good time together," Leone breaks in. "I looked forward to coming to work because of him! He made my day go by easier."

"We talked about everything. Race. Religion. You name it, we talked about it. Everything. And candidly talked about it!" Mecca adds.

"We could joke around. I would tell William, you are so black, you're purple!"

"Blurpurple. Very rude. Lotta words I wouldn't say in private. Wouldn't say in front of Simone."

Leone leans back and laughs. "This is probably the longest conversation he's ever heard me talk that didn't have so many expletives in it! I'd ask him, 'What about Black Jesus?' I don't care about race. I joked all the time with him about white, Black and everything like that. That's why I think that when jokes come from me about race, they didn't bother guys. Out of somebody else's mouth? They'd have been stabbed. There were a lot of officers who were racist, so there was tension. Salisbury was maybe eighty–twenty. Eighty percent Black. There were two Mexicans, the father and the son. Two Mexicans in the whole prison and no Asians. But we understood each other, and we had a great time."

Mecca leans toward me and says in a conspiratorial whisper, "When Leone comes back to work Monday, everybody's setting up. This is when Obama was president. He would say, 'Mr. Elmore, I gotta ask you a question. I was sitting at home this weekend and I heard this song come on the radio, and the song was like– "My president is black, my Lambo's blue." Do you know anything about that Mr. Elmore? What kind of bull crap is that? Do you listen to that?'"

They are both laughing all over again at the old joke. Mecca puts on his professor's hat and says to us, "My lambo is blue means the Lamborghini that I own is blue, and my president is Black. That's how the song goes. It's by Young Jeezy.

"People would hear us talking like that and they would say Leone was a racist. If they heard me talking back, then that would make it more confusing. I'm an inmate so if I do have an opinion, I'm not supposed to say it out loud. But my point is, Leone would always play it like I was some kind of authority on everything Black people did. So I shifted on him. Whenever I found something with white people, I say, 'Mr. Leone, I got something for you. What's up with this?' Now if Donald Trump was in office then and we were in the clothes house, it would have exploded. He would have had to answer to all the crazy stuff that Donald Trump says and does."

They begin to recreate their banter, going back to the one good thing in that bad situation.

"All day long back and forth," Mecca says. "Except when it came to Tom Brady. That's one thing we have in common. We both like Boston."

"Greatest Quarterback Ever."

"The Celtics and the Patriots."

"Larry Bird wasn't white; He was clear!"

We all laugh and then the room gets kind of quiet. Mecca breaks the silence, "But how we got along also could be a problem. I think that they – the administration – felt like, because of how Leone pulled me out of the kitchen and kept me out of there, they always felt something else was going on. Nobody ever gets out the kitchen like that. The kitchen is like..."

"It's Fort Knox."

"And once I was in the clothes house, all those years, if I stepped out of line, Leone would always tell me if there was a problem. He might say, 'You have too many pair of shoes. The captain said something about it.' And Leone would have my back.

"It worked real well for maybe seven years, and then it didn't. I got transferred, pulled out, and even my mom calling him, nothing could make it work."

Because, as Mecca keeps reminding me, prison is prison and the whole point is to never let you forget that for a minute. Which is a huge paradox. How are you going to survive a long sentence, a life sentence, unless you find a way to comfort yourself, to make your peace with the situation. But the whole point of prison is too keep you uncomfortable, on edge, clearly in the hands of the state.

"Yeah, I tried, but it got out of my reach. I was good in the camp, but when they transferred him, there was nothing doing," Leone says. "I didn't know Ms. Elmore. I've never met her yet, but I talked to her on the phone, and she was not going to let it go easy. She kept calling, and I kept trying to get him back. Then he got honor grade, but she still kept calling. That's how I followed him. Knew when he got his MAPP and moved to Orange. When he got his release."

Leone surveys the room. The place is quiet and safe. He leans in close and wraps it up: "And now William is out and I'm not doing that job anymore and it's a new day."

Chapter 9: The Law From the Outside In

Doing time is more like a maze than a straight line. It's a vast field filled with different mazes that intersect. While Mecca is struggling to manage himself inside prison, Bessie and Cheryl are struggling on the outside. What exactly are you responsible for if you are not the person who committed the crime? What are the boundaries?

They make a pledge to visit Mecca every week. Bessie sets up a mini university for Mecca with reading lists and discussions to keep his mind alive. But good conversation and deep thinking do not solve the bedrock problem: how do you get a man out of prison when the official sentence is life with no option for parole? Difficult question, but as Bessie and Cheryl insist, "From the beginning we knew Willie would get out; we just didn't know when."

I got to know Bessie at a meeting of the Straight Talk Support Group where she sat in a circle with friends and family of people in prison, and they talked about the logistics, emotional and technical, of staying connected. That group became a school for me, a class room where I learned about the other side of incarceration: the people who are not in prison but are fiercely bound up in the system. Cheryl and her husband David were at that meetings. I also met the parents of one of the men attending the prison workshop and a woman trying to shepherd a son with mental illness through his prison time. Moved by their struggles, I joined the group's board, and, when Bessie decided to open the Straight Talk Transition House in 2018, I served on the advisory board.

It's February 2018 and I'm sitting with Bessie in her office at the Transition House. I've been pushing her to talk for some time, but she keeps putting me off. Now I've decided that there are too many missing pieces in the oral history's chronology and I need her to fill them in. I am at the point in my chronicle of Mecca's saga where he has been to Central Prison, Caledonia, Eastern, Nash, Texas, and Salisbury. In 2011 Mecca is shipped from Salisbury to Brown Creek, where his petitions for honor grade are turned down again. I want to know how they finally moved from this limbo to Mecca being the man with a MAPP I met at OCC in 2013. What did the legal battle for Mecca's freedom look like from outside the fence?

Our conversation begins at the beginning, when Bessie leaves Georgia, moves to Raleigh and starts looking for an attorney to take Mecca's case. "I had chosen Carlton Fellers, who was in Dan Blue's office, but he was asking twenty-five thousand dollars, forty-two thousand in 2018 dollars. That's a lot of money. Or seemed like it was a lot of money. It's hard to look back at that decision from what I know now, but back then I didn't know how the system worked. There was also a part of me that did not want to believe that William could be charged with murder. I couldn't accept that this was happening to us."

When I hear Bessie say "us," I am reminded that Mecca's arrest, legal case, and incarceration is definitely a family affair in her eyes. Never for one moment do she and Cheryl treat this as Mecca's problem. But didn't Mecca dig this hole for himself?

In his book *The Master Plan*, Chris Wilson describes the way his own family slowly dropped out of the legal battle. His mother hires a lawyer, but Wilson thinks that being strong means being tough. Most of the other young men have a public defender. Isn't that the cool thing to do? His family gets worn out.

I was going down and I knew it. My family knew it too. My mom visited less and less, and she started complaining about the money. She had to double–mortgage her house because of me. She had to pay for prison phone calls. It's *a burden*, she was saying, *having you for a son.*

She never brought Darico [Wilson's younger brother], like I was a burden on him too.

I called my father three months in. I don't know why. I needed something, I guess. The first thing he said to me was, "How could you kill somebody, Chris?"[9]

Wilson's story reminds me that there is a wide arc here. Some families double down; some families cannot. At Straight Talk Bessie encourages people to give support, but I see that she also respects their need to establish limits. For Bessie and Cheryl the limit to what they will do is barely visible. Bessie resumes her narrative.

"Susan Edwards was the D.A. and when she discovered that I was entertaining hiring Mr. Fellers, he told me that she said to him, 'If you are going to take the case, then I know I'm gonna lose.' But we couldn't come up with the money to hire Mr. Fellers, so we were assigned a public defender, Joe Knott."

I drift off for a moment and think about Joe Knott. The summer after Mecca was released, I made an appointment for us to go to Knott's office in Raleigh. By then he was no longer a defense attorney and had made a place for himself on the conservative side of North Carolina politics. The first time I called, he told me he didn't even remember the case, but I said, "Think on it." When I called back, he reluctantly agreed to meet, saying, "Yes, I remember the case now. He refused to take the plea." The day before the meeting I read in the news that Knott had been a force behind closing down the UNC Center on Poverty, Work and Opportunity, headed by law professor Gene Nichol, whom I ran into one day at a coffee shop in Chapel Hill. I was curious what he had to say about

---

9   Chris Wilson, *The Master Plan* (New York: G.P. Putnam & Sons, 2019), 64.

Joe Knott. I told him about this oral history project, summed up Mecca's story, and explained that Knott had been Mecca's public defender. Nichol pushed his chair back and said, "Joe Knott, a public defender? I don't believe it!" He was not surprised that Mecca's case did not go well.

When we got to his office, Knott met us dressed in a blue and white striped seersucker suit that reminded me of a character in a Tennessee Williams play. Tall, built strong and thick, and with a firm handshake, he was polite and told Mecca he was glad to see that he had done well. Knott said he admired Mecca's community work, talked about his own church work, and then repeated his disappointment that Mecca had not taken the plea. Mecca repeated his refusal to plead guilty to intent. Knott repeated his opinion that a plea would have been the way to go. He refused to talk on tape. We took a photo and left.

"Do you think I'll hear from him again?" Mecca asked. He still wanted Knott to see the case from the other side.

"He talked a lot about God. Maybe he'll rethink it," I said dubiously. We never heard from Knott again.

Bessie pulls me back into the present. "So now, post conviction, I had to figure out what to do. I wanted to look for any loophole. One of them was a Motion for Appropriate Relief. I wrote a letter to Judge Prior in the Court of Appeals and spent a lot of time talking to different attorneys, to anyone who would listen to my theories. I had my own little criminal law book, but it was just theory and hypotheticals. What if?"

In her research Bessie pulled together a picture of the night of the crime, looking for missing information, new evidence. "My theory was based on all of the confusion that was going on that night: other people firing a gun, the back door of the van coming open and the evidence that someone had removed the gun William was supposed to have fired from where it was. The gun that they had in court was not *the* gun. Some guy got rid of the gun, moved it from where it had been left after the shooting.

"I was becoming like a Columbo looking for anything to prove that my son didn't do this. And I think my ego got in the way, because I just couldn't imagine that my son could do what they were saying that he did. I needed to satisfy something in me. To say, no, not my son. He's not this person that you guys are portraying him to be. He's just this innocent kid.

"It took me five years to get to the point where I knew we could not reverse the verdict. It cost time and money, because even when I went to talk to some of the lawyers, I had to pay them. Thomas Maahr charged us seven hundred and fifty dollars just to read that transcript. I hired a forensic pathologist to refute what the pathologist had said in court. Dr. Radisch was her name. Amazing I can remember that. In her report she proved that it was a clean entry wound. Bullet went in and came out. And she showed that this injury should not have led to this man's death. I couldn't understand why the other man in the van wasn't charged with anything. Because he created this situation."

Mecca has talked about this before. Why didn't the man driving the van go directly to the hospital? Probably because he stopped to get rid of the drugs and guns first and by the time they got to the hospital, the victim was dead.

"I was trying everything." Bessie says, her voice growing frantic. "We hired a private investigator to do a re–enactment. William had to relive the whole thing, and I think that was very hard for him."

"How did you find the private investigator?" I ask, remembering that Bessie did skip tracing in Georgia.

"North Carolina made it really clear: even being a skip tracer you have to work under a private investigator who's licensed. So I looked in the Yellow Pages for one and hired Mr. Hilton. He was from New York, so I figured he would know more angles than a private investigator from here. For the Motion for Appropriate Relief – it's almost like habeas corpus – you are seeking relief based on new evidence.

"I am doing all this to keep our hopes alive, but Cheryl is getting annoyed. She didn't feel like Hilton was getting enough 'loot.' We have the bone, but he's not putting enough meat on it. I told her, 'Yes, he is. And it's not your money. It's my money. I'm paying for this.' We didn't argue over it, but her point of view was that she knew more about her brother's activities than I did. To be honest, some stuff I didn't want to know.

"When I came to Raleigh to prepare for the trial, I talked to another attorney, Butch Wilson, about the case and he told me about Thomas Loflin. He was an attorney, someone who might be able to help me with my case. After the trial, I would drop by Loflin's office and talk to him about my theories He would give me these little assignments, and I would go back and pull out my law book and look at different cases. I would go to Central's Law School [NCCU] and engross myself in reading about different cases."

"Was Loflin doing this pro bono for you?"

"Yes. I think he was curious about me. 'Who is this woman that comes in my office? She really doesn't know what she's talking about, but it's piquing my interest. Motion for Appropriate Relief – how does she know about that?' Butch Wilson kept pushing me to use Mr. Loflin, saying, 'If Loflin can get it back in court, then I know I can win it.' Cheryl was the one that finally hired Loflin to work on William's case, gave him the money.

"So now we had hired Loflin, and he needed more information from Danny, the young man who got rid of the gun that was supposed to have been used to kill the man in the van, and so the private investigator, Hilton, had to go interview him in a prison up in Morganton. Loflin wrote out a series of questions, and if Danny answered correctly, then we had a very good chance, because in the trial they never did produce the actual gun to do the ballistics. But Danny gave the wrong answers, so that was more money wasted."

I can see that going over all this not easy for Bessie, but she is determined to get her side on the record. In addition to the ongoing legal battles, there was always more to do to advocate for Mecca in prison. It was at about this time that Mecca got shipped to Texas, and that experience provides a very clear window into Bessie's juggling act.

"When William calls me about Texas, I go to Loflin and I say, 'Do something!' But he tells me he can't do anything. I'm angry. 'Why you can't do anything?' And he says, 'There's a lottery and they can pick whoever they want.'

"So I decide to call Raleigh. I called Franklin Freeman's office, because he was head of the Department of Corrections at that time. He wasn't in, so I got George Lyndon. George Lyndon turned out to be the best thing that could have happened. I told him why I was calling, who I was, my son's name and what I knew. George was looking at his computer the whole time I was talking, and he had pulled up William's record. He says, 'I get calls like this all the time.' And I said, 'Never mind that. William shouldn't be going to Texas.' And he said, 'Give me your number and I'll give you a call back.'

"The dates are very important to me. I remember it's August because I am taking care of my nephew Jamar, who is hearing impaired. I have Jamar and his sister Keisha, who is only four. They are my sister Cora's children. Jamar wanted to go to the model secondary school for the deaf in D.C. and the school wanted to interview him. I need to take this kid up to the school, but I need to deal with George, too. So I take Jamar and Keisha and we drive up to D.C. I can check my messages, but that's all. This is before cell phones. They interview Jamar and we drive back. When I get back there's a message from George, but it's too late to call him back.

"The next day I call George and he says he is working on the Texas thing. Then I get a message from the school saying that they have accepted Jamar and he has to be back in D.C. Now I have to run around to get all of his stuff ready. It's like enrolling in college. You need clothes and things for your dorm. So now we are all headed back up to D.C. They give us a little hotel–type room so we can stay there while we get the Jamar enrolled. It's part of Gallaudet.

"But I ran into a snag because Jamar had disability, so he gets Medicaid, but they won't accept that at the school. I call my job at the women's shelter and tell them what's going on. They know about Jamar and Keisha and everything. My supervisor was extremely good to me. He said, 'Okay, Bessie, what we are gonna do is, we'll add him to your insurance, fax the paperwork, just so he can get into the school, and then we'll take him off.'

"That was a whole day of running around. And all the time I'm calling home to check for messages from George on my answering machine. It was crazy!

"After I leave Jamar in Washington, it's September and George and I are talking every day! He would say, 'How are you doing?' I would say I'm doing good and ask how's things going. And he would say, 'I'm working on it.'

"William is calling me from Texas every day! 'Mom, what's going on?' He's telling me how terrible it is. They have to bring in water. And it's hot there. And *aarugh*!

"Finally George calls and says, 'William's going to come back.' And I'm, 'George, that's so great!' And, I love this part he says, '*Don't tell him.*' But when William calls me, I say, 'Don't tell anybody. Don't say anything, but you are coming back.' Bessie laughs as she says this.

"Now it's October, and George asks me, 'Where do you want him?' And I say, 'Outside of my apartment?' And we laughed. I said, 'I want him back at Nash. Same place he was before he got shipped to Texas.'

"George called me back to let me know that William was on his way back, but he would go to Lumberton in Roberson County, but to be patient and William would get back to Nash. I think we visited him one time in Lumberton, but before the second time, I said, 'Cheryl, you know, I'm gonna call, because I don't think he's gonna be there.' And he wasn't. They said, 'Elmore got shipped out.' They don't tell you where, but I knew it was Nash so we went to

Nash, and sure enough, he was there.

"As soon as we got in to visit, I said, 'I just want to know what cell you are in.' And he said, 'I'm in the same cell I was in when I left here! Everybody was so shocked.' That's because they don't know how that happened, but I did. That's why I say George was another mistake that turned out to be lucky."

Bessie looks proud of that success, but that's hardly the end of it. She returns to the legal battles.

"Next I'm looking at a writ of habeas corpus, because now I've had the chance to meet Hurricane Carter[10] when he was speaking at North Carolina A&T in Greensboro, and that's how he got out of prison. I go to Loflin's office and tell him my new theory: habeas corpus. And he says, 'It has a time limit.' 'What do you mean? Hurricane Carter was in prison twenty-five years and that's the writ they used.' 'Yes, but after that they put a ten year time limit on it.'

"Oh man, I gotta really work now, because we are close to getting to ten years. Well, my time ran out. What's next? Where do we go from here? The writ for appropriate relief is gone. Habeas corpus is gone. Okay, Bessie, forget all of that. We have to find the key. I had to really – Oh! You are taking me to a place I haven't been for a long time. I hadn't given up. We had to work at honor grade. So, what does that mean? What does that look like?"

Bessie swivels in her desk chair in her Transition House office. There's a beautiful quilt on the wall, and she seems to be probing it for an answer. During the day most of the residents are out, at work or looking for work. The place is still, but their presence leaves an odd echo as Bessie thinks about how much she is willing to tell me.

"William was at Brown Creek and I was working at GoodWorks, a nonprofit in Durham," she resumes, keeping a bit of distance. "And I met this gentleman at one of the round tables that Dennis Gaddy used to do. I was Dennis's supervisor when he was on work release at GoodWorks. This is before he got

---

[10]   Ruben Carter's story is told by James S. Hirsch in *Hurricane: The Miraculous Journey of Rubin Carter* (Mariner Books, 2000).

out and started CSI.[11] That's how I knew him. This gentleman had gotten a MAPP, and I had never heard of a MAPP.

"I felt like Loflin had let me down, and Cheryl was really pissed. He was just listening to me pro bono, but then we paid this twenty-five thousand dollars for him to investigate and talk to this guy Danny about the gun and try to get a new trial. I feel I don't need an appointment. I'm just showing up at Loflin's office. I tried to talk to him about the MAPP, but I don't know if he knew a lot about it. I'm sure he had heard of it, but I think sometimes I would be so pissed with him that my tone was not nice. He could tell that I was becoming very agitated.

"Finally I just take a break, because it seemed like I had run into too many stone walls. I needed to do something else with my energy. I decided to start an organization: Mothers Against Racial Injustice. I found someone to do this website for me. I'm going to really push this injustice that's done to Black men. I started a little newsletter and the newsletter was going around to all these different prisons in California. People were saying, 'Oh, Bessie, you are too radical. This is not going to do you any good. Even the name, Mothers Against Racial Injustice, is too radical. You sound like a Black Panther.'

"It lasted about a year. Then I started getting more involved in re-entry councils. I met Nicole Sullivan and Shashana Parker through John Parker at GoodWorks in Durham. They came to a meeting at John's office to talk about re-entry, and I presented my own theory: re-entry starts the moment you enter prison.

"After that meeting, I was invited to Raleigh to talk about re-entry. The more I got involved in it, the more people would ask me different questions and I would think, 'Maybe I'm on to something with this re-entry thing.' But then I got frustrated, because it was always just talk, talk, talk. We would have these great meetings, and parole officers and all of these people were coming, but they came to just chat, chat, chat. Nothing solid about what we are going to

---

[11] Community Success Initiative, a nonprofit in Raleigh, NC, works with men and women in prison, former prisoners, people in transition, and their families as they transition back into family and community life.

do. I had all of these things in my mind about what I felt re–entry looked like.

"Sometimes people would say, 'Oh you are only saying that because your son is in prison.' Well, exactly! My son is in prison and someday he is going to get out!

"I decided to start my own business, Turning Corners. I wrote a grant, my first grant, for Mission Tree. I told John Parker at GoodWorks, 'I don't know anything about writing a grant.' He said, 'Just write and then we'll help you work on it.' They were only going to fund twenty-five recipients, but they sent me a letter and said that they had made an exception and I was number twenty-six."

Bessie is excited. She is going to turn this nightmare of a prison experience into a meaningful life, not just fighting for Mecca, but focusing that energy and knowledge out into the world where it could help lots of people. Remember, Mecca is coming to Bessie with the problems of the other men, like Scott-so and Frank. She's no longer just a victim of the system, she's becoming an advocate and advisor for people in prison and their families. The private family study sessions are expanding.

"The mission for Turning Corners," Bessie continues, "was to create change in a person's life, to actually teach men to fish instead of giving them the fish. I developed teaching modules and my first one was Personal Growth and Development. They were tearing down Few Gardens, the Hope VI project,[12] and they asked me to take a hundred participants through a class of home ownership. I did that using my ideas on personal growth and development. Everybody kept saying, 'What does personal growth and development have to do with home ownership?' And I said, 'Everything begins – we have to change the process of thinking.'

"I gathered my ideas from books – Frankl's *Man's Search for*

---

[12]   Few Gardens was enabled by the Federal Housing Act of 1949. Durham's first housing project, it was completed in 1953. Demolition of Few Gardens occurred in 2003. In August 1992 Congress created the HOPE VI program designed to address the problem of poor living conditions created by the combination of Title I and Title III of the Housing Act of 1949. Hope IV was initiated in Durham in 2000 and became a part of the preparation of families being displaced from Few Gardens to rent or buy housing elsewhere.

Meaning, Nelson Mandela, and Hurricane Carter. They changed their lives while they were in prison. But I was also naïve. I had to take one hundred people through the class, so I thought I had to graduate one hundred people. Nobody told me that they only expected thirty people to graduate. I did ninety-nine! There was one woman I just couldn't break through to.

"And that's how I got my job at the Troy House, right where we sit today, only now it's Straight Talk Transition House! Those years of trying to prove William innocent; I thought that I had wasted the money, but the time after that was a growth period for me. In addition to reentry and the personal growth and development classes, I had the opportunity to volunteer at the American Civil Liberties Union. Now I really understood briefs and writs, and that's when I went back to Loflin and I apologized. I realized how unfair I had been to him, thinking anyone could just do a writ. All of that was a learning experience for me."

We are moving along through Bessie's story, but while she seems to be wrapping up with a gesture to the Straight Talk House, we are both aware that something is going unsaid.

"Was that also helping you to visualize that William could get out?" I probe.

"I don't know," Bessie says reluctantly. "Now you are making me go backwards in my mind. I was still angry at the fact that everything I thought would work didn't work. So I'm at a place and time where I have to figure this thing out again, but from a different angle. I know I can't look at any other legal things to do. That's not going to work. We started working on getting him honor grade, but he kept getting turned down, coming up every six months and getting turned down. I would be so pissed, and I would want to cry but I was, like I can't. I gotta get up and dust myself off. Because through it all I gotta keep William's spirits up!

"Now this is a part of the story that is very hard for me to tell. It's hard to talk about it because it involves a very difficult time for me. I have only told the story of that time in my life to a couple of people – to my sisters, Brenda and Karen – and I did not tell them until a long time afterwards."

We are very quiet while Bessie's weighs her thoughts. She glances briefly at the recorder and then looks me straight in the eye.

"I was feeling so depressed when I saw that we could not win an appeal, that I just didn't know what to do. I was desperate. I just called out, 'Lord what else can I do? Where to we go next?' It was so bleak and there seemed to be nothing else I could think of to do. I had just wracked my brains. Nothing.

"That's when I went for a visit and William told me about this book he had seen on Oprah, *The Secret.* I said I wasn't watching Oprah anymore; I wasn't interested. But he kept talking about this book and saying I should read it.

"I was on duty at the group home where I was working, Alpha Omega in Durham. I was on all weekend, so I thought maybe I would buy the book and see what William was so excited about. The women there always love an outing. First I took them to Barnes and Nobles but the book was twenty-six dollars. So I took them to Walmart, and I bought it there for thirteen and brought it back thinking I would look through it.

"I ended up reading the whole book that weekend. It really got me thinking. There was something that was holding me back, something where I was stuck. And then it came to me, about the thing in my past that was holding me back: I had been raped. It was after I had Cheryl and I gave this guy a ride home. We used to just talk, and I thought it was friendly, but then he raped me, and I got pregnant and I gave the baby up for adoption."

I'm quiet. I'm shocked but not shocked. I remember that Bessie had never told me that Cheryl and William had different fathers. After Cheryl told me, Bessie said, "Oh, I never told you?" As if keeping secrets was a slip of the tongue.

"When I remembered this," Bessie goes on, speaking very quietly, "I even called up my cousin, because I wasn't believing my own memories. I hadn't seen him in a long time, but he was the only person who was there after it happened. He said, 'Yes, I remember it as clear as when it happened. Your dress was torn, and you were bleeding. Your face was all beat up.'

"I have not thought about this for a very long time." Bessie's hands are fisted in her lap. "I didn't tell anyone. My parents died and never found out. I put the baby up for adoption, and I put it behind me and never told a soul. I thought, 'That's it. It's over.' But reading that book, I saw that I was going to have to do something. I was going to have to face this.

"I got in touch with this woman, Gloria, at an agency that searches for birth mothers. She and I did the paperwork and filed to say that my child could contact me. I thought, That's it. I'll never hear from that child. I've done what I had to do."

Bessie's confusion and grief are palpable. I carefully turn us back to a more concrete anchor. "How did you find that agency?"

"I have no idea! The place where I went for the interview to start the process of adoption no longer existed. It was at the YMCA in Orange, and that Y was gone, so I had to find someone who handled it, helped you give permission to release your name to your child. Today, I could just google stuff.

"When you were pregnant," I ask, "you just went in there on your own without your parents or any friend or anything? Where were you living?"

"At my house!! With my parents."

"And how pregnant were you when you went to the Y? Were you showing?"

"No, I wasn't showing, because my parents would have known something was going on. I was probably like I am now but skinnier! And my saving grace was that I was in a car accident and hurt my back, so periodically I would have to go to the hospital because of my back; so I could go to have the baby and my parents would think it was for my back."

All of this is slightly incredible, but I remember the descriptions of that household, and I picture baby Cheryl absorbed into the flow of all the other kids. I also remember Bessie's shame when her marriage started to fall apart and her inability to leave. We look each other in the eye but don't say anything. Bessie has spent many years working in shelters, working with women who are abused. She knows it's a complicated universe with an infrastructure built of shame.

"I was always tomboyish, so I wore a lot of sweatshirts." Bessie explains. "And I stayed in my room. I was never a big eater, so I could skip dinner. I wasn't missed at the table or anything like that. They could say, 'Oh, Bessie, she's in her room, listening to music.'

"And after the birth, my brother came to pick me up. He didn't know what happened – only my cousin knew – but he figured out that I had had a baby because he had to come to the maternity ward. He's deceased now. I wrote about this, about my past, about my family and my life in a book I call *Secrets and Lies*. It's not a published book, but something for myself and my family. I wrote that I'm sorry I put my brother in that position, because he never, never told anyone.

"I did finally tell my sisters, Karen and Brenda. They came down to North Carolina for my other sister's fiftieth birthday – that's Keisha's mom Cora. I picked them up from the airport and we stopped at Cracker Barrel and I told them."

Bessie begins to laugh. "Now I'm laughing thinking about it, because it's so crazy. But it was also sad. I told them, and they said, '*What?*!' My sister Brenda and I are extremely close. Even to this day when we get together, we'll spend hours at night talking about stuff. She couldn't believe I kept that secret from her. She was hurt, and they were both in shock. Total shock.

"She contacted me, the daughter. Her name was Chrystal. I didn't want to see her. But Gloria said, 'You have to do this.' So I did.

"My baby had been adopted by people with money, and they gave her everything, but she got things instead of love. I went up to New Jersey to see her. She told me that she had been abused when she was seven years old. She was very angry, and she was jealous of William and Cheryl, that I had raised them but put her up for adoption. She's was forty and she has two children but no husband. She still lives with her adoptive parents! She had one baby when she was nineteen and another when she was in her early thirties.

"After I met Chrystal, I had to tell Cheryl and William. I did it on a visit to the prison so that they would both hear it at the same time. They were shocked by it, but they felt that I was... They told me there was always something secretive about me. I had some issues with kids. Babies and kids. I didn't like the little babies. I wouldn't hold a baby; I still don't like holding a baby. Oh boy. I don't know. I don't even like to think about it now. I try to forget that man, but his face is there. I can see it so clearly. It was awful."

We look at the floor, Bessie's secret curled up there between us. Then she rescues us and turns the story back to Mecca.

"So I did that and then I could move on. I figured, okay, I got that over with. I did what was asked of me to do. *Now give me what I want.*"

The Bessie I am more familiar with reenters the room, her expression moving from sadness to indignation.

"By 2011 William has been moved out of Salisbury and he's at Brown Creek. Oh, if I could have broken him out of prison, I would have done it then. I called James Leone, his boss at the clothes house in Salisbury, to get William back on the transfer list. I'm calling Leone all the time. You have no idea how stressful that was. Leone would say, 'On the list.' And William would call, 'Ma, I got to get out of here. It's terrible.'

"And there's the whole–day journey going up to Brown Creek for visits. It was just awful, awful, awful. *But,* if he had not been at Brown Creek, we would never have met Charles Cromer! Cromer is a lawyer who helped men get a MAPP. William said, 'Mom, this guy here told me about Cromer who helps guys get MAPPs. He used to sit on the Parole Board. I want you to call him.' And I did, and Cromer was taking just one last case because he was in ill health.

"He told me what his fee *used* to be, but because this was going to be his last case, he was only going to charge us three thousand. But then he told me that fifteen hundred is the initial fee, just to go interview William. And I was like fifteen hundred just to interview! Here we go again. Cheryl said, 'Ma, I don't know. That's a lot of money.'

"By now Frank Walls was out of prison, so everybody came over for dinner, Frank and his wife, Bridget, Cheryl and her husband, David. And I was telling them about Cromer and his fee. Frank was clear, 'If you have the money, Mom, pay it. It's a shot.' Cheryl was still saying, 'I don't know. We've paid out a lot of money to lawyers.'

"I said, 'This is William's money.' I had been saving this money for William – for anything that could help him. 'So if he says, yes, we'll do it.' But inside I was still thinking, 'Fifteen hundred just to go interview him!'

"William said yes, so we paid Cromer. He went to interview William and liked what he heard. Then he starts adding things William is going to have to do. He has to go for a psych evaluation. He has to take these classes. William calls me and says, 'I gotta get in this domestic violence class, and the guy in charge is not a nice guy and he says the class is full.' I said, 'Okay, I'm gonna call him up.'

"So I call up and I tell him – let's call him Mr. Peterson – who I am. And he immediately says, 'I'm tired of you mothers calling up here always wanting to get your boys into a class.'

"And somehow this idea just came over me. I said, 'Oh, that's not why I'm calling you. I'm calling you to inquire about your domestic violence classes because I teach domestic violence classes and I was wondering if I could *assist* with the person who teaches the class.

I've been doing this for fifteen years.'

"And his whole attitude changes. Peterson says, 'That would be something to look into.' I knew it would be a conflict of interest, because I couldn't come to that prison if William was there, but we talked for about twenty minutes. He even connected me to the woman officer who was teaching the classes. She asked me several questions, which, of course, I could answer because I didn't make this stuff up! I have taught these classes. I've worked at the women's shelter and the Troy House."

Like mother like son. Nothing makes them happier than a victory built on a shrewd move.

"William calls me back in maybe a couple of days and says, 'Guess what, Mom?' And I said, 'You're in the class, right?'

"I called Peterson back, but I couldn't thank him directly. I said, 'You know, Mr. Peterson, this was a wonderful opportunity, but I think it might be a conflict of interest. When my son leaves Brown Creek, I wouldn't mind coming to do a class, free of charge.' And he said, 'You would drive all the way up here?' And I said, 'Of course. Domestic violence is something I'm very passionate about.' He said that would be wonderful, but we never spoke again.

"Now we have to go to the parole hearing, for the MAPP, but we have Cromer with us. After the hearing he said, 'You all did a great job.'

"They said it would be sixty days before we heard, but that time passed, and William didn't hear anything. I would call Cromer, but he would say, 'I can't talk to you. I'm not your attorney. I'm William's attorney and I can't talk to you unless William gives me permission.' I said, 'Well, he'll give you permission.' Buy really, Cromer didn't know any more than we did.

"I remember the day I heard. I was out in Morrisville with a girlfriend of mine and I was coming back home when I got a collect call from William Elmore. I didn't hear where he was, just the recording that asks you to accept a call from an inmate. We pull over and I accept the call and hear William say, 'Guess where I am? I'm at Hillsborough Orange Correctional.' Which is an honor grade camp, and if he was going to get the MAPP that was one of the places he asked to go.

"I was just frozen. I was sitting in the car and I couldn't cry. I couldn't speak. He said, 'Ma, are you there? Are you there?' I was just frozen! Because it had been such a long journey and we're finally at the end.

"After I hung up, I called Cheryl, and that Sunday, as soon as we could, we went up to see him. I thought, 'Finally I'm going to see him have on some different colors!' I was just so tired of looking at those brown clown clothes. I was finally going to see him in green.

"When I saw Cheryl, we both started laughing. It was a long journey, but now we just have to wait for that specific day. Nothing mattered anymore. I didn't care what people thought anymore. At one time it really mattered, to prove him innocent, but now I could care less.

"And then seeing him in street clothes when he got his Level Two and he could go out on pass, that New Years Day 2013 – the picture you took of him with David. That was so unbelievable... because Cheryl had taken that old coat of William's to the tailor to get the lining fixed. That was something that he had had *before*. But I still didn't cry when I saw that picture, because I was always afraid that if I started to cry, I would never stop."

I don't want her to start crying now, and I lean over to say, "I remember feeling so ambivalent when David got to take William out on his first pass and I was there. I remember telling you that I felt like you should be there."

"It was okay," Bessie says. "I knew he was going to need to be on his own now. I remember a telephone conversation I had with him. I was telling him I wasn't going to visit as often. William asked why, and I said, 'Because you need to meet other people. You need to have other conversations, to have social interaction with your sponsors when you go out on passes. This is going to be your real life.'

"It was good for me because I was tired of the visiting. Then a funny thing happened. Oops... what do I do with my Sundays? I would still visit twice a month, but two Sundays were for me. For all those years, two decades, if it was a Sunday, no matter where I would be, it could be D.C. or Baltimore, I would leave two or three o'clock in the morning so I could be back for the visit.

"Time to time we did have our differences. Sometimes I used to think that he thought I could pull a rabbit out of my hat, and of course I couldn't. Maybe I gave him the impression that I could do anything. And then there was one time when I had the opportunity to become an informant for the FBI. I could have gotten him out of prison. But when we talked about it, William said, 'Oh Ma, you can't do that.'

"But I would have, because that's how badly I wanted him out of prison."

Chapter 10: Opening My Heart to Hope

The connection to Charles Cromer opens the door to the MAPP, to honor grade, a parole, and finally, a release date: December 19, 2015. But being in prison serving a natural life sentence, each stroke of hope is tethered to caution, and Mecca approaches his MAPP and his release carefully, aware of the precarious spiritual balance involved. The MAPP hearing occurs while Mecca is at Brown Creek, but in 2011 he is moved to Caledonia to wait for the state's decision. Caledonia is where it all began in 1994, first stop on his North Carolina prison tour. Now he is going back there to wait for the outcome of the MAPP hearing, an ironic symmetry that is not lost on Mecca.

Looking a little bit sad and a little bit uncomfortable with the memory, Mecca tells me, "I had in my mind that when I got to Caledonia, I wasn't going to let myself get assigned to anything. I'm gonna do the best I could to mirror a vacation from any type of responsibility to anything other than to myself. A part of that was also conditioning myself for the possibility that I didn't get the MAPP.

"In prison – I say in prison, but I think it's in life – people spend so much time busying themselves to distract themselves from something negative. They don't want to think about that reality. You get so good at it in prison 'til a point where you are not present with the good either. So when I went to Caledonia my mindset was: I'm going to be still enough to accept the possibility of getting my MAPP and really celebrate that – or to be prepared to endure the possibility of them saying, "No, you didn't get your MAPP." Either way, I was going to sit still and embrace whatever was coming down the pike."

This sounds okay to me, but I want an example. How does this look on the small scale of daily life?

"What I see happen across the board is that when you don't deal with what is on your mind in prison – something negative like if I didn't get that MAPP – if you don't deal with it properly, you get up the next morning and you get into a situation. Because your mind is not clear. You get up and you go to clothes exchange or to the canteen or to the yard to exercise, somebody may bump into you by accident. Normally, it's nothing to you. But when you have some bad news and you don't deal with it – instead you are trying to distract yourself by busying yourself – and somebody bumps into you, it can be lethal in prison. You overreact and you can end up in segregation or worse.

"I give you a real scenario. A friend of mine is trying to get to minimum custody. He's been in prison thirty years and every six months he comes up for the possibility of a promotion to minimum custody and, for the last ten years, like it was for me, they keep saying, 'No, not yet. No, not yet.'

"Say this guy and I are playing Scrabble and they say, 'So and so report to program office.' And I say to him, 'I hope that's it.' He goes in there. He comes back and it's obvious in his face and on his shoulders. He's tense. They turned him down yet again. Then the conversation – I have had it so many times – goes like this:

'What's up?'

'Man, they turned me down one more time. I'm so tired of this.'

'What you want to do? You want to talk about it or what?'

'Naw, I'm good. I be all right. I come up the next six months.'

And he wants to resume playing Scrabble.

"Then maybe while we are playing someone walks by and they brush up against him. And instantaneously – there's no words – he's out of his seat. It's a fight. I'm just getting out the way 'cause I don't want any blood to get on me.

"They lock him up and he goes to seg for a while. When he comes out of seg, he's lighter. His energy is lighter. When I talk to this friend about it, he admits that's what happened.

'Yeah, you right. I should have just dealt with it.' So I have to prepare myself, because in prison it can go either way."

Caledonia also puts Mecca in close quarters. He had a single cell for seventeen years because of his job. Now he has to deal with a dorm. His shoulders drop a bit when he talks about this.

"I don't know, man. Prison is so..." Mecca searches for the right words. "Everything can be so offensive. I like anonymity. Love it. I always did. You don't get that in prison. Today, out here, I get up early in the morning to be out and about and I can go out for a run, and that's how I know it's not prison! It's perfect for me.

"For me, prison represented so much of what I tried to get away from in my *life*. I grew up in a household where, in my grandmother's house, there was a lot of people there. It was seven kids that she had. Add in my sister and me. My grandparents. The house was full up. I didn't like that. I loved being around my family, but it just never was enough space. Fast forward to prison. There's not enough of my own personal space!

"Single cell is bad enough, but Caledonia is like forty-second street. Also I was in the worst place in the dorm when I got to Caledonia, meaning where my bunk was in a blind spot. Officers can't see back there, so all the lasciviousness, smoking, and gambling and things go on there. I won't even say on tape what's going on.

"But then there is this part of my life... In the middle of all the chaos I always find these little rays of hope. My buddy, the one I used to play Scrabble with, I hadn't seen him in maybe fifteen, maybe twenty years, but there he is at Caledonia. He was glad to see me. I was glad to see him. We were like sounding boards for each other.

"I saw my buddy. He asks me about my bunk, and he says, 'No, no, no, no. We gonna get you off that bunk. You don't want to be back there.' There was another guy who was in the bunk on top of my buddy. This guy was interested in everything I hate. So we went to that guy and my buddy put it like this, 'What would it take to get you to request to go to that bunk so my partner here can get this bunk?' And he said, 'I wouldn't...Maybe go to canteen and get me soda or something.' And we are, 'What you want, two sodas? Three?'

"So I stay there, in the bunk above my buddy, and it's maybe almost the full ninety days, and then they tell me I have the MAPP."

At this point, Mecca's recounting is catching up to what Bessie told me in her office at the Straight Talk house. Mecca tells his mother and sister not to visit him in Caledonia. "Caledonia was where it started, and now I'm back there again," he explains. "And at Caledonia everything is like you going back in time. You got all these cotton fields. And these old, old, old, what they tell me are tobacco houses. I call them slave houses. You see 'em and it's just like a real prickly reminder of how it used to be. Takes two hours to drive from Durham, and then you have to go through all the security measures. I wanted that to be over for them."

When Mecca gets his MAPP, he's transferred to OCC. I coach him back in time. "You get on the bus. You have all your junk with you. Your books. Your journals. Your shoes! You ride over to Orange and what do you feel like when you are on that bus?"

"I'm overwhelmed with everything. It's a surreal experience, and I'm just saying to myself, 'Wow, I'm really taking direct steps towards going home! This is really happening.' Bus from Caledonia goes to Sandy Ridge where they coordinate all of the transfers. You get off.

There's all these holding pens. You see guys maybe you haven't seen for years. But I'm too keyed up for that. They holler, 'Everybody going to Orange. This is your bus.' So I got on that bus and it's just so overwhelming. This is really happening. I'm really going to what they call minimum custody!"

As a rule, Mecca likes to be in command of his story, the wise man playing chess, and his body language when he talks reinforces that. He sits back in his chair, legs set wide on the floor. Deep, steady eyes. But when we get to this point in the story, he falls back in time. He's a small kid receiving the best present ever! It's as if he is in front of me in two layers: the man in consummate control and the child running free.

"Now most of the guys who I've heard say things about minimum custody, it was always negative," Mecca, my instructor in prison decorum, tells me. "They say that the officers are going to gouge you, because they know that you don't have any room for error. One slip up and you could lose honor grade or worse, your MAPP. There are inmates also that gouge at you, try to get you to do something stupid.

"But other guys who know me better told me straight up, 'Look man, you gonna be great. It's the best thing you could ever experience. You gonna be going out the gate. Trust me. You gonna be just fine.' And to me it didn't matter. Knowing that in three more years it's over, I even could have did that time at Caledonia. Just knowing this is over, I can endure."

I have talked to a lot of men and women in prison and after release about the place of hope in the delicate balance of doing time. The stakes are high and the opportunity to yank hope away is one of the tools used for social control. It's most extreme on death row, but it's there at every level of the system. Every day is simultaneously dull and similar and daring you to hope for something better.

"I don't know if anybody else would admit this out loud, but it makes me mad that I can figure out how to endure something," Mecca admits. "I don't like that, but I can. It was like the suicide, when I told my mother, 'I don't want to live. I want to die.' When she convinced me not to die, I just decided I was gonna live however long that was. And I was kind of mad at myself, because I know that to decide to figure out how to live meant that I was gonna do just that. I was going to have to do this time and live my life inside of a prison. And when you figure out how to endure in prison, you are in one hundred percent. Even when you're dealing on the street every day, you can take a vacation if you want. Take a week off if you want. Take a month off if you want. The difference with prison is that there is no *off* switch. It's always *on*. You can't quit prison unless you die."

We sit in silence for a little while. Mecca takes a long drink of water and moves on.

"So here's how it is when I arrive at Orange. Buses stop in the back by the Peace Center. You can't see the camp. Just the big brick seg unit. They march you from back there to this dorm. Used to be the only building at Orange when it was first built. So old it looks like it could fall down any time. They strip search you. They go through your stuff to inventory what you have.

But I was saying to myself, 'Man you in minimum now. You just got three more years to deal with this.' I don't even know at the time that they had other dorms. That's how it works. They don't give you any information. You gotta figure everything out for yourself.

They do send me to a dorm a little bit better. It's newer and more modern, but they are smoking in there like crazy, and cigarette smoke really bothers me. I can't breath around it. And cigarettes also mean there's gonna be a lot of policing activity 'cause they want to know who's smoking. And a lot of police activity means a lot of rummaging through your personal property. Now I have to be forced to figure out how to co–exist with all of these guys once again but I'm reminding myself, three more years. You can handle this. Three more years.'"

Mecca turns away from his frustration and moves back into instructional mode, walking me through the process of establishing a routine in a new camp.

"The first thing I always decide is let me carve out spaces to be me and do what I do. Exercise. Reading. Jogging. Journaling. I need to pay attention to the ebb and flow, to the movement. For example, I need to find out if this place allows you to get up and go in the day room early, before everybody else, to get the solitude so I can do my journaling. A guy or two used to be in there early. See that's a tricky thing about prison. Is this guy supposed to be in there? So if I start going in there, would I bring the heat with me? And then we both get ran out? Did I mess up his sanity? His peace of mind?

"I took the chance and I went in there and asked the guy, 'They don't say anything about being here?' And he says, 'No man, it's honor grade. You stay in here all night if you wanted to.' So I go in the day room really early, four, five AM, and I do the things I do to kind of prep me for the day. And then they do count time and you gotta go back to your bunk."

Several times a day, depending on the camp and the security level, all prisoners must stay where they are or return to their bunks and cells to be counted. When the count clears, if it's not dark or stormy, the yard is open.

"Lemme go to the yard and see how the movement is in the yard." Mecca continues his lesson. "Who comes out here early in the morning? What kind of energy is on the weight pile early in the morning? Do I want to tackle that and interact with that or do I want to wait? Some people are just more social. They want to go when everybody is there. I don't want to do that. I want my anonymity. You spend a lot of time figuring out, according to your personality, what's the best time to do what *you* want to do."

What I really want to know from Mecca is how does minimum custody change things. Clearly a lot of the old rules and cautions still hold, but I'm looking for something that is totally different about minimum custody, so I ask, "What's it like to start seeing people go out on work release?"

This gets the rise out of him that I want. Mecca opens his eyes wide as if he is seeing the whole thing right in front of him for the first time.

"*Strange!* It's really strange. I got into the work release dorm. The dorm janitor job came open and a guy that I knew for a long time, Melvin – he and I were at Salisbury together. He said, 'Hey man. I got a job for you and you should take it. It's gonna get you out of that dorm. The dorm janitor job is open. I don't know why they didn't fill it, but you can have it.'

"And I was like, 'Naw. I had my days of cleaning up behind people.' He said, 'I understand. But this dorm, it's practically self–kept, 'cause nobody's really there. Everybody is on work release.'

"He took me to the sergeant's office and said, 'This is the guy we want as the dorm janitor.'

'I don't even know this guy. I'm not giving him the job because there's other guys on the list.'

'Listen we don't want those other guys. You want him. You want to send somebody in here that's bringing in contraband and cigarettes and then you got to do your job and come down here and shake it down?'

'You got a point with that.'

"And he gave me the job, moved me to the work release dorm and I got to skip all the intermediate steps. Melvin was right. Guys are gone all day so it's real quiet in there and clean. And I got my bunk. My bunk was on top of my friend Angel Sanchez, who I've been knowing for just as long as I've been knowing Scott-so; and Scott-so is at Orange too. I'm watching guys get up and get dressed and go to work. I can see guys go on home passes. I see sponsors picking up guys for CV passes. I see work release guys getting in vehicles. It was therapeutic to watch that. I could visualize myself going in and out. Everything was prepping me for what I was getting ready to do, which is get out of prison."

The MAPP contract is usually a three–year program. The first year you are Level 1 which means no movement outside the camp unless it is for a Department of Transportation job – Mecca is assigned to road crew for a while picking up litter, which he loves, because you just spend the day walking outside along the highway. Level 2 is where you can go out one on one with a community volunteer/sponsor who has been through a training program and a background check. At Level 3 you can go out with a sponsor and two other prisoners and leave the camp for work release. Whether you are on a MAPP or have a sentencing limit/date, if you earn the levels, going out with a sponsor is a way to prove that you are trustworthy.

"Scott-so pulled me to the Tuesday meeting with volunteers who come to the camp through Yokefellow Prison Ministry," Mecca resumes his lesson on managing minimum, "I didn't like it at first. I didn't like what I saw, how it worked. Looked like speed dating. There are these volunteers who have been approved as sponsors so that they can take men out on community passes (CV passes) sitting at tables and guys sit at the tables and try to sell themselves. I saw a lot of games being played and I thought, 'I'm not doing that.' But if they want you to do this, go out on passes to show you are trustworthy, so you gotta figure out how to do it."

Yokefellow Prison Ministry is an interdenominational, racially diverse Christian ministry of reconciliation that began in 1969. It is founded on the idea that people's lives are changed through committed relationships. At OCC many of the community volunteers belong to Yokefellows, but everyone who has completed the volunteer training can attend. In a way, I have my own private Yokefellows table every Thursday, sitting for two hours with up to a dozen men, so I don't usually go on Tuesdays.

"Another thing is, most of these volunteers are older white people," Mecca says, giving me a sideways glance. "What in the world? That's strange. You don't have anything else you can be doing? Then there are the Quakers. I was seeing, listening with my ears and my eyes and realizing that coming to OCC is important to these people. It's what they were gonna do hell or high water. And at the end of the hour everybody held hands and they said the serenity prayer. And they gave you hugs. They shook your hand. I know it sounds crazy, but I had not seen anything like this in twenty-two years in prison."

Mecca was approved for Level 2 on January 1, 2014. David and I decided to take him to a New Year's dinner at the house of some long–time sponsors, Larry and Nancy Bumgardner. New Year's Day is a quiet day, and visiting a private home seemed like a low key way to step off the prison grounds for the first time. David and I have taken many men out on their "first pass," but each time I am reminded how radical this experience can be. For those of us who come and go, who often think our lives are just too damn busy, it's impossible to feel what it might be like to go nowhere at all for decades.

"And that was my first time meeting David," Mecca reminds me. "You said, 'David is coming to get you.' Real easy, but I was nervous."

"Do you remember what it was like that morning when you got up and put on civilian clothes?"

"I said to Mom, 'I'm getting ready to go out on these passes and I need some clothes. I'm sure to be a trial and error with size. You get some clothes. Bring it on visit. Whatever doesn't fit you can take it back.' She had to take all my underwear back and some of my pants that fit in the waist, but they didn't fit my legs.

"Mentally, I was imagining what that would be like. But actually to put on the regular clothes; you feel like a weirdo. I think I got ready maybe an hour before. Gave myself enough time to pull on my shirt a thousand times. See if my pants fit right a thousand times. And that's one thing I don't deny. How awkward I felt. You don't have a full body mirror in prison. So you gotta keep looking at yourself in little pieces. Does this fit right? Is it feeling right? You constantly looking down at yourself from that angle. And it felt restricted, 'cause prison clothes, they all loose, never any real sizes.

"I had on some jeans. I had on a sweater. I had on a brown leather jacket that Cheryl brought me. That jacket gave me a little bit of comfort because it's something that I remember. That jacket was twenty-five years old. Cheryl got it fixed up for me. To put it on gave me so many memories... one of my favorite jackets. And for her to bring it, and have it fit me right – and I'm thinking, 'How big was it on me then?' 'cause I was very skinny before prison."

"You had a lot of dope and drugs to hide!" I tease.

"You don't take dope everywhere with you!" Mecca rebuts.

Truth be told, Mecca had definitely bulked up in prison. He has a lanky feel to his walk, but his shoulders and chest are strong. His skin has stayed smooth, giving the impression of a much younger man. As soon as he gets his Levels and he is allowed to wear a baseball cap, he wears it everywhere, like the kids I taught in high school in Brooklyn. All day long, telling kids, "Take off your hat in the classroom." All day long doing battle with their identity.

"Then Scott-so sees you and David pull up, 'cause the yard is open," Mecca picks up the story. "I'm the only person dressed like I'm going out, the only person going out on pass that day, so everybody can be looking. And Scott-so is out there talking to everybody. And you and David pull up and Scott-so's starts in on it, 'There you are. There's your ride.' And I was like, 'Okay.' Trying to sound like me. And then I hear, 'William Elmore report to the gate.' They announce it even if you are already standing there.

"I see the officer open the folder and all that for signing me out. And the gate was wide open. Scott-so's like, 'Go ahead. Go out to the gate. He had a ball with that. 'Go out to the gate. You scared to go out there?' He had me, but I tried to sound real calm. I ain't going until the officer flags me to walk through the gate.

"Now the officer is looking right at me, 'Elmore come on. You ready?' And then I walked real slowly to that gate. I looked back at Scott-so. If this ain't right, I'm in trouble. I'm trusting you man. That's what my look said. I crossed out the gate and I shook David's hand, gave you a hug and we got in the mini van. That's when I knew I wanted a mini van. I sat in the back by myself. The space. And the ride was good."

The mini van becomes a running joke when Mecca is released. His sister sets him up with a Honda sedan. At least it's black. But as soon as he has pay in his pocket, Mecca trades in the sedan for a mini van. Doesn't care if it's a soccer mom car. In fact, he enjoys that, playing with people's preconceptions.

We drove to the Bumgardner's house, Mecca looking a little bit stunned. He says, "I know now we were just driving on I–85 to Durham, but that day I didn't know where we were. Hadn't been anywhere except in a prison van and prison and jail for twenty-three years. It was surreal."

Looking back on it, maybe we should have just sat for a couple of hours at the Weaver Street Food Co–op in Chapel Hill, looking out the window at the world, holding it at arms length. Instead we were walking up the steps and Larry was opening the door and giving Mecca a big welcoming hug and it was New Year's Day at the Bumgardner's. There were children and children's children and a couple of men who had already been released from prison who were also part of Larry and Nancy's flock. Nancy was in the kitchen preparing a mountain of food for all these people. It's the kind of household where everybody is welcome, and nobody stands on ceremony.

"It was almost too much," Mecca recalls. "That movement and activity was too much. Having you and David making sure I was all right was kind of like an anchor for me. And that was good. But Ms. Bumgardner, she just wanted to talk and ask a lot of questions and get me involved."

Mecca laughs. At Yokefellows, Nancy is known for her exuberance. "And I'm following David around, 'cause I'm in somebody's house! You don't just roam around somebody's house, that's what I think. But at their house, they tell you to roam around. Go downstairs. Go upstairs. Go over here and go over there. They act like everybody's been to their house before. You just in the house. Do what you do. Be who you are.

"And I was like, 'This is strange. Very strange. This is what passes are like?' I remember Scott-so was saying, 'You gonna like the Bumgardner's. They're cool people.' And Angel had told me that he was gonna get me on their list for passes. So they had been vetted, but I would have to describe it as a little bit of chaos, a little bit of confusion, and a little bit of awkwardness. A little bit of all of that kind of rolled in a burrito. Surreal.

"After a while, Nancy comes over to get me and she says, 'Come here and set the table.' I'm wanting to just sit down and take it all in. Let me be invisible. Let me watch how this goes. But she says, 'You gonna fix the table. Come on.' And in my head, I say, 'Oh man, how you gonna do this? I don't know how to set the table! Nothing but a spork and a prison plate is all I can remember. I probably told her that. But she goes, 'Don't worry about it. I'm gonna show you. You gonna learn. Come on in here.' And David came in and I kind of followed him around the table doing what he told me to do."

We are both laughing. Throwing men into these situations is fun. I have gotten used to watching David coach a guy through the self–checkout at Walmart; let them sit in a Starbucks and figure out if any of this is really a cup of coffee; make pizza at home and serving it with special pizza knives we bought in Spain. The first time Mecca came for pizza I remember looking over and seeing him wrangling with the knife. I said, "Forget the knife. Just eat it like pizza." But Mecca answered, "No, I'm gonna figure out how to use this knife. I can't believe I forgot how to do this."

Prison is about the small things, too. "Did you realize that you hadn't really remembered what the outside world was like?" I asked.

"Yeah. And I realized that even more when I got in the car and we were coming back in the night. To be out at night was very, very disturbing. In prison you are never out at night. You don't want to be out at night because they could assume that you are trying to escape. Even now at night I really struggle with my sense of direction. It's as if... it's like I lose my vision."

"When you got back to the prison and you had to get out of the car, what did that feel like?"

"It felt... that I was going back to familiarity and coming from unfamiliarity. Everybody that was up was kind of staring at me. They kept asking, 'How was it?' And I was like, 'I don't know yet. I ain't sure yet.'"

Mecca did get used to passes. In addition to Frank Walls, he also went out on passes with Chris Agoranos, a Duke Divinity School student, Tom McQuistion from Quaker Meeting, Chris Ringwalt, and Bill Cook. Frank was the closest, a soul mate and buddy, but even when out with Frank, Mecca would tell me, "He's on his phone all the time. I ask him what's this all about?" Frank and Mecca liked to go to the Chinese buffet where they could sit for hours and talk. Sometimes I would come by on a Sunday afternoon and it was just like we were regular friends in a regular world. CV passes from OCC are restricted to Durham, Orange, and Alamance Counties, but Frank would drive Mecca over to the Durham/Wake border where they could see Frank's house just across the road. Another of Mecca's favorite sponsors was Bill Cook, Mr. Bill, a retired white man. It was Mr. Bill who Mecca chose to bring him to the library when we first started recording our oral histories.

"I don't know if you know this story," Mecca said. "Mr. Bill knew of sponsors, some of his church friends, and they took the guy to their house and the guy killed them. I asked Mr. Bill one day, 'What gives you the courage to try this?' And he said he knew Stanley, who used to be at OCC, from outside before he was incarcerated. Stanley recommended me, so Mr. Bill, he took a chance with me and we really hit it off.

"You might think it's funny. A Black city guy like me and Mr. Bill, white guy who lives in the country, but some of my passes with him were probably the most fun. He's older and it's a lot simpler. He wants to just sit down. He used to say, 'I hope this isn't boring.' I'd say, 'No, this is perfect.'

"He would drive to Walmart and we would sit on the bench and just talk. I used to tell him all the time, I don't think he believed it, 'Mr. Bill, this is what I need right now.' I told you this about me before, I'm a guy that's always looking for a father, so even though Mr. Bill would be more like my grandfather, we just fit, just like that. It took him some time to really grasp that, but when he did, it became more fun because he could be himself. And he liked to talk about religion and politics."

Another thing Mecca likes to talk about when it comes to passes is the way they can mirror prison. Mecca would tell me, "The sponsor decides where to go, sets up the pass, and the inmate checks the board and goes to the gate at the right time, mostly not even knowing where he is going or maybe knowing because it's church and it repeats itself. The inmate is passive. Yes, you go out in civilian clothes, but your mind is still like it was in prison."

Mecca decides he's not going to follow that pattern. If passes are supposed to get you ready for the outside, you better be able to be part of the organization of the pass. That's what is going to prepare your mind for release, for making your own decisions.

It began like this: "After we got back to camp, Mr. Bill said, 'I really enjoyed the pass.' And I said, 'I did too.' And then I said to him, 'Let's experiment. Let's do something neither one of us have done before.' And he was like, 'All right. Let's try it. You think of some things and let me know.'

"So I would get the *INDY*[13] when you brought it to your workshop, and I would think of some things and say to him let's try this and let's try that. Let's ask Simone about these places on Franklin Street and see if she can help us put together an itinerary. We did that, and whatever we liked, we would do it again. Whatever we didn't like, we wouldn't do it anymore. And going to stores on Franklin Street in Chapel Hill, just walking on the street, I could really grow

---

13   *INDY Week*, formerly *Independent Weekly*, founded in 1983 and currently owned by ZM INDY, Inc., covers the arts and politics in the Triangle NC area.

with that.

"One other thing, from the inmate's side. Knowing what happened to the people from Mr. Bill's church, that intensified my appreciation of him. We talked about that. But I would say, 'You know, believe it or not, Mr. Bill, there's some risk on my end too – with you, with any sponsor. I don't know you either, so I'm taking a chance with you, too. How you going to drive? Are we going the places on the pass itinerary? Are you going to be fair to me? I have no choice if something goes wrong. I am signed out to you. I can't just walk off or it's attempted escape.' And he said, 'Yes, thinking about it – you are taking a chance with me.' Which also put us on a more even footing, made us more equal."

I've seen this too. People don't think of it that way, but being a sponsor, taking an incarcerated person out in your car, you are totally responsible for taking care of them, for making sure they are safe. If there's something there that's a temptation, something they shouldn't be around, it's your responsibility to get them away from it. So you are simultaneously introducing them to the outside world and remembering this is still part of prison. Each time I see an someone return to the gate and I watch the officers' hands run over the man's body, I remember we are living in two different worlds.

"Now another thing," Mecca picks up, "I have told Scott-so this, I ask him, 'What does a CV pass prepare you for? Release? *No*, it prepares you for the next CV pass. It's not like I would have given up any of my passes. They were real valuable to me, but getting outside, even with a lot of passes, you are going to find out there are parts of yourself you do not know about that are going to present themselves. Out here, sometimes you just be so overwhelmed with everything, you don't know what's going on. You say to yourself, 'What *am* I doing?'. Those are the times you have to know to sit down and be still and let everything settle. You know those things where it's a glass and you shake it and snowflakes fall on a little city in there. Those times come, and I say to myself, you gotta let the snow fall. Be still. Start all over."

Chapter 11: Fire! One More Lesson in Humility

Orange Correctional Center allowed Mecca to come to a place of comfort. His soul could rest. He had his volunteer passes worked out. He had his friends Scott-so, Jeff, Justin, and Angel. He had time to journal in the day room before anyone else got up. Sunday visits happened outside at a picnic table with a spread of home–cooked food.

On Saturday June 21, 2014, Mecca woke up and watched all that unravel. I'll let him tell it.

"I get up every morning between three and three-thirty, go in the day room, do my journaling, watch the news, get ready for my day. Where I'm positioned in the day room, at the window, I look directly at the kitchen. About four-thirty I am looking out the window and thinking I was seeing dark clouds out there, unreasonably dark. In prison, there is always some light. There's no pitch–dark areas on the facility at all. Around five-thirty I hear sirens. I see a fire truck and the truck is going behind the kitchen. Back there, next to the prison fence, there is an area with a lot of equipment, trucks and riding lawn mowers, stuff like that, sheds. I figured something back there might be on fire. Then two or three other guys in the dorm got up getting ready to go to work in the kitchen. Then they say, "Man, kitchen is on fire!' But we don't see any flames.

"As we're talking, more fire trucks are coming. Then the fire chief comes. And maybe twenty minutes after that we see more fireman. It's getting light enough to see a fireman on the roof of the kitchen with an ax. He's cutting into the roof.

"Now it's about six-thirty and I have a pass with Mr. Bill. I say to myself, I'm gonna get in the shower and I'm going to miss all this drama 'cause I'm gonna be gone on pass. By the time I get back, they'll fix it, and everything will be back to normal. About ten minutes after that comes the announcement: 'All CV passes have been canceled due to an emergency.'

"Everything's exaggerated in prison so I'm still thinking it's no big deal. I didn't see any flames. Can't be that bad. The shifts change at six o'clock, so you have all of this activity going on anyway. Guards going out have to do a count before they go. Guards coming on have to do a count to start their shift. But then I see the superintendent, Mr. Hodges, and the assistant superintendent, Mr. Marion. That's when I see that it's serious, because it's a Saturday and they don't work on weekends, *ever*.

"Everybody is still in the dorms. No movement. Dorms are never locked, but nobody leaves the dorms that early. And now guys are gettin' up that are supposed to go out on work release, and they know if they aren't allowed to go to work that it is serious. They are thinking, 'I'm leaving the facility. I won't be here, so why can't I go to work.' Work release has to happen because the employers are counting on these men, but the camp canceled everything.

"Maybe twenty minutes after this Marion goes in all the dorms and says, 'Everybody pack up lightly. Get a few cosmetics. Get some stuff, because you all are going to be transferred out to Johnston. You need to be ready soon. Like yesterday.'

"Next, we saw some people from Raleigh, state officials, and they surrounded the kitchen. Now there's smoke, more smoke, more firemen on the roof, but still no flames. We found out later it was an electrical fire. They are going to have to transfer everybody out because if you can't use the kitchen, can't feed people, you can't keep the camp open."

"Everybody got packed," Mecca continues. "They are telling us, 'Lock your lockers. Nobody's gonna be here at all to bother your stuff. Lock it and take your key with you and you guys be right back.' This is in their favor, because the less you take with you, the less they have to inventory when you come back. They are going to have to search everybody when we come back. That's protocol.

"It was maybe thirty minutes later that they came with a roster and they called your name, and everybody goes to a bus. One by one, the buses left. They didn't wait for everybody to fill up all the buses. As one bus filled up, it left."

I heard about the fire later that day and drove by the prison to see what was going on. There was damage on the roof of the kitchen but not much to see from the road. By the time I got there, all the occupants of OCC seemed to have disappeared. The camp was empty, fire trucks gone, place deserted. I called Bessie to see what she knew, which was not much.

"Now this is where it really begins for me," Mecca says. "We gotta get in those big school buses with the bars on them; buses that I hate so much! As I was getting on the bus, I was saying to myself, 'Man, I promised myself I would never ride these buses again. That was over with. Once I got to Orange, my next stop was home.' But things happen, and I get on the bus.

"Next they told us, 'You guys are going to Johnston County because they have the space.' I'm sittin' on that bus, and I'm thinkin', 'You guys have no idea about where we are going!' A couple of the guys said to me, 'You real quiet. You all right?' And I say, 'You'll see. You'll see.'"

Mecca had been to Johnston County for a short stay back when that camp was medium security. Just a short time before the kitchen fire at OCC, Johnston had been reclassified as a minimum–security camp. To me that would mean clearing out all of the controls required by medium custody. I would have said to Mecca, "Calm down. It's green clothes now." I would have been wrong. Nothing in a prison changes that fast.

"When we got to Johnston, we sat on the bus for about forty minutes. And it's no A/C on the bus." Mecca slumps, miming exhaustion and wiping his face. I want to laugh, but he is not laughing. "It's like a prelude to what Johnston gonna be like. No A/C. It's June. It's gonna be summer. No windows. They've got that grating and you can't touch the windows. They're welded shut. Thinking about that, it's a tough ride.

"Another thing is they're really serious about security at Johnston. When we pulled up to the facility, they had officers out there with shotguns. In medium and close custody that's mandatory. They don't do that in minimum custody anymore, keep inmates under a gun. So when we got to Johnston that was stunning, officers outside the bus with the shotgun telling you to exit. You have to have experienced it to understand the silent communication amongst what we call old–timers, guys like myself. It's looks we give each other –We gonna be okay. Don't lose it. This is just temporary.

"Place looked exactly like when it was medium. No difference except we have on green clothes. And even though I knew what to expect, I wasn't ready for it. I'm the type of person, I want to check with myself and see if I'm thinking straight. I got with a couple of older guys who had been to Johnson also and they were feeling the same way. Not this again. I can't do this again! I just don't have what it takes to deal with this again!

"Finally we exit the bus and they take us through a shakedown room. We are asking, 'Why you shakin' us down? We just came from another prison. We haven't been outside with the free society. We don't have any contraband. We haven't been around anybody but each other.' And they say, 'Well that's how we do it in Johnston County.'

"They were real nasty that way. We had to go there and get strip searched and we hated that, because they don't do that at Orange. I thought I was done with that. Take everything off. Six or seven guys at a time in a eight by ten room with three or four officers, everybody stripped down, all the way down, full body search, cavity search. And you gotta stand there and witness this until the last guy got his clothes on. I am not feeling good about this."

When Mecca mentions the weapons, the body search and that jolt that reminds you this *is* prison, it tripped a memory of a visit I made to the warden's office at OCC. I was waiting outside the office when I noticed a frame on the wall. It looked like a picture, but when I got up close, I saw that it was a display of confiscated shanks. When I said something about this to the men in the OCC workshop group, they asked, "What did you think?" And I said, "To be honest, it worked. It scared me. I know it's not going to happen for real, but it sent me the message that any one of you could have one of those drill bits or chiseled pieces of metal with a plastic wrap grip right now, in your pocket."

They laughed and assured me that's not going to happen in minimum. Men have too much at stake. But that "artwork" gave me a flash of the officer's mentality that is at work during the strip search; that mentality, and an opportunity to pull a man down a peg. To deal with this, you need to have your defenses on duty. When I visited Scott-so at Wake Correctional – this was when he was working at the governor's mansion (for a dollar a day and the right to consideration for a MAPP) – he would always leave the visit ten minutes early so that he did not have to undergo the strip search with fifty other guys. I felt a little humiliated myself; that he had to pay that price just to be allowed to visit with me.

But back to Mecca's experience. "Guys from Orange looking around and thinking, 'What kind of crappy place is this? Look at all the concertina wire.' They are looking at the rec yard, which is big but kind of bare. Everything about it is so different from Hillsborough. No trees. No koi pond. No picnic tables.

"Myself, I go, 'Oh no. Oh man, I'm feeling this again.' I'm having recall of how the place is run. How they do counts, how they expect us to be, because I can sense it hasn't changed in how it's run. We're just wearing different colored clothes, but that doesn't mean anything at Johnston. So I'm pulling up all of that information in my head and exploring how I am going to cope with this and trying to deal with what to expect next.

"Then, the next day, they give us our ID cards. They tell us, you gonna have to have this on all the time. You gonna have this little clamp thing and you gonna have to wear this on your clothes. Something they never had at Hillsborough! Made me think of the yellow star in the concentration camps. You always have to have it on. It says William Elmore, minimum custody, and my opus number. And never be caught without it, because it could be an infraction.

"And you have surveillance cameras. Cameras in the ceiling and on the yard. They had so many cameras around that if you happened to take that ID badge off, sit it down for a minute to brush something off, the camera zooms in. You hear, 'You, in the black hat who just took your ID card off your shirt. You need to put that back on. You with the dreadlocks. You with the bald head. You with the soda and the chips in your hand. Put that ID back on. Standing to the left of the pole, you need to put your ID back on.'

"Now here's another thing. They have one dining hall for maybe thirty dorms and it's very small. At Hillsborough, when they call chow, you have a window of time and they are very gracious with you. You don't have to rush at all. You can pick where you want to sit to eat. You can pick who you want to sit with to eat and that's fine. No pressure.

"Johnston County, they call you by dorms. 'F thirty-six report and line up for chow.' And line up means line up in a single file outside of the chow hall, because the previous dorm has been called and they already in there eating. No more than ten minutes for each group to eat. As ten guys leave at the exit, the officer will come and peek out the door. 'Ten more guys come in.'

"Even the serving is worse. You have a tray with slots, and you have your spork already on your tray. That's a spoon with slots. Tray is up on the rack and they slide your tray down and they pack on your tray what's in front of them. They slam the food down. Real unpleasant. Like they are feeding animals or something.

"Next thing is, you look around a bit thinking maybe you'll sit with a buddy, but the officer is right there. You gonna sit where the officer tells you to sit. Try to look around for a buddy, the officer is going to call you out and you are going to be embarrassed. They are never nice about informing you about what you don't know. Johnston is making me remember that.

"So we try to settle ourselves. Can't be here but for a few days. We don't have enough rations to be here longer than that... We were there five and a half months.

"After the second week approached, they started calling off six or seven names. 'Listen up. Listen up all guys from Orange County. So and so, so and so and so and so report to operations!'

"OK. Maybe they getting ready to tell us we're leaving. We get to operations, all our personal property, our clothes, our shoes, our books, were being brought to us from Orange. They cut the locks. They packed our stuff up and they drove it to us. But next thing is that everything we had at Orange was more than we are allowed to have at Johnston! They told us to go through our personal things and get whatever we wanted. And no civilian clothes because there was gonna be no passes or work release.

"I got my journals, a couple of ink pens, couple of writing pads and I said, 'that's all I'm gonna need. We not gonna be here long. I get an extra bar of soap or two.' I told myself, I can do this."

There was never any solid information for those of us with connections to the OCC prisoners. The staff had no more information than the chaplain or the volunteers and families. When the possessions were shipped to Johnston, it was disturbing for everyone. Every few weeks there would be an announcement that it would be a few weeks more. Rumors began to circulate that they were going to close down OCC. Even the chaplain felt the stress.

Mecca told me, "Chaplain Nickel from Orange came three times, and each time he told us two weeks. So he was put in the position of giving us false news. When we got back, Chaplain Nickel said, 'I've learned some hard lessons. They didn't communicate with me, and that bothered me. It hurt me to come down there and tell you two weeks more, but I told you that because that's what I would get from them. I was putting my integrity on the line. I could see it in your eyes at those visits. Each visit, guys are going to believe me less. I can see now that administration didn't care how I felt about that.'"

All of this uncertainty is starting to wear people down. Staff at OCC are not sure what's happening, and families are in limbo. "My mother refused to come visit me at Johnston!" Mecca exclaims. "She said, 'Don't even ask. I'm not coming to Johnston County.' And I said, 'What about my stuff?' 'cause they said families could pick up the extra stuff we were not allowed to keep at Johnston. She said, 'Just let them hold it and you'll get it back when you go back to Hillsborough.'

"Jeff Willis had visits a few times at Johnson, and I asked him what's it like. He said, 'They are not nice. You don't want her to do it. I keep telling my mom not to come, but she keeps on coming. Man, I love to see my family and know that they love me, to touch them and hug them, but I don't like how they treat them here.' I asked several guys, and they all said the same thing. So I told Mom she was right. Didn't want her to put herself where the officers could humiliate her. Don't let them do that anymore. Five months. In all of prison I never went that long without a visit!"

This was a very hard decision for Mecca to make. I spoke to Bessie about it, and it was hard on her also. But she was fed up with the petty harassment. Maybe you get to visit and they won't let you in. Or they don't like what you are wearing. When I visited Scott-so in

Wake Correctional I learned to always have a change of clothes in the car in case they didn't like what I was wearing. T–shirt too revealing. Skirt too short. Dressing improper. Let us search you again. So Bessie put that release date in front of her eyes and did visits on the phone. "Anyway," She told me, "It was time for William to be on his own. It was time for me to let myself rest, 'cause now we have an end date."

The men from OCC stayed close at Johnston, trying to make sense of it. I had a steady correspondence back and forth the whole time. They bundled their letters and hired one of the prison artists to decorate an envelope for me.

The cheerful image did not disguise the struggles they were all having. A lot of prison stories paint the path from incarceration to release as a steady movement forward, but Johnston helped me see that days in prison can beat you down quickly, and there is very little about a bad day that you have the power to change. Chris Williams wrote, "The guys hope that all is well with you, because it certainly isn't all well on this end. I'm sure Mecca has described this as eloquently as he can. This has to be the place that Dante was referring to when he said, 'abandon all hope, ye who enter.' What makes it so bad is the fact that after experiencing oppressive regimes like this for eighteen years, I got drunk on the liberating culture at OCC, and now we are forced back into the sobering reality of our current situation. I thank God for Scott-so and Mec'; otherwise this would be downright unbearable."

Jeff Willis does not have a MAPP. He keeps getting turned down, so sometimes he can be bitter, and sometimes the privileges at Orange could seem like a scam. But he writes to me that Johnston has been "an eye opener for me," that even in prison he should appreciate good things when they come. "I try to begin to cherish the moments of going out the gates at Orange for litter crew. And just the overall concept of how I was treated and the little things that count... That's all. I'm losing my soul in this place."

Mecca writes that they often sit around in silence, on their own, in different parts of the yard. Maybe he'll get up and cross the yard to say something to Jeff or Scott-so, and then he'll retreat. I write and suggest that they put pencil to paper and see what happens. Mecca catches me off guard with a long emotional letter in reply, the ellipses are in the original:

> I want to run through the halls and scream at the top of my lungs... Bang on all the bars demanding that everyone wake up!... It's blindingly sunny & bone dry compared to all of the tears mothers have cried about this machine that has swept up their sons in droves... I've seen those tears... I've watched them drop like bombs over Baghdad... But they made no noise, no explosive sounds...They didn't lite up the sky... Now it's raining. It's raining hard. Harder! Harder! I plead. Bring it on! Finally the rain has cooled us off. There is no A/C, but my bunk is by a fan... I'm still aware enough to appreciate & recognize subtle respites & sips of relief.
>
> It smells like apathy here, tastes like a bitter dry loaf of loathing... I've had some serious unraveling to do, some serious reprogramming... I've had to dig really, really deep & find some stuff that I've busted up and put far away... Ah! I've found it & it was in shambles... Humpty Dumpty would have been easier to put back together... But guess what, my life is on the line. If I don't figure it out my mom & you Simone & my sister & my sponsors, David & Tom & Chris Ringwalt &

Mr. Bill – They'd kill me...

I've decided to suck it up and endure... I've made up my mind. I'm gonna make it & do it cheerfully and graciously... I'm a lion... It just gets tiresome sometimes.

Love, Mecca

I have a big stack of letters from Mecca and the other men in the workshop. It's hard to reread them, but it's also clear that writing and staying in touch was important. Looking back, Mecca says that it was the sponsors and the letters that kept him going.

But not everything went smoothly. Mecca said later that he had two close brushes with disaster there.

"Listen to this," he began. "At Johnston they have so many people on medication call you wouldn't believe the line," He waves his arm in an arc across the room. "It just as long as the chow line. It really is. It's kinda sad. Med call three times a day. Sometimes the officers right there watch them take them, sometimes not. If not, they can go sell them. Which mean more drugs everywhere. And lots of stuff I never heard of. And the reaction from the drugs. I sold drugs, so I've seen the response. Now I call what I sold basic drugs, because this new stuff... I had never seen how people behave on this new stuff. Frightened me because they are so far out of it, they're dangerous. You don't know what they are going to do. You gotta take care of yourself. When you in these dorms, say thirty-five or forty guys, and the officers are not in there, you gotta manage the house as best you can.

"People get in fights. Beat somebody else up. I'm being really objective when I say there's a prison etiquette. Being nice, being a gentleman, that's only appreciated by administration. If I'm acting like a nice guy, I'm making your job easier. But in the population, they gotta see you in action or have heard about you. I thought I had moved off of that when I got to Hillsborough, but oh no, here we go again. Almost got in a fight two times at Johnston.

"First time one guy actually stole something out of my locker. It was a bag of cereal! Right before we left Orange, we had an order..."

Sometimes things seem so obvious to Mecca he forgets to explain. I stop him and ask, "What's an order?" He looks at me patiently and sighs. It's hard to get momentum going in a story with an audience that's asking questions.

"You use a form and you order food. That's a privilege," he says, meaning it's something earned by good behavior. "I had ordered my stuff and I got my cereal and they packed it up in my stuff when they brought it to Johnston. So I said, 'Okay, I'll keep some of it and see how I eat it.' At Hillsborough, you want some milk, you go to the kitchen, you bring a milk back and you eat your cereal. You can't do that at Johnston. At Johnston I ate my cereal dry. Put it in the cup and ate it dry. I grew up doing that. That's not a big deal.

"Problem comes when they brought a guy who had some real mental issues into our dorm. After he got there, another guy, Adam, lost his soap dish with expensive soap. Dove soap. This guy slept directly across from Adam and myself, and his locker door was open and he had Adam's soap dish in it. Adam went and got it. Should have been the end of it, but then Green, who slept above this crazy guy, came off the yard and saw the crazy guy piddling around in his own locker and saw other people's stuff in there too."

Mecca leans in, determined to keep me on track in case my lack of experience in prison etiquette fails me again. He already taught me this lesson way back when he talked about that move where he left his stuff unguarded on his bunk at Caledonia and went to chow. "Now you gotta understand, locker is personal space. Like your bunk. Nobody messes with anybody's personal space."

This is an interesting phenomenon for me, and I've discussed it with the workshop group. How is it that people who felt perfectly comfortable breaking into another person's house, holding up a Quick Stop, or living by robbing other drug dealers (used in a discussion as a mere description not worthy of any special note) can come to prison and feel entitled to set very hard and fast rules on personal property. "It's no way the same," they explained. "Now, say you need some money, say you need it to buy drugs. Stuff you are stealing is just stuff. Doesn't belong to anybody. It's just stuff that will get you money to buy more drugs. You are not thinking about anybody owning that stuff, but in prison, it's different. Stuff in your locker, on your bunk nobody should be messing with that stuff."

If this is hard to grasp, try explaining the difference between tax avoidance, tax evasion, and tax fraud. As an accountant would say, "Well, this is a gray area."

But back to Mecca, who is trying to manage his own despair and frustration while keeping an eye on the man in the bunk across from him.

"The crazy guy is sitting on his bunk with that look in his eye. I've seen that look before in the street. So I say, 'Come over here for a second.' And he comes over. I sleep on the top bunk so I'm standing looking across my bunk and he's on the other side of the bunk and he's not even looking at me. He's looking at all my snacks that are on my bed. I'm saying, 'Hey, you listening to me?' He nods. He never breaks his gaze off my snacks. Like he's countin' the calories or something!

"So I say, 'Look, you understand what I'm saying?' This guy he never talks. Never heard him say a word. He shakes his head. I say, 'Listen, are you hungry? Do you want anything to eat? I know that you are a thief. I don't want any problems. If you want something, I give it to you. You want a soup?' I gave him the soup. I said, 'You got a cup and a spoon?' He shook his head No. I gave him a spoon, "Here. Enjoy it. If you need something else, ask me. If I have it, I can give it. Don't steal anything.' So he nodded and he went and he ate the soup.

"Two or three days later, I'm not paying any attention. I'm out on the yard. Kalib says, 'Did you have some Fruit Loops?' And I say, 'I think so. Why, you want some?' And he says, "Naw, but you should check in your locker 'cause I seen crazy man with a whole bag of Fruit Loops.'

"When I came in, I checked my locker three times, just to make sure I wasn't crazy. And soon as I finally realized that he had been in my locker and stole my cereal, they called count time. 'Everybody get on your bunks for the count.'

"I'm brewin' on it on my bunk. I'm livid. And he sleeps right across from me so I'm lookin' at him. I'm lookin' so he'll look at me, but he won't look at me. Now somebody else says, 'He been in your locker.' That starts a roller coaster. He went in my locker. But it's just Fruit Loops. Man, chill out. It's not that important. It's not gonna be any big problem. He's kinda crazy. But he went in your *locker!* You don't do that. He's kinda crazy. But he went in your *locker!* You don't do that.

"Here's what worked for us both. They had three recounts. That gave me time to come to myself. I mean I was ready for this fight. Fight about Fruit Loops!

"After about an hour they announce, 'Counts clear.' I jump off my bunk and I go over to his bunk. He's laying down. I say, 'Hey, can you hear me?' He don't say anything. I say, 'I'm talking to you. Can you hear me?' He won't say anything. I say, 'Open your locker.'

"Now he has a lock. He didn't come with us; he been in Johnston from before us, so he still has his lock. When we left Hillsborough, they cut our locks, and thinkin' we are only here temporary, we don't want to waste money on a lock.

"I said, 'Open your locker. I think you have my cereal.' He shook his head no. So I went back on my bunk. Yard is not open yet. And I can't go anywhere with myself. Everybody's watching and they're getting riled up. We not having no thieves in here. We don't do that in Hillsborough. Back there, if you went in my locker there would have been no conversation. I would settle it fast. I wouldn't even talk to you!

"So I started to pray and settle myself down. They opened the yard, so I went on the yard and I walked laps. Jeff can tell you. He walked laps with me. I just walked and prayed and worked to settle myself down."

It's astonishing to me that a man as composed as Mecca can be tossed around by something like this, but it also demonstrates how unhinged he had become. Without visits. Under close watch. Yes, he said he could have done the three years of the MAPP in Caledonia, but that's just talk when you are in an open camp like OCC. Now he's back at Johnston.

"I was ready for this fight. Fight about Fruit Loops!" Mecca says. "Could have lost everything. Could have lost my MAPP."

After he left prison, one day when he's out riding his bicycle Mecca calls and texts me a photo. "It's the Fruit Loop Guy, Simone. He's right here getting on a bus." And there he is, hopping on the free bus in downtown Durham. By then he's become a watchword between us. Unanticipated chance to mess up: Fruit Loops.

"That was the first thing," Mecca resumes in a slightly confessional tone. "Next thing that happens is this. Guys who are on work release at Hillsborough get moved to Wake and Dan River so they can go back to work. Places they work are waiting for them. Can't hold the jobs open forever. That leaves space in the dorm at Johnston so the dorms are blended now. Gentrified, Ha! They bring in all these guys on ninety day parole or probation, guys that violated it to get off of it. You see, that's a thing to do. When you get on these curfews and rules and drug tests while you are on probation, guys maybe can't operate without breaking the rules. So they will violate, come back to prison, finish that time, maybe only ninety days, and when they get out, they are off everything. They won't have urine tests anymore. They don't have no curfew. Same time, inside, they can do what they want. Drugs. Whatever. Their date doesn't move. It's gonna be ninety days no matter what.

"So the atmosphere in the dorm is changing. There's a whole motley crew of guys living in with us. This day, it's time to take a shower. At Hillsborough the shower time is relaxed. You just go to the shower. There's not a line or nothing. Johnston County, whole different set–up. Guys are responsible to call their turn. You form a line.

"Make a long story short, this is what happens. Once they clear count at four o'clock, the showers open. Every day, this guy is always asking who is last in the shower. He would always get told some position after the last guy. For some reason, this particular day, he come straight to me, not looking for the line or nothing. He says, 'Who's last in the shower?' And I say, 'I think it's the guy way down there.' And he says, 'What's his name?' I say, 'I don't know, but he's right there. He's has a beard and a bald head. I think he's last. I'm not sure.'

"He keeps repeating, asking me the guy's name. Finally I say, 'Hey man, I don't know the guy's name. What do you want with me?' And he leans in, 'I'm asking you a question! Why don't you know his name? I'm tryin' to find out who's in the blankety blank blank shower! Man, what the blank is wrong with you?'

"He's talking to me while I'm sittin' on my bunk. I'm in the top bed where you can pretty much stand and talk to me and I can see the shower line from there. He keeps on me, 'You actin' like you don't know nuttin'. I'm sick of this. Every time I ask something, you act like you don't know nothin.'

"So I jump off my bunk and he's headed to his bunk and I walk to his bunk and we nose to nose. I say, 'Man if you ever talk to me like that again, that's going to be the end of you.' He's just standin' there and he's kind of shakin'. I said, 'Do you understand me?' And he says nothing. Then we hear, 'Recount! Recount. Everybody back to their bunks.'

"Same as before. Luck for me! Recount. So I go back on my bunk. He sleeps on the top bunk too, about three or four down from me, and I'm just as mad as I was with the guy with the Fruit Loops. It compounds the place to me. And I'm saying to myself, 'Oh Lord, man what is going on? I'm too close to everything to lose it here over nothing!'

"They recount and then they go to another dorm. After the officers leave, this guy jumps off his bunk and he starts heading towards my bunk. Then five or six guys from Orange jump off their bunks and they're trailing behind him. He says, 'Whoa everybody. I want to apologize. I'm sorry. I'm sorry. I want to apologize. I shouldn't have talked to you like that. Man, I'm trippin'.' I said, 'I understand.' And we closed it like that.

"These meds that they are getting and trading, for me it's not like the street. And even more, when I am on the street I can move away. I'm not living with those people. They are just my customers."

We pause and there's quiet in the room. Mecca leans back and looks out the window at the trees, like he is trying to settle himself again. I ask, "What's up?" And he takes a long time to start talking again.

"What did I learn from all this? What I learned is that I am a poor sufferer. I really am. Even after more than twenty years in prison, in that instance, at Johnston, I suffered terribly. I whined. I was angry. And I felt like I deserved to be angry, because I felt like all of this time I did a really good job of dealing with things, and that's how I got to Orange. When I found myself back in Johnston, my anger about having to get back into those tools that it took to cope was so strong and so intense, I could have ripped those two guy's heads off – over Fruit Loops and a shower line. I would have thrown everything away.

"That was a heck of a punch on the chin where I was in my sentence. It was also a beautiful thing. I needed it, but I wish I would have dealt with it better. My anger made me feel entitled. I wasn't angry with God or nobody. I was angry with the situation. Man, I'm not going to deal with this again! I dealt with this for twenty-two years and I finally made it to Hillsborough. I can exhale a little bit. Now I'm back at square one. Man, I'm not ready to go through this again. Everybody pretty much better leave me alone. I deserve this time to sit down and lick my wounds or pick at them and pour salt on them. I deserve that. Just leave me alone.

"Was it humbling? It was like being gutted. I was empty. I knew when I got this time, life sentence, that this was gonna be a marathon, not a sprint. When I got to Johnston, I took a respite from that marathon, and I didn't have a way to get back up. I hit a hill and I'm thinking, 'No, not at this point in the race! Not at this point in the race!'

"I didn't suffer as well as I thought that I should have. Yes, I'm a tough critic on myself. Nobody going to be harder on me than I am on me. And I would say, 'You not dealing with this well. You gotta be better than this. What's wrong with you?' I would ask myself was I suppressing? Was I not really dealing?

"And then I would say to myself, 'No, you need to see this, because Hillsborough put you to sleep about what prison is like. You going out on these passes. You puttin' on jeans and stuff. You think you ain't in no dag-gone prison. You can easy get lost in that.

"I been to camps five times worse than Johnston has ever been, but I didn't know any different, so I had a different perspective. Every prison is tough because every prison is prison. When I got to Hillsborough, after all the time I done, I made a shift and I dropped my vigilance.

"I asked Scott-so, he's done a lot of time. I asked Jeff. I asked another OCC guy, Bobby Brown. Bobby's been in prison twenty-nine years. He's been at the worst prisons you can think of and was in prison before they integrated. He's seen it all. But when I said, 'What's the hardest time you done?' He said, 'This right here in Johnston. This was a torture camp for me.' Bobby's seventy-three years old. The man was once on death row. It don't get no worse. He said, 'This is it.'

"It's not the worst prison, but after Hillsborough, then going back, that really put the dagger in us all. Everybody was heavy, heavy. Men walked slow. They moved slow, lethargic. They were heavy with grief. I would ask people. Is it just me?

"Scott-so said, 'Man, you can't never see the stars or anything.' I could tell he was obsessing on it. And I said, 'Man, don't you lose it.

You come too far! Somebody got to hold it together. Let me lose it. Don't you lose it.' He was fasting, Ramadan, but it wasn't the fasting. He was right; you didn't see stars. You didn't see squirrels, not one squirrel. It was like toxic waste. Like Chernobyl had happened there and everything was *dead*. Nobody could write this stuff. It was that ominous.

"I'm not gonna lie. The first part of that duration had me in a stupor. I didn't want to eat. I wanted to shut everything down. I didn't want their food. I didn't want their weights. I didn't want to use their water, their microwave, the news on their TV. I didn't want nothing they had. Just leave me alone. Let me sit here and sulk. Took me back to that place when I went to CP. Way back.

"But the good of it, which is not the kind of good you want, came when we were about halfway through. It finally dawned on me, like I had an epiphany. I wrote it to a sponsor, maybe to you. I said, 'I refuse to let the light of Hillsborough and the darkness of Johnston County cheat me out of figuring out how to find a lesson in this.'

"And I did figure it out. Johnston let me know that I can still make it through whatever they are going to throw at me – in prison, in the world after prison. I just don't like that kind of test with no room for error. I don't like that. But that's what it was for me."

Chapter 12: What Can You Learn While Butchering Hogs?

When Mecca finally returns to Orange Correctional, it's less than a year until his release date. In the MAPP contract, firm dates are set for moving up the ladder of levels. When Mecca was sent to Johnston County, he was at Level 2 and allowed to go out on passes one on one with a sponsor. Mecca returns at Level 3, which permits a single sponsor to take out a group of up to three men. Level 3 is also a requirement for work release, and Mecca is supposed to get a job. While Mecca was at Johnston County, Bessie was trying to find him a job. She hoped her connections would get him work with a re–entry organization where he could move from work release to permanent employment status. But nothing is happening, and Mecca is getting nervous. The program office is not happy that Bessie thinks she can do their job for them, which may be why they seem less than enthusiastic about working the placement angle on their side.

The first offer Mecca gets from the program office is for work at K&W, a classic southern cafeteria chain where you slide your tray past service stations and self–seat at a table. There's cooking to do, but most of the job is scooping food, clearing tables and cleaning up. If Mecca hated it in the kitchen in prison, he does not see why he would like the work at K&W. He turns that down. The next job interview he gets through the program office is with Chem Strip, "The East Coast's Largest, Full–Service, Metal Stripping Company." They want to offer him a job, but there's some unexplained delay and nothing is happening there.

The purpose of the job is to allow men approaching release to earn more than the prison wage (capped at a dollar a day) so that they leave with some money in the bank. Since Mecca has good family support, he's not worried about the length of the job, but he's getting the message that the parole commission wants to see a clear six months of work. Mecca is in the OCC program office one day talking to one of the programmers, Mr. Ashley, about Chem Strip when Ms. Hughes, the head programmer, turns and asks, "Is he trying to refuse a job? Because if he is, I have to put it in my report to Cheryl Bell, who's the coordinator, and it's not going to look good."

That tone of voice is really familiar. When the recruiters show up from Neese's Sausage, Mecca puts in his name for an interview. Neese's is a hundred–year–old family business with a manufacturing and packaging facility and a slaughterhouse. If stripping chemicals in protective gear sounded like a less than ideal job, working in a slaughterhouse was not a dream job either; but as Mecca is going to learn, you never know what color your good breaks will be wearing.

His interview is conducted by Thomas, a fifth–generation member of the Neese family whose mother, Andrea, is running the business, including keeping an eye on the slaughtering facility. Thomas is accompanied by Chris, a man Andrea and he are training to take over the slaughterhouse. They are doing a second day of interviews when Mecca shows up. This is a private meeting, but later in the year, I go out to Neese's and get to hear the story from both sides of the table. On one side, boy from New Jersey, now a man in his forties who has served twenty-three years in prison for murder. On the other side, the folks from Neese's. They are there because Andrea Neese heard about the work release program at her church and decided to offer men from OCC work in the slaughterhouse. This is a charitable proposition, but to do the job men need to be qualified and strong.

Andrea Neese is not officially at the interview, but she is the force behind every major decision. She's an attractive woman, straightforward, and totally committed to the business. "I began working here when I was in high school," she says. "As soon as I could drive, I would come and work in the summers. I worked during college, but then I got married to Thomas's dad and moved away for ten years. When I came back Thomas was just six months old. I started back in January 1987 and I've been here ever since."

"I started working here a little bit after that!" Thomas looks at his Mom and laughs. "No, really, I guess I started when I was thirteen or fourteen. I couldn't be around the equipment then, so my cousin and I would come out during the summer and help out in production, boxing, and cleaning up around the old house in front. After I graduated from college, in 2010, I came back full time."

Chris adds, "I started working here on May 1, 2013. I found out about it through a mutual friend. Before this I worked in a totally different business, a chemical company and warehousing carpets."

"Right." Andrea leans in. "This job, there's nothing like this in the world." We're talking in the plant's office and there is a steady racket coming from other buildings on the site. As I drove in, I could see the barns in the back, the building with the kill floor, and the processing area. Andrea looks out the gritty window and tells me, "The men that work here, they're not like anybody else. It takes a certain breed of person to work in this atmosphere and this job. We ask people when they come in the same questions: Do you hunt? Have you ever shot a deer? Have you ever gutted a deer? Do you know how to field dress?

"We start with those kinds of questions because if you don't know, if you've never been exposed to those sights and sounds, it's not gonna work. When you first walk on this floor, at the slaughtering plant, you have no idea what you're going to see. So this job is not for everybody. We tell that to the people who come in. It's a bloody, very wet environment. In the summer it's very hot – you can lose twenty pounds. In the winter, it's very cold, because the kill floor is not heated. If you grew up on a farm, if you slaughtered animals as a child, you'll fit in great! But if you're a city boy and that's all you've known, you might not work out here. We need people who are prepared for that."

I try to imagine Mecca as a candidate for this job. He's strong, but if he was not prepared to pick cotton at Caledonia, how and why is he going to work in a slaughterhouse? Leave it to Mecca to surprise me again.

When I ask him about the Neese's interview, Mecca explains, "Somebody gave Neese's Sausage my name, and I go in the multi-purpose room and Mr. Ashley's there. He introduced me, and I shook their hands. There are two of them there, Thomas and Chris, but I didn't get any names then. They just tell me to sit down and they find my name, last name on their list.

"They asked me, 'What do you know about animals?' And I was truthful. I said, 'I had a dog before.' And they said, 'Na, we talking about like farm animals like pigs.' And I said, 'I've never seen a pig in real life. If they not at the zoo, never seen 'em before.' I didn't even tell them about my turtle.

"They said, 'That's all? You never done no farm work?' I said, 'I've never had a job before. I've never worked before.' And they sat back and they said, 'That's interesting.' It did not look good. I didn't want to sound desperate, but I said, 'I need to work and I want to work. The one thing that I can guarantee you is that I know how to do what I'm told. I know how to follow instructions. I won't bring any strife to the workplace, and if there's anything I don't know, I'll be the first one to raise my hand. And I do want this job.' So he scribbled something down and said. 'Good interview.'"

Mecca was not sure what that meant. He does not feel like a man who clinched the interview. Good interview. Good–bye. Don't bother us anymore. Thomas and Chris have exactly the opposite take. Sitting around at the plant office, Chris tells me, "We had a list and he was one of the guys already on our list before we even left the prison. Some of the guys that we interview both in the prison and here, they come here for a job. They want you to think that they know how to do everything here. William was honest. He said 'I've been in prison since I was twenty. I have no skills, but I'm willing to learn.' And that was it – the fact that he was honest and that he was eager to learn how so that when he did get back out in the real world, he had some type of skills. That really got me."

Thomas sighs and explains that men who are desperate for work in a slaughterhouse are not going to be the pick of the litter, but they want you to think that's just who they are. He goes on to say, "A lot of the other guys that we'd interviewed at the prison had been through shop class or some type of technical training or cook school. William hadn't done a whole lot of that, so I asked him what he had done since he's been incarcerated. The thing that he told me – I still remember – was 'I did a lot of reading and soul searching.'

"And I thought, 'That's a vague answer.' So I asked, what he'd read about, and he said, 'A lot of psychology and sociology subjects.' I kind of turned my head and asked why he was researching that. And he said – I still remember exactly how he said it – 'I wanted to know what made me tick so that when I got out I didn't commit the crime again, go back to my old ways.'

"Nobody else that I've interviewed, has said anything like that. That really impressed me, that he was that dedicated to bettering himself. More than twenty years is a lot of time to sit around and either better yourself or make yourself worse, and he chose the better path."

"Another thing," Chris says, "We got back and a day or two later his mom called up. She said, she hoped we would give him the opportunity and he needed to work because he's never been working a job in his life. And I said. 'Me and Thomas are talking about it; there's a pretty good chance that we gonna hire him, but we've not made a decision yet.' And she thanked me for listening to what she had to say."

"That impressed me," Thomas said. The fact that his family moved down here to be closer to him, to support him. That's something special. I don't think there's a whole lot of people, especially that are in his situation, that will stay with someone for that long. Most families, you know, they disown 'em after they do something like that."

I'm reminded of Bessie's call to Brown Creek, her offer to volunteer to teach and reach out to the men. She has quite the stomach for risk, but this is different. She's sincere and definitely in the saddle with Cheryl on this one: Mecca needs to get some skin in the game and learn how to hold down a job.

Mecca is both offered a job at Neese's and finally invited over to Chem Strip. Now the dealer, the businessman from the street resurfaces. As Mecca explains it, "I researched it and Neese's would get me more money. I get eight twenty-five an hour. I pay eighty for room and board. Now there are guys that make twelve an hour, but they make less because they pay for transportation, sixteen dollars a day. Neese's, they pick you up. No charge. And the room and board, how they do it is based on your hours. Guys taught me to keep my hours below thirty-six. Thirty-five hours and fifty-five minutes. Anything over forty, they take out a hundred for room and board. So I got to work at least forty-two hours to make up that difference, and work is supposed to be forty hours and some days it's shorter, so maybe I can't make up the difference. End of the day, I end up with more money at Neese's."

So everything's set? No. This is prison. Murphy's Law is always in force.

"Before all this can happen, there's another problem," Mecca recounts. "Mr. Ashley starts the paperwork, and he says, 'Where's your social security card?' And I say, 'I don't know. You tell me.' He says he can't find it, and, 'I can't let you go to work without the social security card.' Tells me it could take four to six weeks to get a new card. I haven't got that kind of time. Neese's, Chem Strip, they are not obligated. They could back out any time.

"I left his office very upset about it. I called my mom and said, 'Here's the deal, I don't trust this process. I feel like I'm getting sabotaged. I want you to call Neese's and explain to them that I do want the job. I want them to hear that from you, because I don't really know what they are being told at the other end of the phone.'"

That's the phone call Thomas and Chris remember. "She asks what's the problem, and I say, 'I don't have no social security card.' And she starts panicking. 'I don't have your card. I haven't had it since you were twelve years old. Do you know your number?' And I say, 'Yeah, I know my number. But they want the card.' She says, 'I'm going to call this Mr. Ashley. All this time they had you in prison. Where am I supposed to find it?'"

"She was livid. She called Mr. Ashley. And you know how I know? 'cause ten minutes after that I hear that squawk box, 'William Elmore report to Mr. Ashley's office.' I get in there and he says, 'Tell your mother to calm down. Explain that we're going to work this out. We're going to get your social security card. We just need to fill out some paperwork first.' We do it, and he seals it in the envelope and says, 'Please call and tell her I put this in the box today!'"

"This is the first day of work in my life!" Mecca explains. His eyes are wide, not narrowed down the way they are when he slips into a monologue about dealing. Unlike the prison kitchen, gym, clothes house or cleaning the dorm, a job in the real world in unknown territory, and if there is one thing Mecca does not like it's walking into a situation without information; maybe he's putting himself in a spot where he could easily be blindsided. But the social security card has come through and he starts at Neese's on Monday. "All that Sunday I'm worried, and I'm thinking, do I pack a lunch? I'm forgetting everything I saw everybody else do. Do I need to go the canteen and get some stuff? Right, they gonna get us a lunch to pack out.

"As soon as the shift changes, six o'clock, the car drives up and I go out the gate and I get in. The same guy – one of the guys who interviewed me – drives us to Burlington, me and a couple of other guys. Now I know that was Chris, but that day I didn't know any names. I didn't know anything about where I was going. I was clueless.

"We get there and first thing I go to the break room, and there is Ms. Neese, the heir to the throne. She's got all this paperwork for us to fill out. That stuff is like foreign language to me. The other guys have done this before, so they get busy right away. Ms. Neese, she's telling me step by step what to write down. Finally she says, 'You've really never worked before? How did you do that?'

"I had been in prison twenty something years. That's how!"

"That was long and tedious and boring, all that paper. Finally we were done, and she says she's going to walk me around. Now everyone else is familiar with farms and chickens and killing, but she's got me singled out. She says, "You gonna see some things you've probably never seen before. If you get queasy or weak, let me know and we'll cut it short and I'll take you somewhere else. Put on this smock and tie it and put this rubber suit on and these rubber boots and this hairnet, this hardhat and these long gloves.' I'm like, what's going on?

"We went and toured the whole place. We started on the kill floor. That was very hard, and Ms. Neese, she stood beside me and she held my arm and she kept patting it. She said, 'You gonna be okay. Keep this in mind. I've done everything in here. If I can do it, you can too. Is your stomach queasy? You're not going to fall down are you? That floor is wet with a lot of blood, but it's not gonna get on you. You got on rubber boots. You gonna be okay.' She actually talked me through the whole thing.

"I told her, 'I love animals. This is not easy for me to see.' She said, 'I understand. You let me know. If you can't handle this, we will find something for you to do.' Then she made the call. Probably saw I did not look right! 'Okay, let's go.'

"But I did go back in and work on the kill floor. Only for a day. Worked with the chitlin's. Cleaning them out. They have a machine that does it, but it doesn't take the smell away. I have never seen anything like this. The machine's like blowing up a balloon, blowing up the intestines! And Ms. Neese says, 'Never apply any more than about twelve inches of intestines on the machine. Don't be greedy like me. I slid maybe twenty-four inches on and what happened is when it hit that level it blew up and I got it on my hair and my shirt got covered. I had to go home and take a shower and it was not pleasant. Don't let it blow up to more than twelve inches. We gonna start you here. You won't be here long.'

"And so for the whole day, that's what I did. Now my back was to the kill floor so I couldn't see what was going on, but I could hear them, the hogs. They don't make a noise when they get electrocuted, but they make this noise before because they're in a small space and they get on each other's back. They make this squeal that you will never forget, like 'Get off of me! Get your six hundred pounds off my back!' And you hear the buzz of these big giant saws and these water chutes, the sound of machinery working along with the squealing pig, and the floor is always wet and bloody. Blood is dripping from the ceiling. It shoots up there and somebody's always hosing it down. I felt comfortable because the inspector was right there, so it has to be up to some standard. But it looks terrible. It smells terrible."

Mecca stops his story to take a break. It's hard for him, but that MAPP is holding it all up, floating freedom right on the other side of this job. Andrea and Thomas and Chris all remember trying to decide where to put Mecca. As they are talking this over, they can feel the beginning of something different in their relationship with Mecca. They are working their way into a personal investment in his success.

"I told him we'd put him on the kill floor," Thomas explains. "And he was, 'I'm going to be honest with you. I don't think I can take it back there. You have anything else?'"

"We were going to put him there in the beginning because of his strength," Andrea adds, "but then he said he couldn't take that floor."

"Right," Chris says. "We only have a couple of positions that require a certain body type or person, a couple that require picking up thirty or forty pounds repetitively all day long with one hand." Chris makes heaving motions, tipping forward in his chair. "Most of the positions here, we have equipment that does the lifting for us. So a strong guy like William, we're gonna try to put him on the kill floor.

"But, also, he was the first guy that we had hired that has been in there for violent crime. One of the things I asked him was if he was going to be okay having a knife around other people. Looking back on it, I probably shouldn't have even asked him, because once I got to know him better it was obvious that he wouldn't hurt a fly. I didn't know anything about what he had done in the past. I didn't want to bring up bad thoughts for him. But he handled it, and we learned something ourselves."

"Now here's something funny I remember," Andrea shifts the tone. "I said to everyone, 'When you come to work you punch in and when you leave work you punch out.' I could see he didn't really understand, but everyone else seemed fine, so I forgot about it."

"That's funny we still say that," Thomas says, motioning his hand up and down. "We haven't had a mechanical time card in twenty years, twenty-five years."

It's a card scan now, but Andrea was right. Punch, scan, swipe – those were nothing Mecca had ever seen before. He hasn't earned any money at the camp, so he hasn't been given a debit card to use in stores when he is out on a pass. Looking back on this clueless moment Mecca says, "Ms. Neese, first she showed me how you take this thing and you do that with this card. I didn't know what she was talking about. Punch a clock? I didn't know it was a real punching of a clock or swiping. I seen it maybe on TV. Never seen it myself. So I don't do that for a whole week! I'm lucky they have the hours from transporting us or I would have lost a lot of pay." He rolls his eyes. "And I'd never seen a paycheck either. Got my first check, had to show it to someone. All this stuff on it. I'm asking what all these things? FICA? All these numbers that show what you get paid. And then what you not gettin' paid."

It's fascinating to watch Mecca move into the world of paid employment. Yes, he's had plenty of cash flow through his hands, but money hand to hand, on the street, is different. It's a different way of earning and it breeds a different way of spending. He gives me a blow by blow of his first few days at work.

"First day was horrible. Working on the kill floor. Second day they figured I needed to recover from that, so all I did was take the trash out and hose things down. Third day I go to the processing room. That's where they gave me my knife, plastic shield so I don't cut my arm, and my cuttin' glove. They showed me how to sharpen my knife. Then you go in the processing room and when I get in there, they just tell me these guys will help you. They say, "Don't worry about speed. It's more about knowing what you're doing. Speed'll come.' It's kinda chilly. Kill floors are hot. But in the processing room they got fans running. It's not like see my breath cold, but nice and cool.

"I'm in there I have this long thing for sharpening my knife, and everybody's doing it, so I'm just kinda watching them. Ksshh. Kshhh. They're making small talk about getting drunk and all that stuff. And I'm watching what they do and next thing I know I hear this noise, sounds like a train. Like somebody says, "Whoo-hooo'. The second after that I hear this shshshsshh. These half a pigs are on this hook with a wheel. They're coming in along the ceiling, hanging down, and the whoo-hooo is a heads-up, because if you're not paying attention, if you coming out of a hall or a bathroom or an office, there's not a lot a room to negotiate. The half a pig is over half the size of the hallway. That thing hits you, you goin' to the ground. It's on this thing and it slides – shshsssh – and it hits the doors of the processing room. *Boom.*

"I used to call them "cows," and they kept remindin' me, 'they not cows, man, they're pigs.' But they so big, bigger than cows, and they comin' one after another, one, two, three... six of 'em. Really it's three, but they cut in half. Somebody climbs on the ladder and takes the knife that's hooked on this Achilles thing and they slice it and the half–a–pig is fallin' down and you push it to get it on the table. Table is long enough for six halves.

"They tell me how to start. Cut the shoulder off first. They are very patient, very kind. I cut the shoulder off first. Then they say, 'Now you gonna cut the ribs out. Then you gonna cut the tenderloin out. Then you gonna cut the ham out.' We are dissectin' these hogs."

I remind Mecca that's called "butchering." He nods but his expression makes it clear he has never seen meat before it got packaged in cellophane and put in the cooler at a supermarket.

"Yeah. I'm a butcher," he concedes and plows on. "We get 'em fresh, right from the kill floor. They still being doing this twitching. The nerves are still jumpy. I'm thinking they've been bled before they get to us, but after we finished cutting and slicing, I looked at my smock and it's bloody. The blood is still in the pig, but I'm thinkin' I'm cut! 'cause this knife is so sharp! I see these nicks. And I'm saying to myself, I don't want to tell anybody. I don't want to be a liability. So I say, 'I'll be back. I'm going to the bathroom.' Because after these pigs are cut up, we gotta wait for the next six to come in so there's a break.

"I go bathroom and I gotta take all of that protective stuff off and put another set on. When I go in the bathroom, I see all this blood, but I don't feel anything. Now, you the first person I told about how nervous I was – because it's embarrassing. In the bathroom I look see nicks in my gear. I see these cuts. When I got back, I didn't say anything, but I guess the guys can tell. They seen all this before! One guy says, 'Don't worry. Everybody's smock has that blood on it.

You want a breast plate?' And I say, 'What's that?' And he says, 'The breast plate, you know, 'cause sometimes you cuttin' that meat you come near your chest.'

"They're not laughing at me, just offerin'. But I said 'Naw. I'm good.' And he says, 'You sure? Look man, don't cut yourself. Not worth it. You got everything else on. You can add in the breast plate.' I got more equipment already than everybody else. But the guys all say, 'Don't worry. As you get better, you'll start to shake that stuff off. We all started that way. Look, I don't even have a cut glove on.' Then he showed me his hands and he got these marks all over 'em. Now I don't want any of that so you not gonna see me cuttin' with no glove on.

"Next thing is I'm tired in my arms and my shoulders 'cause I'm wrestling against the meat. I'm trying to cut with my strength. I don't have any technique. I'm cuttin' zig zag. I'm cuttin' triangles. It looks so ugly compared to their meat cuts. They're cuts are neat and symmetrical. Mine, looks like I just grabbed it, like I was a wolf eating." Mecca gives me that shrug of survival. He flicks his head as if he's tossing something out of his brain. "I made it through, and now I kind of know what I'm doing."

It's the end of the second week of work when Mecca shows up at the OCC workshop group. He's looking troubled and asks if he can take some of our time to talk about something at work. Everyone's curious. What about work release can be troubling a man like Mecca?

"There's this guy at Neese's, JB, who works in the processing room with me." Mecca checks the room and it's clear everyone is on alert. "I'm not sure what he wants, but I'm watching. The second week, we're in the processing room sharpening our knives. And JB says, 'You know what? I can't believe that she did that.' And he stops cuttin'. That's what gets my attention, because he's not talkin' to nobody. And he looks at me. He says again, 'I can't believe she did that.'

"I'm still cuttin' 'cause I'm the slowest guy and I don't have time to not cut! They so fast. They cut three times faster. But I can't be ignoring him. So I'm trying to figure this out. I say real neutral like I didn't hear him, 'What's that?' And he says, 'she just cheated on me. And she told me to my face. I can't believe it.' The other guys are just cuttin'. Maybe they know about JB. Not going to get sucked in, but I'm new, and he's telling me this stuff and it's confusing to me.

"I'm saying to myself, 'Why did I even open up the door for him to talk to me?' 'cause now he's not cuttin' anymore. He's just standing there. Remember, all these knives are all around. He's looking right at me now and he says, 'I just can't believe it man.' So I said, 'Well, sorry to hear that.' Which is lame, but this is new situation to me.

"Just then it's break time and I'm glad about that! JB smokes so he goes in the break room. I don't go in the break room 'cause everybody there smokes so I can't breathe. I'm sittin' on the steps in front of the establishment when he's headed back to the processing room and stops. JB, he's the head of the processing room, so we can't get started until he says the room's ready. If the inspector comes in and something's wrong, that's a flag on JB, so he's the one sets things up.

"So, JB, he's leadin' the pack back to the processing room but he stops in front of me. He says, 'Can you believe it man? Out of the blue she just cheated on me. I never cheated on her. I got a fourteen–year–old daughter with her.' I'm saying to myself, why does this guy keep tellin' me this? None of the other guys he's tellin it to. I'm startin' to think I might look like the guy his wife's cheated with? There's something about me. Maybe I'm a good listener."

Mecca laughs and the atmosphere in the room at OCC softens down a little. Mecca has been in this workshop for two and a half years, and everyone knows he is a good listener.

"When we get in the processing room, I hear the sound *wheoooo, wheoooo!*" Mecca smiles when a few of the men jump in their seats. "And the pigs start coming and we starting to butcher them, and he does it again. This time he's sharpening his knife. And he was like.

'Man I've been with this woman twenty–something years, and any time I think about it I get so angry I don't know what I'm going to do.' He's right across from me. None of the other guys respond. They doin' their work. He's lookin' right at me and I'm saying to myself this ain't good! I'm really uncomfortable. I don't say *anything* this time. I assume position like everybody else. I'm just cuttin'.

"Next JB starts singin' some song and somebody else says, 'JB, why don't you knock it off man and come on? We got two more drops.' That's our quota. How many pigs we gotta butcher? We got do two more drops and then we done for the workday. Then they gotta clean out the room for inspection the next day.

"Now someone else says, 'Chill out JB. Let the man do his work.' And JB goes, 'I'm not doing nothing. I'm just talkin' to him.' It's not really tension. These dudes all know each other. I'm the new jack. Eventually he quiets down. We finish the last two drops and we strip down, throw everything away, and I'm thinking I'm okay and that was over with.

"But the next day JB's talking to other people, but he stops when I come by and he says, 'Where you from? From the prison? I actually used to be a correction officer at Hillsborough. How long you been there?' And I say, 'About two years.' And he says, 'No, I was there before you.'

"He knows some names from Orange. He tells me how he lost that job and why he's not there no more and how his life has been, what he's been going through, drinking. He tried to kill himself when his wife left. He took all these Xanax or pills and his daughter found him and he has to go see the psyche now 'cause he's suicidal. And he's just pourin' it out on me and I'm saying what is it about me this guy wants to share this stuff with me? And I don't know what to say about none of it. So I'm assuming a position of listening and hoping this workday gets over with. 'cause where I'm from, prison, weapons mean something and there's buckets of knives everywhere. They get dull and you just take a new one. And he goes on and on and there we are across the table and the carcass between us and

I'm lookin' at him every chance I get because I don't know. He might go postal."

There's a strange silence in the OCC classroom. A story like this is usually about looking for advice and everyone is eager to present their analysis. For example, Mark Hall, an older white man with a white–collar crime and a firm release date, got charged with "possession of contraband" because he was wearing running shoes in the yard. The shoes had been brought in by his wife and inspected, but one of the officers who resented Mark stopped him, pointed out the "illegal" shoes to the superintendent, another person with no love for Mark, and they brought up a charge. The debate in the room that week took up the full two hours. Should Mark try to talk one on one to the superintendent? Should he wait and see the outside mediator who visits the camp a couple of times a month? Would he just get a slap on the wrist? Would he go to solitary?

So if a topic like this comes up, they can keep a heated discussion going for a long time. But JB? There's no wiggle room. Make the wrong move and a man could lose his work release, burn his MAPP. Keep cool was the best advice anyone could offer. Mecca said that was enough. He just needed to get this out, air it, and settle himself down.

The next week Mecca tells us what happened. "Next day JB is gone. He quit. I come in and he's gone. Never saw JB again. Nobody's seen him."

When I asked Thomas about JB he said, "I don't want to say that I'm glad that he left. He wasn't a violent person, but he had so many emotional problems that every other day it was something else. But I think that was probably a good thing for William to see so that he knew how *not* to act."

"With the type of people that we have here, that's important," Chris adds, "A lot of our employees have been in fights before. They come off of the street here in Burlington and they've done bad things before, but in the three, four years that I've been here, I've never ever seen anyone pull a knife on someone to actually threaten them. The guys know that if they are going to fight, they are going to go outside and fist fight. I tell them; you guys want to fight, you clock out. You walk across the street. Take your shirt off, drop your keys, drop your knives, drop your phone, and duke it out and then come back over here and settle your differences. These guys understand with the type of equipment they are working with, they can't come at each other with knives."

Butchering hogs is not ideal, but nothing about prison is ideal, so why should work release be any better? In that spirit, Mecca finds some unusual ways to amuse himself. For example, nobody at Neese's works out. You get a break, you get something to eat, you smoke a cigarette. You do nothing. Unless you are Mecca. He decides he wants to get in some exercise since there is not going to be any time in the day for hitting the weight pile. After prison Mecca joins Planet Fitness. One day there's a forecast for temperatures in the 20s and as he's leaving my house Mecca says, "Think I'll go running early tomorrow morning. Know why?" He laughs. "Because I can!" That's freedom.

"I asked my supervisor at Neese's and he said it was okay for me to go outside and do some push–ups or pull–ups during break," Mecca warms to his story. He knows I'm already amazed anyone can get through a workday at Neese's. Who needs to workout?

"So at break time I'm getting ready to start my routine and this dump truck pulls up. It's the guy who brings the corn that they feed the pigs. I asked him, 'Do you mind if I help you unload the corn?' And he says, 'You want to help me?' Guys looks like he's about seventy years old. I said, 'I don't mind helping if you don't mind.' He said, 'Sure.'

"So I help: hundred bags of corn, fifty–pound bags. Good work out for me. We unload the corn and soon as we finish the PA system says. 'Processing Let's go'.

"I go on up there and I'm dripping sweat. The guys say, 'Got your workout!' And I say, 'Yeah I been unloading the corn.' And they say,

'He let you? He doesn't let nobody touch that corn!' It's kinda cool in the processing room and I'm trying to dry out. They watch while I put on two smocks and they keep sayin', 'The man let him unload the daggon' corn! I can't believe it.' That's the talk of the day. Guess it's like prison everywhere. People got their turf and people gotta talk.

"The corn guy comes once a week. The next week when he comes, I miss him. I catch him as he's pullin' out and I say, 'I would love to have helped you.' He says, 'I'd love to have your help.' Which means we are on good speaking terms. So I say, 'Can I ask you a question? You wouldn't happen to have a tractor tire, would you?' And he says, 'Funny you mention that, 'cause I was about to take all our old tractor tires to this place in Greensboro. What size you want?' I say, 'the biggest one you got.' He says he can just drop it by Neese's.

"Lo and behold the next week, he brings a *monster* big truck tire. About six feet tall, a three–hundred–pound tractor tire. I'm in processing and my supervisor says I gotta report down to the pig pen – that's where he drops the corn. He's there with the tire, so we both get up there and we muscle it off. Now I can't wait 'til we finish in the processing room and it's break time. When we pushed it off, I got a feel of it!

"That day I had about an hour to myself. I went out there and I couldn't budge that tire at all. Man, this skinny dude, been workin' on a farm all his life, who works on the kill floor comes by. He says, 'What you tryin' to do with that thing?' I said 'I'm tryin' to flip it.' Outa prison, people probably just look at YouTube but can't do that at OCC. Skinny Dude says, 'Let me show you something,' and flipped this thing like it was nothin', said, 'Man, I been doin' this all my life. It's nothing about your strength. It's your technique.'

"When he showed me, I was able to flip it. He got all the way under it like this and then get it standing up and then you turn it over. And also, I was trying to do it with gloves on, and I didn't have the grip. I took the gloves off, and I flipped it once or twice just to get the feel of it. And then that was it, so I left it layin' on the grass.

"Next day during break, I'm still strugglin' with it. It isn't easy. Thomas walks by and sees me. He's a big guy, about six four, three hundred pounds. He sees the tire and asks, 'What the heck is that doin' here?' I explained to him how it happened.

"He says, 'Man, let me see that one time.' He's got some old Crocks on, kicks them off and flips it like flippin' a slice of pizza. Like it was nothin'. He said he has a nice gym, so he knows about technique and all of that. He said, 'You should see how we beat it with the sledgehammer.' He goes to this tool shed, comes back and says, 'That's only a six-pound sledgehammer. I'm gonna bring you a real sledgehammer.' The next day he tells me, 'You get through processing, come see me.' When I stop at the office. There is this day-glow orange, twelve-pound sledgehammer, still got the tag on it from the store. Thomas goes, 'Here, that's yours!'

"A week after that Ms. Neese pulls up and she sees me beatin' that tire. Now she gets into it. 'What the heck are you doin'? Everybody else is in the break room or on the steps smokin'.' I explain I'm workin' out, and she kind of laughs, but then she says, 'At my Greensboro plant, we got a semi-pro body builder named Willie that I want you to meet. I'm gonna give him a day off, bring him down here, and I'm gonna give you the day off and you two can sit and talk, workout, do whatever y'all want to do.'

"Next Thursday, he came with his photo album, and we just sat and talked, and I showed him my toys. I told him what I do, and he does similar things in Greensboro on his breaks. And Ms. Neese was just beaming, watching me and Willie talk. Then the machine broke down, so I got a chance to spend a lot of time with Willie.

"I'm telling you all this because it was a lesson to me. People can surprise you. I thought Neese's gonna be the end of me. Screaming pigs. That guy JB. But I got to meet caring people. I even got to drive a tractor! Now, all these guys been tellin' me about Caledonia and lovin' being in the field. Not me; but one day I see this tractor at Neese's. It belongs to the guy Frankie who mows the fields.

Technically doesn't belong to Frankie, but guys tell me, 'Don't mess with the tractor. That's Frank's tractor and nobody can mess with it.'"

When I ask Andrea about Frankie, she tells me, "Frankie has been here with this company and in the slaughter business for over fifty years. He came to us from Chew's, which went out of business. Nobody knows how old Frankie is, and he won't tell you. He could be fifty; he could be eighty."

Thomas adds, "Frankie doesn't talk a lot, but when you get him talking, he's a smart guy. The funny thing is, he's smart with life experiences but he has only a seventh or eighth grade education. He actually couldn't read when he came here."

"We sent him to ACC to adult reading class," Andrea jumps in. "He did that, but he still couldn't read past the sixth–grade level. He said his greatest thing was reading the Sunday paper. So he doesn't read like we read but enough that he can get by."

"But he knows everything," Thomas sweeps his arms toward the office window, out toward the rest of the plant. "I've worked just about every piece of equipment in this plant and so has Chris, but at least once a week we've got to ask Frankie about how to do something around here, because he's just been around it so long that he knows every little nook and cranny of this place. I told him he's not allowed to die or retire 'cause I don't know what's gonna happen without him." Andrea and Thomas are definitely surprised when they hear that Mecca rode on Frankie's tractor.

"Mr. Frank has a tractor he uses to mow and stuff," Mecca tells me. "I see that tractor and I'm real interested. I've never seen none of this stuff up close. I went and sat on it, but the guys, like with the corn, they go off on me. Right away a guy said, 'You better not let Mr. Frank catch you sittin' on his tractor! Mr. Frank, he don't play no games by that tractor. Get off it.' So I got off of it.

"Day or two later I saw Mr. Frank hook the bush hog to the back to cut the grass. And I had the gumption to say, 'Mr. Frank, I got a question for you. Man, the only time I seen a tractor was in the TV show *Green Acres.*' He laughed, right? I kinda left Caledonia out of this. He said, 'You serious? Where you from?' And I told him, and he said, 'Oh, you the city boy they been talkin' about.'

"I don't know if I like that, but I say, 'Mr. Frank before I leave this place, I want to say I rode a tractor!' He says, 'You do, huh?' He talks real slow. 'Maybe we see if we can work that out.'

"About a week later, I'm at work. My supervisor says, 'Mr. Frank wants you down there.' They send me down by where they park the tractor. When I get there Frank says, 'I'm gettin' ready to cut this grass and if you want to ride this tractor come on with me.' So he pulled the tractor out. It's runnin' and he put it in neutral.

"He says, 'Go ahead and sit down right there. You see that pedal by your right foot? You see that pedal by your left foot? That's the clutch and that's the gear shift and it's in neutral. If you bash the clutch and you put it up to your right, that's in first and that's gonna go. Not gonna go real fast. Put your hands on the steering wheel. Just settle down. I'm gonna stand right here besides you on a little running board and we gonna roll. Put it in first and hold the clutch.' I put it in first and it wasn't going nowhere. He says, 'You gotta let your foot up a little off the clutch. That's what you gonna control it with.'

"I let it up too quick and it jerked. But when I let up on the clutch slower, around the compound we went! And it happened to be break time, so when everybody came out, they could all be lookin' at me and sayin, 'How in the world does that happen?' It's a very big, powerful machine, and it's loud, and it's intimidating. But we goin' real slow. And I am driving.

"Mr. Frank, he's up behind me, guiding me. 'Turn it a little harder.' And I'm turnin' the wheel and I'm tryin' to look at Mr. Frank and he's pointin', 'cause it's the narrow part of the grass area that you gotta really navigate through. We went through there and we went around cuttin' the grass. And then he was like, 'You had enough?' And I was, 'Yes, that's enough for today.'

Mecca is literally glowing. "I'm having a ball at work." His black skin shines. "It's an adventure for me. I love people, all kinds of people. That's a feeling from before prison, and at Neese's I'm feeling how that is still alive in me. And I can do my daydreaming about freedom from there.

"One more thing; I have to tell you about the day Ms. Neese thought she had lost me. She was looking for me and I'm out back, and she goes around the building but not all the way around. And when she finds me, she is frantic. She said, 'Where were you? I asked all the guys, "Have you seen William? I don't know where William is." I was frantic, but for the life of me I could not imagine you leaving.'

"I said, "Listen Ms. Neese, if it matters anything to you, you can go get that little rifle, shotgun they use to put the pigs down, put a bullet in my leg, and tell me to climb that fence, and nothing is going to drag me across that fence. Nothing is going to keep me from not messing up my MAPP. Nothing."

When I ask Andrea about this, she gives me a very serious look. "That was a hard day for me. When William came walking around from way down below the barn, I was so relieved. Angry and relieved. We are liable for each of these men, responsible for their safety. We had a man from the prison go missing one day. He went out and got drunk with his girlfriend and came back so drunk he could hardly climb the fence to sneak back in. We had to let that man go. That's not something I could ever imagine William doing, but I was worried."

"We want to know where all the employees are all the time," Thomas explains. "Just being down in the barns can be dangerous. Thankfully, every time I've slipped and fallen down in the barns, I've never hit my head or anything, because with those animals it can be a problem. Our hogs weigh five hundred to seven hundred pounds, so if you slip and get knocked out, there's a possibility they can hurt you and more. That's always our worst fear, that somebody was down there slips and can't get up. It's never happened, but we worry."

"And those hogs down there, they are all female," Andrea tosses her hair back and laughs. "You get eighty females in one place! They can be fighting. You get in their way... We try to keep our eyes open."

"That day, later," Andrea continues, "William came into the lunchroom and came over to talk to me. He said, 'You were pretty mad.' I said, 'Oh no. You've never seen me mad! I was concerned. You will know when I'm mad. I am *red* up the arms, *red* up the neck. I was concerned when I could not find you.' He said, 'Well, I'm down there flipping the tire. Or I'm down there exercising.' And I said, 'You need to tell me. Let me know where you are.' And he said, I remember his words real clearly. 'I'm not going to leave. I can see the other side. I can see my freedom. I'm not messing it up.'

"After that, sometimes I would see him sitting on one of the pickle buckets. He would sit at the fence and watch the cars going by. Finally I asked, 'What are you doing, watching the cars?' And he said, 'I'm projecting myself, for when I get out... I'm in one of those cars. I'm just watching the people. And some of the people that go by, they wave at me. And I wave back.'"

Andrea leans back in her chair. "There's a lot of guys that we've had here – and actually a couple that we still have – you talk to them and you realize that when they get out, they are going to go right back to their old ways." She looks genuinely disappointed. "They haven't learned anything from what they did. But there's absolutely no doubt in my mind that William was good to go. When he left this job, I said, this is what I will do, I will be watching you. And I've already called him a couple of times. I expect good things of him." She leans in close to the recorder and cups her hands. "We love you, William!!"

Chapter 13: Stepping into Freedom

Saturday, December 19, 2015. That's the official release date. But the week before, the prison informs Mecca that he cannot be released on a weekend and will have to wait until Monday. It's only two days, but it sends everyone spinning. Bessie's sisters, Karen and Brinda, have flown down from New Jersey. Cheryl and her husband David have prepared Mecca's room. Even more important, Mecca is ready. "That's prison," he tells us. Just one more test to see if he can ready himself for the next test.

We all get together to keep Mecca out of prison for as much of the weekend as we can. On Saturday David takes Mecca out on a pass to a coffee shop where they can sit and talk, while I stop by Bessie's apartment where everyone is gathered to wait out the countdown. We sit in a circle in her living room with the little recorder on a coffee table in the middle. It feels a little like a ritual, a closing ceremony to this phase of the journey.

Bessie is the first to speak.

"This morning I was talking to Karen, just going back in my mind to some of the experiences that I have had here in North Carolina and how good people have been to me. And I almost started crying, so I stopped talking. I've always been afraid that if I started crying, I wouldn't stop. It's just been a long journey. It's something that we prayed for and hoped for and now it's happening. It feels like I'm going to jump out of my skin. And all the people that are wishing me well on Facebook and – it's just – I don't know. I don't want to talk about it too much because then I'll get so emotional."

Coming up beside her mom, Cheryl is also on an emotional ledge.

"I've been thinking about it as each day goes on, and this morning when I got up, I was thinking to myself that right now it's still unbelievable. It will be that way until Willie gets into my car and we drive away and I exhale. It's remarkable and I'm just grateful that the time is here."

Even though she's watched a lot of this from her home in New Jersey, Brinda is right on track with her sister and niece.

"What I'm feeling is pretty much similar to what Bessie said. It looks like I'm watching it from the outside and I'm seeing everything come to a conclusion. It's the ending but yet a beginning – not for me, but for Willie. I'm watching this story unfold and asking myself, 'Honestly, did I ever think that it would come to this?' I had faith, but you can have faith and even so, with the way things are in society... to be honest, even now that everything has come together, I am wondering, 'How did this happen?' And only thing I can say is: by the grace of God."

"I didn't know you felt that way!" Bessie touches her sister lightly on the arm. "I never, I never felt it wasn't going to happen I just didn't know *when* it was going to happen."

Karen turns to them both,

"For me, I felt that with every start there's a finish, so I knew that as diligently as Bessie had been working, there would be a conclusion to this. I just didn't know when it was going to happen. My feelings are also different from Bessie's. Maybe it's because I still live in the area where we grew up. A lot of people, his friends and peers are no longer around. A lot of them are either deceased or incarcerated. So

I felt – as weird as this may sound – I felt safer with him being incarcerated than him being a young Black male out on the streets."

"We talked about that during visit," Bessie says. "First traffic stop, and they want to know who you are, and they'll see, *convicted murderer*. That could be very deadly for him. We talked about him walking the fine line, being compliant as far as probation is concerned. Being over the top careful, because it's going to be necessary. Unfortunately for him, because of his color and because of his background, of who he was, a convicted drug dealer, it's going to be necessary.

"Cheryl and I also talked to him about some of the people that were in his path – that he has to sever those ties, because he cannot be associated with them anymore. This is all something he has to do. I can't protect him from that. But William is not the same person now. Well, he's the same person, but he does not have the same lifestyle. But what I want most of all – I just want him to be happy."

"If anyone can transition from where he's been to where he's going," Karen says, "I think that William can, because he's always had a strong personality. He's always been a leader and not a follower. That part of his spirit never ever faded away! If anyone is capable of doing their own thing, finding fulfillment in life, William is that kind of person.

"When I have visited him in prison, he might ask about what it is like to be in New Jersey. You can't bring in a cell phone, but I wanted to show him a picture. This area looks like this now; it's not the same. I've tried to describe things. I've run into people that he knew, and I would tell William, 'I saw so and so, but he looked like this – not like you imagine him. To try to let him know that it is gone. There's nothin' even worth the time to talk about it. Because you have gone way beyond that, and some of those same people that you are wondering about are still doing the same thing, and you have gone way ahead of that.'"

Brinda works with people in the projects, and she is quick to add her authority to Karen's.

"William's situation, compared to the average person that's coming out of a correction facility, is different. I have clients that live in the apartments that I work in – they don't have the support that he has. They don't have the education that he has. They don't have the things that are already lined up for him. And it's not that they can't have it, but they don't have the desire to do better that he has. So many of them are still wallowing in the fact that they have this criminal history and they can't see Tuesday because of Sunday and Monday. They are still just hangin' on there. And they definitely can't see to Wednesday or Thursday. It's unique that he has this vision. It is a blessing."

An important part of the plan that works in Mecca's favor is Cheryl's decision to invite him to live in her home. Maybe "invite" is the wrong word, because in this family it just works that way. Mecca is not going to have to search for transitional housing or worry about paying rent or getting a job on day one. In fact, Cheryl announces, "We're looking forward to it. I know my husband has anxiety, because he doesn't really know Willie that well. He has all these feelings about what we should be doing for Willie before he gets to our house. But I said to him, you don't have to do anything. Our job is to see him through this time period while he's going to be on probation. We're just a conduit to help him get there and that's it!

"He asked me a while back if having my brother – if things are going to change between us. And I said, 'No, but I just want you to know, when you see us engaged in conversation, it may seem like we're arguing, but it's not what you think. That's how we talk.'"

"Yes," Bessie jumps in, pride in her feisty children being at the top of her list of joys. "They have always been like that! They're competitive but in a healthy way. He always wants to be on top and Cheryl always says to him, 'But I'm the oldest.' And he's saying, 'But I'm going to be the smartest.'

They've always done that."

And I remind Cheryl that when she met her husband, Mecca's incarceration was already a big part of her life. She agrees: Willie is part of the package.

There's a little bit of silence, which Karen breaks, "I think that what Willie's initially gonna do is he has to take it all in. He's going to be assessing the situation for himself. One of the worst things anybody can do, and we'll probably all be guilty of it, is ask him, 'Well, how are you feeling?' He is not going to be able to answer that question."

Karen is right on the mark. I remember going back to OCC with Mecca after his first pass. He could see Scott-so in the window of the dorm and said, "Oh, no. There's Scott-so waiting for me, and I just want to be quiet. I just need to sit and figure out what's going on in my head." Mecca has not been one to fool himself, and he's been in training, like an astronaut, ready to be overwhelmed and still remember to keep his hands on the controls.

Another silence. Bessie looks down at her hands as if she can physically move things into place.

"William would say to me – talking about some of the guys like Frank – that they all had end dates and he didn't. Well, in my mind, to me, he always had an end date. My job was to keep him believing in that. No matter where he went, to the worst prison, we never had a bleak conversation about that. He would tell us how bad it was, and we'd joke about it a little bit, but we never, never thought that this day wouldn't come!"

"And it wasn't delusion," Cheryl adds, reaching down to embrace her mother. "I told David this morning that we always knew that Willie was going to get out. We never once expected that he was going to be in prison for the rest of his live."

Bessie exchanges a smile with her daughter and her sisters, then looks straight at me. "No. No. Every time he was turned down for honor grade, he would call us, and there would be silence for a minute. And we would say, 'Okay, we just gotta get ourselves ready for the next time.'"

"Yes, he committed a crime," Cheryl is very serious. "But this punishment, natural life sentence, it did not fit the crime. So there was always something else we could do."

Bessie adds an affirmation, a strong nod of the head like she used to do in her father's church. She says, "We had to step up to this right from the beginning and it was emotional. I remember when Brinda – we were in court and we had to get a detainer cleared up in New Jersey. William was in jail in North Carolina so he could not appear, but we needed to clear this old charge because it could hurt his situation in North Carolina. Brinda was holding my hand while we were waiting for the judge to decide. Finally he called me back in his office and told me, 'It's going to be taken care of.' I had to wait for the official letter and I finally got an email from the judge saying that it was done. I called Cheryl and she said, 'Mom, I have to call you back.' Why? It's because she was in her office and she had to go outside to sit in her car and scream. She was just so relieved.

"That's how it was... each thing we had to go through. And that's why it's special for me to have my sisters here. They have walked with us through all of this."

We are all excited and we are all thinking about how wonderful and how difficult re–entry can be. Maybe it was unconscious, my choice of the word 'astronaut' to describe Mecca, as it's ironic and appropriate that the process of release from prison is called 're– entry'. These men and women have traveled somewhere that the people close to them have never seen.

Jeffrey Ross and Stephen Richards began writing survival guides for prison in 2002. In 2009 they published *Beyond Bars: Rejoining Society After Prison*. It's a manual, a guidebook that I still hand out to men I know who are getting out. In the first chapter the authors ask:

Why do so many ex–convicts fail to succeed? You can bet it's not because they plan to or want to. Despite everything, most people walking out of jail or prison are wildly optimistic. They are convinced that this time everything will fall into place and that their luck has changed.

A big part of the reason that ex–convicts end up back in the joint is that nobody ever really informed them of the perils that await them on their return to the streets. And they also fail to take into account how life on the inside has changed them.[14]

Cheryl has been pacing a little, passing back and forth between the living room and the kitchen. She stops to look at the trees outside. "I was wondering this morning, what is he thinking? Twenty-four years now passing... It's going to be exciting! I don't know if I'll sleep at all tonight."

On Sunday afternoon I head to the public library to meet Mecca, Mr. Bill and his wife, Judy. It's a gorgeous day, warm with soft light, the way North Carolina can shine in December. It's been almost two years since we had our first "oral history" session in this same building. We're going to talk and then drive to my house for a last CV–pass supper. The situation is simultaneously ordinary and extraordinary.

I am going to ask Mecca the exact question Karen has warned us not to ask. I line up the recorder, check that the green light is blinking and open the session, "Can you put into words how you are feeling?"

Mecca looks at the recorder with a wry grin, a flash in his eye, and an intake of breath. He says, "No words!" He turns to look out the window, looking out at the bare branches and the sharp sunlight as if they are something from another world. "I'm up in the clouds somewhere. Numb sometimes. Overwhelmed with everything."

He stops, and Bill and Judy and I wait. We can hear a group of young kids laughing in the room next to us. A mother goes by with a toddler loaded down with picture books.

"I keep getting reminded of it. Guys all day long for the last week

---

14   Jeffrey Ross and Stephen Richards, *Beyond Bars: Rejoining Society After Prison* (Indianapolis, IN: Alpha Books, 2009), 2.

or so saying, 'How many days you got left?' Officers too. There are two guards who work second shift, six PM to six AM. I'm normally up at three AM. For the last three days, I've laid there, as opposed to actually getting all the way out of bed. These two guards, they have come to my bunk and they gently tap on it and say, 'Dang, a few more days and I won't see you no more.' For them to do that, it really gets my attention in a way that highlights it all. You right, I won't see you no more!

"I have trained myself in prison. So my routine would be, when a stranger comes up to me, especially somebody who works in the prison, I do not get called into it. But when these officers who've been paid and trained to disassociate and not get into it, not make a connection, when they come at that hour, it's something different. They don't know that I'm up. I'm just looking at the ceiling and they say, he lowers his voice, 'How many more days? Oh... I won't be workin' that day. I be off. I won't see you no more. Take care of yourself!' That's special to me! And it let's me know that sometimes people be payin' attention and you making some kind of impression and you don't even know about it.

"After that maybe I sit up, and it's dark, 'cause everybody is asleep, and I look around and blink. I do this a lot; I'm taking pictures of the environment, because, like it or not, I grew up there. Twenty-four years of my life has been in prison, and I learned some life lessons there that I needed to learn – about myself, about people, about my family, and about that time that I lost. Oh wow, what would my life have been like if I had not come to prison? Would I be married? Would I have a family? Or would it have been worse. Would I have gotten killed like a lot of my peers did? I entertain myself thinking about all of that stuff.

"I'm always being reminded of where I am in the sense of gettin' out. Just like today when everybody looked at the board with the CV passes and they saw William Elmore and Bill Cook, they said, 'that's all right, Mr. Cook your main man. You on your last pass.' And you can tell when it's genuine. Someone saying, 'You know what, man, this your last pass. No more itineraries. No more checkers comin' to make sure you where you are.' And I say, 'You know, you're right. This is it.'

"Some guys I don't want to talk to because I don't really like them. They go left and I go right. Now those same guys, they corner me off somewhere and say, 'You know what, man, take care of yourself. I know you gonna be all right. You one of the few I seen that's going to be all right.' It's like, wow! Okay, thank you. It's a shock. I appreciate that. These are the guys who have done just as much time as me, whether they done it in increments or one long stretch. When they say that, guys who are so pessimistic, it means something to me."

I ask, "So just by saying something, encouraging you, feeling hope for you, they are exposing a part of themselves that they usually keep locked away?" We talk a lot about this in the workshop group.

"Prison trains guys to harden their hearts so you don't feel nothin'," Mecca explains. "You do years that way and you get real good at it. And those guys... it's in their shoulders. How they move. They numb themselves to everything. They say sentimental things, but they don't feel the emotions that carry the words. In prison, most of the time, it looks attractive to not feel. And it looks like that works, like you can endure it better if you don't feel it. But it's dangerous.

"Here's an example of what I mean by dangerous. If you let down your guard, something can take you back, turn you in some direction you don't want to go. This happened to me maybe sixty days before I'm getting out of prison. There's an officer, real big, Black officer. His name is Nelson. He's just playful like a big teddy bear, and he does not act like an officer at all but like a big kid. He works second shift. When I get up about three, three thirty in the morning, he's doing everything he can to keep from falling asleep. He gets off at six. So I go in the day room and start doing my reading and my writing and my stretching and different things like that. He knows I'm up and he can come bother me. Entertain himself.

"Sometimes he would be joking around. When he sees me, he

would delay the count. He comes straight to my locker and he opens it up and says, joking, 'I need to shake you down and go through all of your things, because you have too many so and so. I'm gonna check your locker now, confiscate stuff and send it home.' It's not funny to me, but I laugh it off. It's part of living in prison.

"Now it's different. I'm looking at the count every day: ninety more days and I'm done with this. One morning he says to me, 'You've gotten another pair of shoes?' Which I didn't have. All the stuff in the locker is the same. I said, 'Come on Nelson; man, you say that every time you see me.'

"He says, 'I don't understand how come they allowing you to get all these shoes. I worked in medium custody, so I know the rules. You only can have state–issued shoes. How you keep getting your personal shoes?' And I said, 'Nelson, you ask me this a thousand times. I show you my paperwork. What's the problem?' 'Cause, remember, I got my medical papers for my shoes. Had them for decades. But he says anyway, 'I'm starting to think that you Marion's boy.'

"Superintendent Marion. You understand that language, Simone?"

I say, "Yes. He's accusing you of being a snitch."

Bill and Judy and I can all see that Mecca is agitated. It's hard to sort out what's part of the story he is telling and what belongs to the general stress of moving his mind back into prison for an extra weekend. He's lifting out of his seat, leaning over the table. His face is dead serious.

"I had my earbuds in, but I took 'em out, and I stood up and said, 'In other words, you think I'm a snitch, and since you think I'm a snitch, and you've been through medium custody and you been doing this for a while and you call yourself a convict officer, and since I've been in prison twenty some years and I'm a convict inmate – I tell you what we do. Me and you can go like convicts used to do in the back and we can get it on, since I'm a snitch.'

'Oh no, man. Why you getting so serious?'

'Because you know better. All your buddies hear you say that, and it's only two more months but I gotta live it right here. Joking or not, you said it twice and you know better. So let's go handle it.'

'Man sit down.'

'No, I'm not going to sit down, 'cause I gotta live here, and you know better.'

'It's getting too thick in here. I think I better leave.'

"And he left. But after the ride came for the guys who are going to work release and the day room's empty again, Nelson comes back in and says, 'Man, I apologize. You want to accept my apology?'

And I said, 'Not right now, I don't.'

"So for the last two months he went from officer to officer and inmate to inmate, and they say to me, 'Nelson, he's sorry.' And I say he can apologize, but he transgressed. Prison is dangerous and he knows that. When he put that out there, he left me no other recourse."

Mecca sits down again and leans back. "Now I say thank God we didn't go in the back of the dorm and fight, because it's clear I could have lost my MAPP. I could have lost everything."

"Yesterday," Mecca resumes, "I was out on pass with David and he asked, 'What are you afraid of? Are there things that might be frightening for you?' And I said that at this point I don't know. I do know that my honesty has always helped me through things, and I will be the first one to say, 'I don't understand.' I have these pillars, my friends, my sponsors, who love me like family, people I can call to say, 'I'm not sure about this. I'm feeling crazy right now.'

"Being in prison for twenty-four and a half years I have a lot of practice paying attention to how things flow, to be where I can be, where I need to be. And I have always enjoyed my own company. What I think I'll have to deal with most often is this: people asking me 'Are you okay?' when nothing is wrong. Because I can sit in this room and look at those trees and I'm good. This is how I was before

I even went to prison. The chaos of my life, living around a lot of people who were confused about their lives, it allowed me to enjoy what it means to also sit still somewhere and just be quiet.

"I've always been like that. My mother says I've been like that since I been a kid. At daycare they used to call my mom and say, 'Is he okay? Is he having some kind of problem?'"

'Why?'

'Because all the kids are over here hula hooping and jump roping and he's in the kitchen with the women that are preparing the lunch.'

'He's like that at home with his grandmother. He's going to sit in your office and ask you all kind of questions. Maybe he doesn't need to be out in the yard.'

'Yeah, that's exactly what he does.'

"So I said all that to say, I've always been okay in my own company. People might think that it's a response to me being in prison. It's not. And even when I am in prison, I'm going to sit on the other side of the yard, with or without my radio, someone see me there and they say, 'What's goin' on? You all right?' And I say, 'I'm fine. I'm okay.' That's kind of strange to the world, when you don't seem to be doing what everybody else is doing. But I'm used to that."

"That may be why people like to take you out on pass too," I say. "Because you can take someone out on pass and they're busy trying to be unnoticeable, and that can be awkward for the sponsor too."

"I talk to guys and I see this too. Guys, they don't allow themselves to be vulnerable on the pass. They are too concerned with how they look and how they are perceived by others. I'm way less concerned about that. I'm like a kid in an amusement park! I'm too caught up in what's going on where I am to think about how I look to people on the outside. I can't be spending my pass thinking about whether I look foolish to someone else. Debit card is a good example. Don't nobody on the outside have to think about how does this debit card work. But that's what I'm gonna have to do, even if there's a line of people waitin' behind me. *Pin?* Damn.

"I do wonder sometimes if I'm giving off any kind of signs that I'm an inmate in prison. I guess that can happen when I'm out, but I got to keep moving through it. I got to a point now with my reality where I got to embrace it for what it is. That can give you a sense of power and you can use it for your benefit. After that? You lord it over that fear rather than it being something hanging over your head. And something hanging over my head is goin' to be too much like prison!

"Now before we turn that recorder off, Simone, I want to say one thing for sure. When I get out, I'm goin' to make time to keep doing our sessions. There are going to be plenty more stories! You know me. Things are going to happen! I want to... that okay with you?"

"That's a promise on both sides."

I push the recorder closer to Bill. He's usually silent during the oral history sessions. I ask him to wrap things up for us.

"I have been thinking and praying for William and Ms. Bessie. One of the privileges in my life has been meeting you, William, and getting to know you, and I sincerely count you as a friend. And it's not going to stop at nine o'clock tomorrow because you are no longer incarcerated. And I appreciate the confidence that you have shown in me. I think much of it is undeserved. I don't know that I'm as good as you think. It's been a real privilege, and I will be there for you. If you talk about words of wisdom, I can't think of any right now. I'm too emotional. But I know that we will continue to have time to spend together."

We are all tearing up now, looking a little bit self conscious about the glass windows of the library study room. Mecca bails us out.

"I teared up this morning! I was looking out the window and the sun hadn't come up yet, and I saw it coming up through the angle of the window. I let myself really appreciate that. I'm blinking my eye and I'm taking pictures and saying to myself that after Monday

I won't see the sun rise from this angle this way again. I know that tomorrow morning, I really might fall out crying. And that kind of stuff is real meaningful to me. The prison environment and setting doesn't dull that. I won't let it do that. I won't let it distract me from the beauty of the world.

"It's going to be beautiful like that in the morning when I get out. People ask me, how I see it going for me. I look up and just say, 'It's just beautiful. So beautiful.' It really is. I don't mean it's going to be perfect. It's going to be life, wherever we are. Challenges. Ins and outs. Ups and downs. As long as you are living, you gonna have that stuff. I don't care where you are. I know that. So I look forward to the everyday things, finding out everything about everything. And I'm looking forward to sifting out what I don't like anymore. You know, my aunts tell me all the time, 'When you were nine years old you liked this or that.' And I say, 'I don't know if I still like that stuff. I don't know. But I'll find out.'"

I meet Mecca at the library again the day after he gets out. Frank has driven him there, but it's not on a CV pass, so Frank doesn't need to stay! We are both a bit giddy. Recording the oral histories has not really been "legal," but now there is no checker and it's a new day. Mecca sits down in his chair. He's clearly trying to – as he says – settle himself. I'm eager to hear but hesitate to push. Mecca already phoned me on Monday night from the restaurant where his family was celebrating to say he was happy but overwhelmed. He's also pissed off at the prison and determined to get the reason down on tape.

"Last day, I woke up at two AM. I lay on my bunk some. Get up. Try to get ready and stay calm. Hours going by very slowly. Even though they had regular count at six thirty, nine thirty they call another count. I have to go to my bunk. I'm kind of confused. I gotta do this one more time? I thought I had done it for the last time. I get to my bunk, but before they clear count the programs officer, Mr. Ashley, he calls me on the PA. Officer says, 'It's okay. They can count you in the office.'

"When I get up to the Programs Office, I'm talking to Ashley, but they have a new programmer in there and telephone is ringing off the hook. I hear her saying, 'I'm not sure if he left yet. He may have. He should have.' She doesn't know who I am, that I'm sitting right there with Mr. Ashley. So when she gets off the phone, she says, 'That's the fifth person calling, a volunteer calling asking about William Elmore being released.'

"Mr. Ashley says, 'Well soon as the count clears, he will be released. This is him sitting right here.'

But he doesn't do anything. Ashley sends me back to the dorm because my parole officer is not there yet. I keep being called to programs and then sent back to the dorm. They did that all morning. Elmore report to sergeant. Elmore report to programs. Back and forth. Back and forth. The idea is to get you ready so that when the parole officer comes to escort you out the gate, you'll be ready, but no parole officer is showing up.

"This is all real confusing. They have let one of the other inmates, Justin Danforth, carry all my stuff to Cheryl's car. Even if the parole officer makes me ride with her, my stuff is going with Cheryl. I can see my mom and Cheryl waiting. Chris Ringwalt, one of my CV sponsors, is also waiting by the gate. He brought some balloons and stuff for me, him and his wife.

"Then they call me to the sergeant's office again. I got to the sergeant's office, and they tell me Mr. Ashley needs to see me. So I go back to Programs, and Mr. Ashley says, 'I think they made a mistake. You might not be going home today.'

"I kind of sit back and I exhale. I say to myself, 'I'm not gonna get into that. I'm just gonna be quiet.'

"And then he's, 'I'm just joking. Let me see your envelope.' He rifles through it. 'I gotta get you to sign some more papers. I gotta put some more papers in. I gotta take some papers out. He's being Ashley. It's not nothing unique to me that day.

'Are we done? You sure?'

'Oh, yeah, yeah, we done this time.'

"So I leave his office. Now I'm really ready to go! More than I thought I could be. And the only thing between me and Mom and Cheryl is the gate. I'm looking at them and I'm sayin', 'Wow. This is really happening. I'm really getting ready to go home.' They're like sitting in the car and then my sister jumps out the car. 'What's up bro? You ready?' And I'm talkin' to her at the gate, from inside.

"Then they called me back to the sergeant's office. Had to give me a card, a debit card or something that I need. And all of that... PIN number and all that kind of stuff. I say to the sergeant, 'Is that it. I can go now?' And he gets on the radio and lets the officer at the gate know. He says, 'You can let Elmore out.'

"Man, music to my ears, to my soul. And as I get to the gate Chaplain Love is coming in. The officer is opening the gate to let me out, but Love has no idea I'm going home. He says to the officer, 'Wow, thanks. You opening the gate for me?'

'Oh no. I didn't even see you behind me, Chap. I'm opening the gate to let somebody go home today.'

'Who?'

'Elmore.'

'Hey man, just want to shake your hand. I had no idea you were going home today. Congratulations.'

'Man, that's a good feeling. Thank you.'

"Then Mr. Ashley called me again."

I'm trying to arrange Mecca's story in my head. "The gate's already open?"

"It's open. But the officer picks up his radio, listens and then he says, 'Mr. Ashley wants you to come back to his office.'

"Oh, man, I'm so tired of this. This guy just won't quit. So what I start to do is I start to jog instead of walk. Too much energy to walk. As I'm trotting to the office, Ashley is coming out of the office and we kind of meet halfway by the canteen. He says, 'Naw, I'm just pulling your chain. Go ahead. Get out of here.' He shakes my hand again. And I turn around and I run out the gate. I say to myself, 'I'm not stopping this time. I'm not stopping! I'm not stopping.'

"And I ran through the gate and I hugged my mother and my sister, and my mother's just overwhelmed with tears. I'm like, 'Let's just go! We can do all of this at MacDonald's down the street. Let's just go. We can stop and cry and do it again someplace else.'

"My sister's filming it on her phone. The officer says, 'Mam, you can't do that.' But I could tell the way she said it, female officer, that she was told to say it. It wasn't her talking. And I keep saying, 'Let's go. Let's go.'

"We left and ate breakfast, and then I went back later because they still had to give me my check for my pay from Neese's. After that we went to Mom's house then... from breakfast? No, after getting the check. I can't remember. It's all rushing me. We were at my mom's house with my aunts and then out to dinner at Maggiano's with all the photos and stuff. Super packed. Shoulder to shoulder. Elbow to elbow. I counted. It was seventeen of us. Cousins that were this big now had kids this big! These are not people I saw regularly, on visit. Kenneth, my uncle, was there. Both of my uncles, both of my aunts, cousins. My cousin's wife was there, someone I never ever met.

"I kept telling myself, this is normal. This is something for everybody. They wanted to see you and spend that meal with you. And I sat beside my mother, and it was more her night. Phones. Conversations. Plates. Dishes. Menus. A bouquet of stuff everywhere. And everybody's like, 'You okay?' 'You okay?' 'You okay?'

"Finally Cheryl's like, 'You ready to go?'

"I'm ready. I've had enough. I'm overloaded. We get in the car – all four of us, David and his brother, who lives at their house, and me. They have to stop at Walmart and J.C. Penney first. It's so crazy there. I needed some stuff from Walmart, but it was too much, all the people rushing around!

"Then we got to Cheryl's, and I was so tired I just dropped into the recliner in the living room. She wanted to show me everything. Here's the kitchen. Here's the den. And I said, 'I know, but I'm tired. I'll look around tomorrow.'

"Then I get up to my room, and now I'm too tired. When I get too tired, I can't go to sleep. This is how I am. So I just put my stuff away, the bags from the prison and stuff. I did that and then I lay down on the bed and looked at the ceiling and stared at the fan. Phew! I got into bed, but I kept waking up every hour and looking at my watch.

"It was too much! I need some time to just take for myself. I want to be with everybody, but I am going to have to manage this. I was like that when I was dealing. I had like fifteen phone cards in my head. Dial a number. That one doesn't work. I've got another. It was like that. But prison has changed me. I'm not like that anymore. People might think I'm still like that, but I've changed. I will have to find a way to manage myself. I'm going to have to find a way to do time management out here.

"I hear about what happens to other guys, and I used to wonder why. They start drinking again or drugs. End up back in prison. Now, I understand that. They are looking for something to take the edge off. I don't drink, but I can see that. What I want those guys back at the prison to know – maybe they can read it right here in this book – is about how it is out here. They need to know to get ready for freedom because it is so different from prison. The time goes so fast and it is not structured like in prison. It's crazy.

"It's a big change for your mom too," I remind Mecca. Bessie is already thinking about what she can do now that she doesn't have to be worrying about the prison all the time. "She has her life back. She doesn't have to be planning every week for her visits to you in the prison. She doesn't have to always be arranging things."

"She gets a kick out of me and Cheryl," Mecca laughs and there's a spark in his eyes. "She says it delights her heart to know that I am here, and her kids are going to do stuff together. She wants to know, 'Where you all at? What you all doing now? What you all doing next?' Like we used to do when we were kids!"

"Did I tell you I drove with Frank to his house on the way over here? I couldn't go on CV pass 'cause it's in Raleigh. We could park and see the house from Durham, but I couldn't go there. We were talking and riding and then I looked up, and he's pulling up to this house. He pulled in the garage and he said, 'This is my house.'"

"Were his kids there? And Bridgett?"

"Yeah. Bridgett was pretty casual about it, but the kids. Oh man! They came running down the stairs and yelling 'Uncle Mec!' and jumping on me, and I got on the carpet and played with them a little bit. We didn't stay long. He just decided to stop there for a second. But when I went to his house, that was like another milestone that I'm really out. And driving over here, I'm looking at the cars with state plates and I'm thinking, 'No checker.' We here talking and nobody coming to check on us!

"And something else – about all the people calling. I never anticipated this. *No.* I'm talking about people I haven't seen since 1987. Haven't seen or heard a word. And when I do talk to them, they talk about some stuff that they remember that was and is important to me. And I'm thinking, 'Wow, you had to be somebody for them to remember that.' I didn't know, or never knew or thought of myself as being as influential as I was. These people say they've always been asking about me, inquiring, but I didn't know that.

"That kinda gets me, because it lets me know that I had some kind of value. When you stay in prison for a long time, you wonder who you were, who you are, if you left anything of significance behind. Especially, I don't have any children. I'm selling drugs in the street. What did I do that was enough for people to remember me? But the responses I've been getting are letting me know that maybe I did leave something of value. 'cause these people, they keep calling back. It's not this one conversation."

I'm cautious when I ask the next question. I don't mean an insult, but I keep going back to that day at Seton Hall. I keep seeing Mecca strutting up and turning in his SAT and thinking about his business on the corner and Bessie waiting, asleep in her car, waiting for the doors of opportunity to open up for her son.

"When you were in prison, did you feel like you had an impact for people like Frank and Scott-so but that that was the limit of what your impact was going to be? Does it make you feel at all spooked into thinking what if you hadn't kept dealing drugs? If you had gone to Seton Hall?"

"Man, it makes me sad and contrite that if had I done better things, what kind of impact I could have had. Like I say, I don't have any enemies. There's no place I can't go. I left no bad blood nowhere. My name is straight with people. I don't owe anybody anything. I don't have anything hanging over my head. However, had I done better things... I can't even imagine what kind of impact I could have had. Instead, I went to prison; I didn't do anything to have no impact on nobody."

"So when you meet a kid like Atrayus Goode, when he came to the prison workshop and talked about Movement of Youth,[15] that must be difficult. It's a mirror. There's the road not taken."

"Here's the thing, before prison every time I did meet people like him, I stayed away from them. I never wanted what I was doing to be attractive to people like him. That was my way of saying I can converse with you about what you are into, but I wouldn't dare want you to think that you can juggle your path and mine. I'm gonna stay away, so you'll never see me again because where I am is over here."

"And why do you think you were so attracted to that other side.

---

[15]   Atrayus O. Goode founded Movement of Youth in 2006 when he was a junior at UNC-Chapel Hill. In 2014 he came to speak to my workshop at OCC about his group's work mentoring youth and helping economically disadvantaged middle and high school students prepare for college. He had some legal difficulties but overcame them to transform a college project into a strong nonprofit.

Was it a money thing? Was it that you were good at it?"

"Initially, initially it was strictly to supplement a lack of income. But then, after I started to get into it, into dealing... I had that aunt, Cora, she was such a contributor to me remaining as long as I could. She knew how badly, how desperately I didn't want anybody in my family to know, and it became a never–ending debt of hush money.

"So you never got to the point of feeling like: I'm just going to cut this out?"

"No, prison did that for me."

"So if you hadn't gone to prison?"

"There's no telling how long it would have lingered on. And my Aunt Cora, she was a master at manipulating, and I couldn't see a way past it. And the dealing – it was also an addiction. Absolutely. The ability to continue to pull it off one day after the other; that is an addiction. It's the risk thing. You get so fascinated with the risk in it, and you think you so good at it. Each day you think, I want to do that again and again and again. Little more, little more, little more. Yeah, little high about it.

"My belief system has changed. It was changing before I went to prison. Morally it was bothering me. Prison gave me a chance to stop spinning around and to be still, allow my contrition to set in with me about what I was doing. Prison gave me an opportunity to get off this merry–go–round and sober up and see things a lot clearer and see myself a lot clearer. It gave me a time to stop dodging and dipping the punches being thrown at me morally for what I was doing with the drugs. I couldn't run from it no more.

"In prison I'm surrounded by people who are exemplifying the effects of drugs. Lot of them still high. Still under the raw influence of these drugs they are using. That's what did it. If I got sentenced to somewhere else where I didn't see that as much, I probably wouldn't have changed. Prison, being saturated with people who not only have done a lot of drugs, but they are not getting healthy.

The effects of drugs are still part of their character. They are living these effects out in everyday life. That was it for me.

"Out here, my energy has to go somewhere, 'cause I still have it. I'm gonna do something with it and I don't have a problem doing something constructive, something more meaningful in the way of giving back to somebody else's life. That's gonna happen. I'm coming in the door with that attitude.

"All night last night, I was waking up every ninety minutes. But it's good. It's fun to feel myself settling into freedom. To be expressing it in real time. Each day I'll get a little bit more balanced. When you been incarcerated and you get out, you are going to feel your body healing itself. Day by day, you just feel a little bit stronger, a little bit more sound."

Part Three: Freedom

Chapter 14: Christmas Holidays

It's Christmas Day, 2015. Day Three of freedom. I am in Mecca's room at Cheryl's house where he's surrounded by a swarm of technology: phone, computer, DVDs. He opens the computer, looking baffled and overwhelmed. None of this existed when he stepped out of the real world.

We're waiting for a call from Scott-so. After the fire and the move to Johnston Correctional, Scott-so transferred to Wake Correctional in Raleigh in order to get a work contract at the governor's mansion. The contract included a guaranteed right to a MAPP hearing, which he got but was turned down. It's another three years before he can have another hearing. I have been visiting him at Wake Correctional, but Mecca has not been able to communicate.

The phone buzzes and Mecca tentatively swipes the screen and hears the recording announce: "This call will be monitored and recorded. For customer directions, corrections or complete procedure, or to block future calls, dial 1-866-230-7761. To accept this call press five now. To decline this call hang up."

Mecca presses five and says, "Hey!"

"Hey, Bro! Hey, how you doing?" Scott-so asks.

I break in to say, "I'm here too. We are in Mecca's new cell. It's a bit up market."

Scott-so laughs and says, "I suppose that's right. He doing nice?"

When I reply that he looks like his brain is fried, Mecca chimes in, "Nobody has any idea, Scott-so! Nobody has any idea what this is like! Listen, CV passes do not prepare you for freedom. You know what they prepare you for? The next CV pass. That's it. Not for freedom. See, in a CV pass you have the barrier of knowing in six hours I'm going back. There's something about that. It's like bookends. But freedom is like being in the ocean with no shore."

Scott-so digests this and says, "I been trying to imagine. Man, I feel for some reason like I just got out as well! Yeah, it's almost like I got out because of the bond that we have for each other, the love that we have for each other. I'm overwhelmed and thankful."

I tell Scott-so that because it's Christmas week everybody has plenty of free time to say, "Oh, what do I want to take Willie to do next?" And Mecca isn't entirely comfortable with that.

"They say that, but they don't mean that," Mecca says. "They say, 'Where you want to go?' and then they make all these turns and GPS is there and I don't know where I'm going. They make exits on roads I never seen and then they park somewhere. And I say I don't remember saying I want to go here. You know how many times you and I said we wanted to go on that Tobacco Trail? I went there today. We walked eight miles. Five on the trail and three miles around our neighborhood. I did it today for us. No question."

"That's good man. Appreciate it, Bro," Scott-so says with a laugh, followed by a sigh.

"I'm holding it down 'til you get here, man," Mecca reassures him. "That's all I want you to know."

"Hey, like I always share with you, you never have to tell me that. I already know," Scott-so replies.

Cheryl comes in to say hi to Scott-so, who asks her if everything is good and is assured that it is. Then he asks where Bessie is, and Mecca says she's at home "resting up."

"I just gotta give her a call and make sure to tell her that I ain't forget about her. I am gonna call her," Scott-so says and asks Mecca to send him some pictures. "I want plenty of pictures."

Mecca doesn't know how to do that yet and says, "Cheryl, take a picture. She's doing it right now. You got everybody? I gotta learn how to go get it printed off the phone. You know I know what you need. I just left, so I know exactly what you need."

When the pre–recorded voice breaks in to announce that sixty seconds remain, Mecca says, "Hey, I love you, man," and Scott-so replies, "I love you too, man, and I thank you all and I give you a call soon."

At the fifteen second warning, Mecca says, "We'll get the money and send it to you on Jpay[16], so you have some money for the phone and whatever. We got you."

 "OK, then, Bro. Appreciate it," Scott-so replies as Cheryl and I say goodbye, take care, and he says, "See you later. Bye," as the call is cut off.

The three of us stare at the phone screen as if Scott-so were alive inside of that little black box.

I break the silence and ask, "What's it like, talking to Scott-so?"

Mecca pushes the laptop Cheryl has given him aside and sets his album of DVDs on top of it as if clearing some of the clutter from inside his own head. "Bittersweet." He walks to the window and opens it despite the cold outside, but he says the fresh air smells like freedom. His cadence is slower than usual when he says, "I know that he's genuinely happy for me – that I'm gone – but, at the same time, it kinda punctuates that he's not out yet. And he doesn't

---

16   Money transfers to the incarcerated are commonly made through the technology company Jpay. Using an internet account or through the phone funds are transferred directly to their prison account for use at the commissary (canteen) or for phone calls. Fees vary. For example at OCC, using the internet the fee is $6.65 to send $20 to $100. Using the phone the fee is $7.65 to send $20 to $100.

know when he will be gone. So it's like he tries to mentally project himself to be where I am. That's what I picture. If I could show him every square inch of this room, if I could send it to him in pictures, mentally he would put himself in here with me. And he would call me and say, 'I was hanging out in your room today.' That's just how the mind does in there. Or how we do our minds.

"It be harder if I couldn't talk to him. So it's hard either way... but way, way harder for him. I got a million distractions on my part. And at this time, him not getting his MAPP, it's very important for me to be there in any way that I can. Would be something if I could've talked to him the whole time I was on Tobacco Road. He'd have just wanted to know, 'What part of the road you on? What does it look like? How many people out there?' And I could say, 'We got two people coming our way. One on a bike and one walking.' He could hear them say, 'Good morning, Merry Christmas.' For him to hear that! Would've been great. I'm an extension of his fingers and eyes. I enjoy nurturing that.

"And it's not only Scott-so. I'm realizing that word of mouth... it's like wildfire! It's nonstop. See when somebody calls from prison at first it reads the same way: 'Call from a correctional facility.' I don't know who is calling. But if a guy doesn't have money on his account, they say, 'You have a collect call from Carl Dunlap 0114150,' or whoever, men from inside. I'm thinking, 'How did he know? How did he get my number?'

"I don't accept the call if I wouldn't even talk to him if we were face to face. But others are guys that I've dealt with shoulder to shoulder; these are guys that I will eventually send money to and pictures. That's what they ask, 'Send me pictures. I want to see you out!' They haven't seen me with real clothes on, they never even saw me in green clothes or heading out on a CV pass in street clothes. And these guys are genuinely happy that I'm out."

Mecca looks out the window again, as if he is checking to see that outside is really still there, then sits down and Mackey, the Jack Russell Terrier, hops up on the bed. He's not supposed to be up there, but Mecca is an easy target.

"I feel overwhelmed just trying to process it all. I feel queasy. Things are moving so fast out here. It seems like everyone is doing so much all of the time. And everybody seems to want a piece of me. I appreciate that they do care about me, but nobody asks me anything. It's more about them and how they feel. At dinner the first night, Mom posted on Facebook that I was out, and she gives out my number and right away my phone starts buzzing.

"Angel Sanchez, on a pass, he tried to warn me. He said, 'Listen, when you get out you gonna be pulled in a million different directions. Nobody means any harm. But it's going to happen.' Angel worked five days a week on work release, had CV passes and home passes – everything you can get to prepare you, and he told me, 'None of that compares to when you are all the way out. You'll see.'

"And I saw. I say to myself, it's like jumping in a pool. You stick your toe in and it's cold. You stick your foot in and it's cold. Then you say, what the heck, I'm going to jump all the way in and just adapt. And it's still a surprise when you hit the water. I'm doing that daily. I tell myself that after the holidays, people get back to their routine, then I can find myself, can create a sanctuary of stillness within. I've done that in the busyness of the inner city and in the way I grew up, in the chaos of my home. Just stop and sit in my room with my dog."

Mackey curls up even closer to Mecca.

"I'm going to scout out some gyms tomorrow. To be able to exercise, that would be an outlet for some of this anxiety. I call it the gift of fatigue. When you fatigue yourself physically, then you are forced to be still and breathe, just listen to your own breathing. That's when a type of clarity kicks in for me. I want to tire myself out and just lay back and say, 'Man, what a day.' And look at the ceiling fan and say, 'Man, I'm really here.' And close my eyes again and say, 'Yeah, I'm really here.'

"Time is funny. All that time away just closes to one point and one moment. You know what? It reminds me of the brevity of life. You look up and you are right there at the end of something. When you are in the midst of your years in prison, it's the longest time of your life. Then, just like that, I'm out and it's over. I tell myself I've only been out four days, but it feels like – because of all the movement – it feels like I been out a year already!

"You go out on a pass and you know you can only do that twice a week. Here I tell myself, 'Wow, it's on again tomorrow!' And then I wake up in the morning and I think, 'Time to get ready for this adventure.' That's a beautiful experience."

The phone buzzes and Mecca says, "It's a text from Mom. She says, 'I am so HAPPY.' That's it and one of those smiley faces. That's enough for me!"

We turn off the recorder and go downstairs to Christmas dinner.

I am scheduled to meet Mecca at Bessie's and encounter a group of men hanging around in front of the building – strong, Black, tattooed arms revealed by the rolled–up sleeves of brown hoodies. Not too many white women coming in and out of that complex, so they are brazen about taking me in. Two or three standing and two more sitting on the truck bed with cans of beer and a lot of attitude. I stop a few feet away. We exchange a solid minute of hard looks, and then they part and let me pass. I am acutely aware that I had learned something about "movement" when going in and out of prisons, something that I wished I did not need to know. I read them and they read me.

Mecca opens Bessie's door with a big grin on his face, waves me in, gives me a hug, and motions to the kitchen table. He goes over to the washing machine in the far corner of the kitchen, tosses in a load of clothes, and then joins me at the table. Doing laundry in your mom's machine can be something really special.

When I turn on the recorder, Mecca jumps right in. "Today is the eighth day, ninth day, and it's like one long day. I have to ask you or look for my watch to come up with how many days. I'm not counting down anymore. That's over."

Bessie takes a seat next to me and says, "I never counted down. You would say, 'Mom, how many more days?' and I would say I don't know because I am not counting. I knew and Cheryl knew that the day was coming. We just didn't know what day. It wasn't like a countdown because, to us, it could be tomorrow.

"But do I feel different now? Yes, for sure. I woke up this morning at three AM and I realized I am not on that grind anymore. Every morning prior to William coming home, especially prior to him going to Hillsborough, every day was a grind. Every day I gotta get up and I gotta figure out everything. What am I supposed to do today to work on his case or do to get ready for a visit or to get that phone call? Now I don't have to figure it out, hold my breath, be go, go, go. I don't have to worry about the mail, about making sure I get this on time, about now I gotta get ready for the visit. What we gonna eat? I don't have to make Christmas packages. I don't have to do that anymore!"

Mecca's eyes are on his mom. He's listening carefully then turns to me and says, "I had no idea. Phone call. I know everybody's got those cellphones so if I call her and she doesn't answer, I don't know why. I don't have any picture of her life. That's humbling for me to realize that nothing is as simple as I thought it would be. Nothing out here is as easy as I thought."

Bessie picks it right up. "He's calling and telling me, 'Now check the mail, Mom. Did you check the mail?' Because some form or notice is supposed to come from the prisons or the lawyer or something. I say, 'Hey, I don't work at the post office! I don't know what time they will put the mail in my box.' And maybe William says, 'I mailed it off on Monday. Mom, get the mail!' Or he's asking, 'That money didn't get on my account. Did you J–Pay it?' And then I got to stop what I'm doing in my day to be checking on that.

"People on the inside, they don't understand that it is not you that's the problem, it's just the circumstances. I'm trying to do something through the prison, and it goes from me to someone else and somebody else and somebody else. Maybe the officer didn't put it how he should have. But the person on the inside can't understand. William would be, 'Mom you didn't...' And I say, 'Yes I did!'

"One time I got into a confrontation at the post office. I had this same P.O. box for twenty-two years. The woman working that day did not put the mail in the correct box and they sent it back to the prison. William had me so upset. My perspective got messed up, and I almost got that person fired. I got so angry. I got so tired. That's what people talk about at the meetings at Straight Talk. They want to convey to their loved ones that are incarcerated: I work from nine to five. I can't be doing this stuff twenty-four seven. Me, sometimes I worked three jobs."

I can see that Mecca is thinking this one over. One of his strengths is the ability to listen and to hear what is being said. For a lot of the time in prison, the discussion focused on how to get him out of prison. Now that he is out, Bessie and Cheryl are more open about the challenges on their side. Mecca doesn't know it now, but he's starting up a new toolkit, gaining the insights he is going to use to advocate for and guide others as they move from the inside out.

"For people on this side of it," Mecca points to himself, "that's what I can bring to the table. It's happening on both sides. The mentality of the person that is in prison is looking at things to try to minimize the frustration. From inside, it seems like if you are not in prison, you should be able to do what I'm asking you. In prison, we have a sense of space and time that is different than out here. Also, on the inside, you can't see outside. It's like you are blind."

Mecca fusses with his phone to check a message from his brother–in–law, David, saying that there is a message on the landline asking Mecca to call his parole officer. He says, "Cheryl showed me how to email her, but I'm not sure it worked. This is all very new to me." He calls and learns that the officer didn't get the email, so he explains:

"My questions basically are predicated on the fact that, as you already know, I'm from New Jersey. Much of my family are from New Jersey. As far north as Newark and as far south as Florida. They in and out of town. Gracious enough to want to see me and want to visit me. And I understand how clear you were about my curfew and that you've made the exception for me to spend time with my family at the restaurant Monday night and that you extended it to nine o'clock. How does that work going forward?...

"Right. Okay. That was my sole motivation to try to communicate with you. As long as I am within my curfew and I'm within the county I'm good? And I need to make sure I am doing this email right because that is a way of contacting you. I'm gonna try to do it again. Please let me know if you get it... Okay... All right."

Hanging up, he says, "She said that for the first ninety days it's going to be tight."

Bessie and I have never seen Mecca speaking directly to someone who is, in effect, in charge of him. It's disarming to hear this slightly contrite, overly polite speech.

After we all take a break to get something to drink, I pick up the thread and ask, "While we are on the subject of supervision, did you pay your parole fees yet?" Just as the incarcerated who are on work release must pay for the cost of their room and board, the formerly incarcerated are expected to pay for the cost of their post–release supervision:

> Payments: A condition of your probation may require you to pay the State of North Carolina certain costs, fees and fines associated with violating the laws of the State of North Carolina. Amounts are specified on your judgment. Your probation officer will total all your costs (including the supervision fee) and divide them by the amount of time you are on probation (minus 2 months). This is the amount you must pay each month in order to pay all the fees owed as ordered. You may pay more on the monthly payment if you wish, but the minimum payment is required. You may also pay all fees owed at one time. Payments are to be made to the

Clerk in the county where you were convicted.[17]

"Here we go again, Simone!" Mecca is eager to air this beef. "My parole officer said you need to start paying that when you can. She's knows I'm not working. So one day I had the heart to go pay it even though I wasn't working. I had the forty dollars, so I go all the way to Raleigh to get the process started. They asked a million questions in the courthouse. I stood in the long line. Got to the teller. She's just as mean as most people who work in those buildings. Here's how it goes:

"My name is William Elmore. I'm here to pay my parole fee."

"What's your name again?"

"William Elmore."

"Where you from? What camp?"

"Before I could finish answering the first question, she's asking me another one.

"What's your number?"

"What number?"

"You supposed to have a certain number, blah blah blah."

"Mam, this is new to me. All this is new to me. And I was told I needed to come here."

"I need your number!"

"So I step out of the line, call my parole office and explain the situation and she says, 'What are they talking about? What number? Who are you talking to?' And I said, 'I don't know.' So I go back up – I'm going to abbreviate this – I'm talking to the teller and my parole officer at the same time. My parole officer gives me the number, I give it to the teller.

"That's not your number! It can't be your number."

"I'm on the phone with my parole officer right now, and this is what

---

[17]   https://files.nc.gov/ncdps/div/CC/Publications/Brochures/Completing_Prob.pdf

she told me."

"That's not your number!"

"So I left. And I got in the car with my mom and told her what happened and said that I'd put forth a perfect effort to do what I was required to do, and I was at peace with that. I got nothing done but I'm at peace with that. It's not on me no more. It's on them. I said, 'If you are all right with it, I'm all right with it,' and she said, 'Let's go.'

"I left and I haven't heard anything back from them since."

A few months later I ask Mecca if I can check out this story. We drive to Raleigh and take a short tour of the facilities there. He shows me the bay behind the jail where he was delivered to North Carolina from Georgia. We walk out to the corner across from the jail and he points way up to the window of his cell and shows me how Bessie could wave while he stood on his bed to signal her through the bars by waving a white sock.

When we go through the metal detectors into the courthouse, Mecca dissolves into that same compliant posture he assumed on the phone with his parole officer. We go upstairs to the window for paying parole fees. I'm asked to stand just outside the door, but I can see the line of similarly compliant people shuffling up to the thick glass teller windows. When it's Mecca's turn, the woman behind the window speaks to him, checks his ID, goes to talk to someone else, returns, takes her time sitting down before accepting his payment, and slides his receipt through. It seems she was surprised he was paying the full amount. Evidently most people negotiate a partial payment.

Changing the subject, Mecca wants to talk about something my husband, David, asked him when they were hanging out the previous weekend. "He said, 'Are you nervous about anything?' And I said, 'No I'm pretty much on an even keel.' He wanted to know if I would feel any kind of pressure, given where I might be or who I might be with. And I explained that I don't drink or smoke or use drugs, so I don't have to worry about getting into any of that. But I did say I'm a little nervous about the dating game. And he said, 'Really?'

"Yeah, because it's not 1989 or 1990. Everybody seems to be more fast. They want to get right to the point. But I'm not really in a hurry to get right to the point. The process is a joy for me. Yeah, I'm not nervous about it, because I'm gonna maintain my position regardless and do things in the way that I'm okay with regardless."

Bessie and I both laugh, and I say, "I think David's worried you might get ensnared."

"Yeah. And he did mention the quality of life that I had become accustomed to from selling drugs and asked how would that work for me. If I would feel seduced by that again. And I told him, 'David, I had twenty-four years of sobriety. Prison taught me how to live with the bleakest circumstances, meager means. I still like nice things. I liked nice things before I started selling drugs. My taste is just like that.'

"And David said, 'Yeah, I know. Every museum we went in, everything you liked was the highest price stuff in the store.' He's right. It got to a point where we would be somewhere and I would say, 'This is nice,' and he would look at the price tag and say, 'It figures.' I said, 'David, that's nothing new. You ask my mom or my sister. My taste just kinda runs that way.'

"But I told him, and I want to say it again here, officially. Nothing material is as expensive as losing my freedom. Or my sanity. Or my peace of mind. I'm not sixteen or even twenty anymore. I'm forty-five and my priorities are different. When I was younger, I liked the Lexis, the BMW, and if I had the money, I would get me one. That's really not that big a deal to me no more. In my former life, I was around people who were associating their personality and their character with how big of a TV you have or how expensive their car was or how expensive their shoes were. Or maybe they have a diamond necklace. The people that I have developed, people that I'm in contact with now, they don't care about that. They don't think that way. I received David's question as genuine concern for me, and that's why I want to repeat it. I'm not above hearing that. I do need to pay attention."

"Speaking of paying attention," I say, "let's go back to this thing about women and dating."

Mecca checks Bessie with his eyes. "My mother told me that. My sister told me that. Five years prior to my getting out they already talking like that. Before I even had a MAPP, Cheryl says, 'I'm telling you little brother,' and Mom says, 'I'm telling you son. When you get out the chicks are going to be all over you.' And I'm smiling from cheek to cheek at that. I'm not worried that way. I've learned in life that when you maintain your position and stay consistent with who you are, it does a lot weeding out on its own. If you maintain your own tempo, if you are okay with and move in that, if she's not the right one to complement that, then she'll move on. Idea is, nobody has time to waste."

Bessie is not going to let this go that easily and says, "There are some women out there who will try to draw you in, and before you know it, it's too late. Guys that I've talked to that have been in prison, I see them, and they have some story to tell me and they say, 'Ms. Elmore, I should have listened to you.' Because, unfortunately, women can set all kinds of traps. If they see something they want, they go after it in a different way than they did twenty-four years ago."

"What I do with that information," Mecca says, "when people I trust, like Mom or Cheryl, start to tell me that, what I do is I flip the question back on them. Particularly with my sister. She says, 'Look, little brother, leave the chicks alone because they ain't about nothing.' But when I flip the question on her, 'Well, who do you know that might be interesting?' she says, 'I don't know nobody.' She leaves me to myself all over again. But I want to know, Cheryl, if you have an opinion about it, who do you suggest? And she comes up empty.

"But I also understand their fears. I figured some of it out from journaling. Having grown up in an abusive household with my dad and my mom at such a young age, it made me lean to being more compassionate to a woman who has a situation. I want to help. Because I couldn't help my mother, I'm drawn to that. I know I am. Damsel in distress."

Bessie and I look at each other and exchange a smile. We are both flashing back to those visits from Annette years ago. That's what we are both worried about. I offer Mecca this warning, "That comes up, you have to show both of us her budget. We want to see her bank account and her budget!"

"The cougars are out there!" Bessie laughs and reaches over to give her son a nudge. "I'm serious. I feel concerned because I don't know how you are, outside of being my son."

"Hold on," Mecca says, offering a bit of push back. "I'm forty-five. I don't have a lot of time to be playing no games. I get you guy's input, but, as my mother knows, my decision is my decision. I know she's chock full of her own opinions and my sister is twice as bad. Cheryl's a pit bull. She runs 'em away. But I know I have missed the things a woman brings to the conversation, and so I'm going to be interested in that.

"You know what I missed most about a woman is the femininity. Living in prison, you don't get none of that. Guys I've talked to about women, guys who have done a lot of time, they tell you and I tell you, the first couple of years inside all you do think about is sex, but as you mature you think about other things. Compassion. How the woman you are thinking about is with a person, what she brings to a relationship.

"Prison is a traumatic experience. It does things to you. So if a guy doesn't do the necessary emotional and mental work, the trauma will stay as it is and he'll respond like a teenager. All teenagers think about is fast cars, money, and different girls. But for the guys that do do the hard work, they see that sex is not the only thing that they miss about a woman. They miss the unique thing that a woman brings to a relationship with a man. It's the female energy that draws you in. Prison plays so many tricks on your nerves. You need to be reminded of the type of person that you really are. You want a female friend to bounce your thoughts off, as opposed to hundreds and hundreds and hundreds of dudes all the time.

"I've talked about Keisha, the love of my life. She's married now, so that's off the table. But I'm still looking for the same thing. I want to connect and when I do it's a whole connection. It's not compartmentalized. I'm gonna really care for that person. Women... this is another time it calls for what I call 'thin slice.' Figuring people out, understanding the situation, that's a skill set that I'm very good at. My lifestyle before prison and in prison demanded that. Slice it thin enough where you could see through it."

Maybe we are looking a little bit skeptical. The jargon sounds good, but women and dating, especially for a man coming out of prison, that's asking for a very thin slice. One of the men from OCC, Mark Hall, worked at the Durham Rescue Mission, and he told me, "More than drugs there's one thing I hear when I ask how someone got in trouble. They are going to say, 'Well it was about this woman' or this man."

Bessie spreads her long, graceful fingers across the table like rays with a definite purpose and says, "Living here has taught me to be more careful, to scan the situation. And going in and out of prisons and jails, I just know it's hard for me to know how anyone, even William, can come out of there unscathed."

Mecca looks right back at his mother, back to the time they exchanged that promise almost two and a half decades ago and says, "Don't underestimate me. Whether it's a woman or whatever, I'm out of prison and I'm not going to be nobody's fool."

Chapter 15: Zelda – Friendship and Love

When we talked while Mecca was in prison, he often mentioned Keisha and showed me his photo of the two of them on their way to the prom. Her dad became his father figure and her home became the home he missed. I think Keisha fit the narrative Mecca needed to hear at that juncture – or needed me to hear.

When he got out of prison, Mecca had a clear feeling that he had pretty much lost touch with the world of love, never mind marriage; then a woman named Zelda appeared on the scene. She was a friend from New Jersey who came to weigh the pros and cons of Atlanta and Durham because she was thinking of getting out of New York. In the fall of 2016, Zelda moved to North Carolina. In five years of conversation with Mecca, I'd never heard of her – he does play his cards close to the chest.

I asked Bessie what she thought about Zelda, and she was, as usual, both protective and skeptical. She said, "I asked Zelda – just like it was a man suitor of my daughter – 'What are your intentions with my son?' And she said, 'I missed my chance before, and I'm gonna give it another try.' How about that?"

Zelda became an active supporter of the Straight Talk Transition

Group and helped Bessie with the opening of the Straight Talk Transition House in Durham in 2018. Once I met her, I could see right away that she is a woman who knows herself and knows how to love Mecca without crowding him. She's as important to him as a friend as she is as a lover; and I soon began to notice that during our conversations Mecca might say, "Funny you should ask me that. I was just talking about that with Zelda today."

When we talk in April 2018, I take it as a complement that Zelda speaks openly to Mecca and to me about her side of the story. Most men in prison have unfinished business with women back home. Mecca is no exception.

I first ask Zelda when she met Mecca, but she says she is not sure. Mecca, being Mecca, jumps right in with the whole story. He loves reliving those memories.

"Oh, man, it's a long story with a lot of twists and turns. You know most cities or towns have something that divides them; the north side/south side, uptown/downtown. I lived what we call "down the hill" in East Orange. Zelda lived "up the hill" and, in my opinion, down the hill was the most exciting part of that city. A lot of action – good and bad – a lot of entertainment. More gritty. More grimy. More everything.

"As a kid, I moved around so much. I rode my bike to other cities, skateboard to other cities. Walked my dog to other areas. And if I lived in this city, I went to school in that city. Lived in Orange, school in Irvington, other way around. So I had my feet in both places." He looks at Zelda, "Correct me if I'm wrong – the girls that were up the hill would get all dolled up and come down the hill."

Zelda is laughing. No correction called for. Mecca is straight on.

"Laughing or not laughing, they would look real pretty, her and her little clique of girls coming down the hill. Now we are talking about my first time seeing her."

"I don't really remember that. I think Swill saw me before I saw him," Zelda says, using Mecca's New Jersey street name. "I really wasn't paying attention to anybody. I just was hanging out."

For Zelda, Mecca is always Swill, his Jersey street name. "Kay Gee of Naughty by Nature, he gave me that name," Mecca explains. "It's a combination of 'Will' and 'slick', cause, back then, Kay Gee said I had a kind of craftiness."

It's also important to note that Zelda is both quiet and careful. She doesn't plunge right in and give out her secrets. She doesn't collect gossip.

"Right," Mecca says. "I just saw her. I actually thought she was much older than me."

"I think I was one grade ahead, but girls mature faster than guys."

"It's not like I had any kind of interest right away," Mecca says. "I just remember you coming down to where we lived with a group of girls. And then it might have been even years later, the next time I remember. It's summertime and – you know how it is? It's like in New York City. People are outside. People are hanging out on the corners. Fire hydrants are open.

"Where we are that day, it's called Grand Avenue in Newark. I saw her walking down the street and I said, 'I know that girl from somewhere. What she doing around here?' I come to find out that her friend Fatima lived on that street. First time we met we are young, maybe eleven or twelve. Now I'm maybe fifteen, sixteen and I know her face. Found out she's sitting on Fatima's porch. I came up to that porch and I think I had the nerve to say something to you. Did I?"

"I remember that, but when we talk you remember more."

"I said something to her, like, 'What you doing around here?' And that was the beginning of me actually having any kind of conversation with her."

"What was your first impression of him?" I ask Zelda.

"Yeah!?!" Mecca smiles and leans back in his chair. Now everyone is laughing.

"I was nonchalant about it. Not speaking back or whatever. My girlfriend would say, 'Who was that?' She knew I like the darker skin, chocolate guys. 'You remember him from East Orange?' And I was just, 'Oh, yeah.' But I noticed him."

"So what was the social scene? Did you ask people to go out? Or did you just kind of dance in circles?"

"You wait for him to give you – to approach you and ask you for your number or you tell your girlfriend and get her to kind of talk to him and ask, 'Are you dating somebody?' and tell him, 'She likes you!' The numbers get exchanged that way."

"I think Fatima got involved," Mecca adds, "because Fatima is very outspoken, brash and impatient. That's Fatima. She say, 'Stop playing. You all talk. I'm gonna go inside for a minute.'"

"I'm shy," Zelda defends herself. "Yes, that sounds right about how it happened! Then we started talking, and I remember the things that stood out to me. This guy Swill, his conversation was a lot different then than guys his age and the guys that I was around. One thing that stands out most is that he had a very spiritual base. He would tell me different things about the Bible and quote different things, and I thought that was kind of... it was sexy, intriguing. It was just like 'Wow!' I remember when I came to his house, and he had his *own* Bible. What? I don't know young guys like that. I'm not a studious type of person, so I thought that was very interesting and intriguing – that he had this whole street persona but underneath all of it he was very spiritual. That attracted me to him a lot."

I have talked with Mecca about faith. He refers to himself as a Christian, but he stayed away from the various Bible study groups at OCC, and his friends are just as likely to be Muslim as Christian. I probe a bit, "You haven't talked about that a lot. Were you reading the Bible literally or more as a spiritual or philosophical text?"

"I was doing both," Mecca says. "My mother's father was a Baptist preacher. He had his own church in Newark. When he got kicked out of Alabama and came to New Jersey, he was a devout alcoholic, but he had a tragic car accident where he felt like he should have died. He didn't die and that changed him, and he gave his life to the Lord and became a pastor.

"I'm his only grandson, so when he needed another male on deck, he would grab me. His sons, for whatever reason, they weren't into the church, so he would take me with him to do things – clean–up something or hold this tool or something. He did construction on the church all the time. He wasn't the kind of pastor where every other word was Jesus this and Jesus that. I liked that, because I had been around those kind of pastors, and it didn't work for me. He was a real practical, down to earth southern guy, hard working, knew how to do a little bit of everything. So I loved hanging out with him.

"And probably the closest person I've ever been to in my family is his wife, my mother's mother. And her being a preacher's wife, she was very devout. In between those two, it rubbed off on me.

"When my mother and father purchased their home, my mother used to conduct a Bible study and I would attend. By nature I liked to discuss things as opposed to sitting in a service hearing somebody tell me what God said. I liked that it was a time we could discuss what we all think that the book of God is saying. That stayed with me and some of that would come out in our conversations, me and Zelda. A little bit spiritual, philosophical, and also literary."

"Zelda, what was your background? Why did this attract you?"

"Not the same as his, but I had studied in various faiths, and I would read the Bible, but I never could understand it – the thou, thee – just not getting past it. So when I would hear him discuss it and he had such a good grasp of it, it just made me look at him differently. It gave me a different insight into it. I told my mom, 'I want to have my own Bible.' As progressive as I thought I was, looking at different faiths, I was like, 'This guy seems to be a little smarter than me!' I really enjoyed that about him.

"I liked to study things. I think that came from my stepfather. He bought an encyclopedia that was like the internet for me as a kid! I'm through every volume from A to Z, just studying. My mother always thought I would be a journalist because I could just write for days about any and everything. So to find and to talk to a young guy that had a conversation outside of music, clothes and sneakers!

"My mother was a computer analyst for an insurance company, Mutual Benefit Life, before it folded. And my father worked at Budweiser. He was brew master. They both graduated high school. She didn't have a college degree, but she had training in computers. Did they expect me to go to college? I don't know exactly what they expected. I was a good student, but I was rebellious. When I became a teenager, they knew that whatever expectations they had they had to put to the side, because I was going to do whatever I wanted to do!"

"Here I am, I'm a kid but I have these liberties like an adult." Mecca explains. "I'm doing so good in school I could take days out and make up for it when I came back. Zelda had a similar capability to move around. That's another reason I thought she was so much older than she was, 'cause she somehow had these liberties to go somewhere and stay out all night."

Zelda is laughing again. "If I did it, I would probably tell my mother I'm staying at my girlfriend's house. She would call my girlfriend and my girlfriend would vouch for me."

I decide to point out the elephant in the room. What about the dealing? Zelda gently provides me with a lesson in New Jersey dating. "I did know. We didn't talk about it. Mostly I assumed it. I strongly assumed it because of the guys he hung out with. That's pretty much what every one of the guys that age in that area did. Didn't seem risky. It just seemed like: okay, that's part of the life in this particular neighborhood."

"I give you an example real quick from my work now with youth, why this develops," Mecca says. At this point, he is working with a nonprofit trying to intercede before kids who have drug problems get into deeper trouble. "Yesterday we went to see a potential client. He lives in a trailer park. His mother is on methadone, which means that she's in recovery from heroin. He's not working and he's not in school. He kept saying he wants to work and get money. He thinks money will change his life.

"In this situation, he's either gonna do one of two things: crime or a low–level job. Say he works. He is going to realize that minimum wage is not a lot of money and he is going to move on to crime. He's probably seen his mother or his grandmother work, but still they don't have no money. He's not connecting it to them using their money for heroin. To him, you work, but you don't have money. You sell drugs; you have money. I can relate to that. I remember that.

"And me, I also managed my money differently from my peers. The first thing they want to do when they get some money is do something that kind of said something about them. Buy stuff. For me, first I took care of my responsibilities, helped out my household. Initially that was my only reason for even beginning to get into that lifestyle. Once I had more money, I did buy clothes, jewelry, cars, but providing money to my family was always the first part of it. That had a lot to do with the personality of the person that Zelda met when she met me."

"We talked about some of those things," Zelda says. "And I was thinking, 'Wow, such a young guy with these responsibilities.' That made me feel closer to him. He had a different mindset. You taking care of home? It made me have a different feel about his character, which stood out from the other guys."

"And Zelda was more adult–like, quiet, see everything but speak on nothing. Saying that, I gotta note she is like that now. You tell her something, you tell her a little bit, she knows the whole story, and if it needs to be quiet, she won't ever say anything. I'm like that too. We have so much in common."

I ask Zelda if she realized how much money Mecca was making.

"I don't think I really knew how much money was involved until we started having conversations recently. I'm like, 'What? You should have told me.' If I knew fully, at least I would have said, 'All right but you need to transition out of this. You need to be putting up a business.' Maybe he even knew what my mindset was, and he wasn't ready. I was thinking let's get married. Settle down. But I was not saying it out loud.

"I did know Cora from coming down the hill, and I knew what she was into. I just didn't put the two of them together. I didn't see Swill being part of that."

"You didn't know that because my movement was like that. I don't like to transfer information. In the culture of drugs, you become more vulnerable when people know your soft spots. If people know Cora is my aunt, that puts us both in a situation. Cora is a drug addict. She owes people money. I'm her nephew. I'm selling drugs. That's a problem. The less people know about that kind of intimate stuff, the better it is for Cora and for me. So with Zelda, we got older and a lot of the time we went out of town. Poconos. Atlantic City. Let's go to Georgia!"

"I might even have asked him to go out of town. I'm private in how I move. I didn't want to be all, 'Hey, let's get the same leather jackets.' I don't need people to know that about me."

With all this talk about trips out of town I have to ask, "Were you doing anything about pregnancy? I ask because so many of the people I talk to at the prison have these babies that came into their lives by accident, 'something happened.' Did you go to Planned Parenthood or anything?"

"I don't know," Mecca says, passing it to Zelda.

"No." Zelda looks back to Mecca and they both laugh. "We didn't think about that."

Mecca tips back in his chair and meets her eyes. "I want to add this: I always felt, from conversations with Zelda, at a friendship level, she was more mature. Her thinking was so much further down the road than mine about everything we talked about. Because of her maturity and the way she thought, I always felt a little bit insecure beside her. A little bit. Not a lot."

"That's unusual for you, yes?"

"*Very.* I'm not used to that. We didn't become competitive. But Zelda was somebody I could bounce my thoughts off of. Then the more turbulent and stressful my life got, the more I shied away from her, because I felt like it might look to her like I can't handle this. It's crazy to think that, but I didn't want her to see me unravel, so I got away from her. I abandoned her. All the way until recently. I disappeared."

I turn back to Zelda. Mecca is watching her too. There's a scent of sadness hovering in the room. "Do you remember that? Could you figure out why he dropped contact?"

"I remember," she begins slowly. "Um hmm. It was very hurtful, and I was just devastated. Swill was out of town a lot. I'm assuming he is just living the life, and so I'm like, 'Really? Okay.' I felt like he had moved on, but we never had that conversation that said I'm moving on. So I was in limbo. We had this great relationship and we had this great communication. When he broke it off and stopped returning phone calls, I just couldn't understand that. It was so out of character for him."

"I drifted off out in the middle of my mess," Mecca says. "My whole life was falling apart and one day turned into a week, one week turned into a month, turned into six months. Six months turned into nine months. I'm on the run for murder. I feel like I'm so far out. What do I do? Tuck my tail? Put my hat in my hand and pop up now? What's Zelda going to think?

"Well, finally I did! I always knew that she was a pillar of stability and there did come a point when I was on the run, I reached out to her." He looks at Zelda with an odd touch of pride. "And then it was as simple as me saying, 'I don't know what you doing, but I need to see you.' And she came to see me."

"I flew down to Atlanta. I had family in that area. At this point I'm grown and I don't need to explain. I'm living at home and working, so I say I'm going to visit my father's side of the family down South. I'll be back. My mom, she didn't really know what was going on.

"I already knew what happened because the word had got around. Once I learned some of the things that were happening, about his charges, on the run, then I understood. I was at a point where I was waiting for him to reach out to me. I wanted a way to reach out to him because I felt like he needs me. He needs some advice. He needs some friends. But also, I was kind of mad. If only Mec' would have called!" She turns to look at him. "I felt like if you had told me where you were, what your issues were, you would have had an ear. I would have helped you with that."

Mecca seems torn. He's a little bit defensive and a little bit sad. He hasn't heard anything this directly from Zelda before. He looks for a rebound, "Remember, I'm on the run. I'm living where I can. Apartments, hotels; any time I felt like the space was shrinking I would leave. Cora still had her hand in it. If she couldn't rent a place or a car for me, she had a friend that would. I learned that people will do almost anything for money. You pay somebody to get you an apartment. Put it in their name. Stay there a few months. Few weeks. Go get another one. I was bouncing around like that a lot."

"Could you tell how bad things were when you went to visit him?"

"It was not like he looked bad or anything. But it's a serious situation. He's on the run for his life. I was very concerned. We discussed different strategies, but I don't think I was ever thinking we need to go turn you in."

"Nobody ever said that."

"At some point, I did ask, 'Are you prepared for when and if the time comes. How are you going to prepare yourself for your case?'

And we had deep discussions about what could happen if he got caught. But I never got from him that he was afraid. He kept that hidden."

"My frustration wasn't about 'What's gonna happen?' It was more about 'How the hell did this happen?'"

"And that's why I was really pissed off at Mec's so–called friends – friends that we grew up with – that offered information to the police. And I remember one time the FBI must have called my mom and she was asking me, 'What's going on?' And I said, 'I don't know. I don't know where that phone call came from.' But I could tell the FBI had information."

"I didn't know they went to talk to your mother. They went to another girlfriend of mine at her house also. Because these guys who testified at my trial, now in prison, they knew me enough to give me up. The FBI wouldn't have known to talk to Zelda or her mother without these guys telling them."

I ask, "How does Keisha fit into this?" By this point Keisha's prom is over. The cover of high school is over. Mecca is a full–time dealer who's on the run.

"Keisha has already segued out of the picture," Mecca says in that way he has of making big events sound ordinary. "Keisha and I broke up, got together, broke up this one last time. During that time was when I met Zelda again. When Keisha sensed that – women sense things – or heard about Zelda, she tried to get back with me, but it was too late.

"In prison I liked to think about Keisha, play with that in my head, 'cause of her and her family, her father, how close I was in their house. Zelda was something else. That's why you didn't hear me talking about her. Not mentioning her that way, in just any kind of conversation. Like I said, I like my privacy."

I respect Mecca's boundaries but also sense that he is letting Zelda take the lead on how far we go.

"When you went to see Mecca, Swill, when he was on the run in

Atlanta, did you just go as a friend or did you feel like your relationship to him was part of it or just see it as his problem?"

"I felt connected to him, and I wanted to be more involved than he wanted me to be. A mutual friend was with him some of the time. He was a loyal, stand–up guy, so I felt like as long as he is with Swill, he's gonna be all right. I wanted to be there for him as much as I could, but, you know, again, he was pushing. He only let me in just so much. I went to see him a few times, and then at some point everything was disconnected. The number or the way I could communicate with him didn't work. He went back to being on zero, on silence again."

"I'm not trying to speak for Zelda," Mecca steps back in. "I know for me to call her from anywhere, I would say, 'Look where you at? What you doing? I'm in Georgia, Tennessee, Alabama. I send you some money. You want to come down here?' I wasn't approaching her like she was still my girlfriend. There's a level and layer of friendship between us that's so solid and strong, I always knew that even if she had had a boyfriend, I could still ask her to come somewhere to see me. We would be intimate or not."

"I know Bessie talked about getting you to Mexico. You didn't have plans like that?" I ask. You didn't talk to Zelda about that?"

"Us running off? I thought about doing a lot of things as a solo act, but I never proposed that to her, because I did care about her enough to know I can't ask you to tag along with me this way. You've got your life. What's your mother gonna say? And I didn't want Zelda to be looked at that way, as this stupid girl running around behind this boy who has nothing. No where to go. But I knew a little bit then and I know a whole lot now; had I asked her to, she would have done that. I'm glad I never asked her."

"And I would have done that because, although you may have been calling me as a friend, come see me on the platonic, I always still had this hope. Swill needs me and I'm going be there for him through this. Our connection was that strong." Zelda laughs. "Well, there would be times he just went into radio silence mode. I'm thinking, he's probably with somebody else. I'm not gonna just sit here and look stupid. So I would date, and I did go out with several people, but it wasn't anything serious."

Mecca turns and leans toward the recorder. "I want to say something. Let the record reflect this. If you are a half decent guy that cares about somebody outside of yourself and you are living a life that is high risk, you have to think about the responsibility that comes with bringing somebody along with you. Imagine if I had been on the run forever and I get to Mexico or someplace, change my identity, I don't want to bring someone else into my life under these circumstances.

"So a lot of my silence and disconnect, whether it felt right or not, was predicated on that. Remember they had me S–O–S – meaning shoot on sight. I'm considered armed and dangerous. I didn't want to bring anybody – especially Zelda – into that reality. Running around with her, it could be real romantic and great, but there's responsibility. I could deal with it for a weekend, three or four days. But than... you go back home and you're safe, and I still gotta keep on figuring out how I'm gonna get away.

"If I had articulated that, maybe she would have felt better. I thought it, but I didn't articulate that. So let me say that now, for the record."

"Zelda, do you remember hearing when he finally got caught?"

"I don't remember who told me, but I do remember hearing. It's not that I didn't care, but I'm just not a person who cries. But I was sad and I was mad; sad for him and mad at his friends, at the betrayal. He came out to help you, did all this trying to save your life, and now you pretty much ended his life. I'm still very upset at those friends."

"Did you have contact while Mecca was in jail waiting for his trial?"

"She came to visit me. I asked her and it was the same. Everything was always on my terms. When I reached out and would contact her, Zelda would be Johnny–on–the–spot to come visit me."

Mecca and Zelda exchange looks. Mecca's efforts to spare Zelda have a bit too much of a macho ring to them. I ask him, "Do you see that as fair?"

He's quick to answer. "*No. No.* That's not fair at all. There was not one time that I ever would question her presence. If I asked, she would figure out how to show up."

I tap the table. "Just clearing that up!"

"Zelda, when you came to visit him in jail or prison, do you remember what it was like?"

"I had never been to a prison or a jail out of state. I always heard that they were a lot worse than it was up North, so I was afraid for him more than anything else. I went to Nash with Frank's girlfriend, Jackie, before Bridgett. We rode down together.

"I remember it was sad. I've never seen Swill in such a sunken place. He's this positive person, upbeat and competent. At Nash, I saw a different side of him. It was a time when I still felt a little angry." She turns to Mecca. "I know when you were on the run it wasn't just about me. But when I got to Nash, I was still a little salty about it. Also, I was at a time in my life where I was trying to get myself established in my career in the entertainment industry. I was more focused on me."

"I liked writing," Mecca says, "so when I got arrested, I was writing her a lot. And then, after I was sent to prison, the roles kind of reversed. I'm writing her all the time and she's only sparingly writing me back."

Zelda hesitates, "I was also thinking, 'Hmm, now you got time for me!' But it was more that I was on a roll with where I was in my life. We were young and our communication was not at a level where we could talk easily about why this happened."

"She's working on her career and I'm working on figuring out how to get an extra blanket! I would write her all the time, and she wouldn't write back that much. I didn't take it personally," He's looking at Zelda again. I'm not even there. "I'm not expecting you to complement my life at that point. I might go a year, two or three and I wouldn't write her, and then I would write again. 'What's going on? What you doing?' She would always respond initially and then she would fade out. Maybe ten years like this. I never asked her, 'Are you dating?'"

"He never asked that. But every time he would write me, it seemed like I wasn't in a relationship. But in those letters the conversation would stay general. I think there were some apologies that we both needed to make. I wanted to give him one and I was expecting one from him, but I never got that in a letter, so I just kept it platonic. I didn't know if somebody else was writing and coming to see him."

"And remember this. We knew a lot of the same people, so there was a lot to talk about."

"And pictures. He was always asking, 'Send me pictures. If you have any pictures send me pictures.' And I sent some books."

I ask Zelda, "How do you finally resolve it? Did you fall in love or did you need to move on? Not a fair question to ask you in front of Mecca, but I'm asking anyway. He's in prison with a sentence of natural life."

I get the same response that I got from Bessie and Cheryl: "I never thought that he was in for life. I knew he was coming home. It just was when. But it's ironic – funny enough – had he asked me for more back then, even where I was in my career, I would have said, 'Let's see how we can make this work.'"

One more person to remind Mecca to hang onto hope. Reading Bryan Stevenson's *Just Mercy* or Laura Bates's *Shakespeare Saved My Life* you learn that there is a very tangible link between hope, redemption, and rehabilitation. It has a deep effect on the way a person does their time. Bates asks the lifers in her workshop, "*Can Shakespeare save lives?*" and a man named Leonard says, "I believe... that there are some people who, if a program has the ability to reach a person's soul to a degree to allow that person to seek healing and redemption, I believe that some – not all, but some

– may be prevented from walking across the line of no return." Another prison student says, "They may see a new approach for whatever it is that they're after." Bates asks, "We've saved a life?" Another man answers, "Saved my life."[18]

When Mecca made his promise to Bessie at Central Prison, he was not collecting a free pass. He was not going to be guaranteed a reversal of his sentence, a commutation, or a parole, but he was guaranteed hope. Zelda's loyalty, her gut instinct about their friendship and his eventual release is another bet placed on hope.

Zelda is aware that she struggled with that commitment; it was informal, unspoken, and came and went. She continues, "In 2005 I got married. I wanted that as part of my life, and didn't think that would happen if I just sat around and waited. That's another sad thing. It was a point where I just didn't think there was a relationship between us; so I got married. I had a destination wedding. In Jamaica. But I couldn't bring myself to tell Swill. And then, before I could tell him, our communication stopped again. He moved to another facility."

"How long did your marriage last?"

"About a year and half. It was brief."

"Sort of a date?"

"It was a long date!"

"One day I wrote Zelda at her house and she told me she was going to have a P.O. box. I didn't inquire, because details didn't matter to me. What mattered to me was the friend that I had in her. I'm smart and I know she's probably seeing somebody. If I really pressed the issue, I would have heard from her. But my letters were general and generic. I never asked or demanded. Didn't need to know."

"Sounds like you were both going around in circles. The part of each of you that is trying to define yourself, you are not sharing that

---

18   Laura Bates, *Shakespeare Saved My Life: Ten Years in Solitary with the Bard* (Naperville, IL: Source books, 2013) 180–181.

with the other." They both look a bit sad but also determined. There's a reason things are working for them now.

"First let me say," Mecca turns to Zelda. "Are you sure with me saying this?" She nods. "I never dated anybody I wouldn't have married."

"What about the woman you were staying with when you were on the run, when you got caught?" I ask. Mecca does not dwell on this detail, but when he was arrested, he was staying with a woman. In fact, her son had wanted to go fishing with Mecca that day, but, fortunately, Mecca decided not to take him.

"That's only one," Mecca says. "You're right, I wouldn't have married her. When I was on the run, I was so out of myself. None of that even counts. Even when I was in prison, I always looked for things, the realest things, the most stable and solid things to get a grip on to remind me of myself. And Zelda has always been one of those people. When I really want to know where I stand, who I am and what I am, I find the realest people, places and things to go stand beside. And she's always been that kind of person.

"When I got my MAPP, when I knew I was getting out, I didn't have Zelda's address anymore, so I asked Frank could he go on Facebook to find her? Did he know how to do that?"

"I think Frank found someone who found my cousin," Zelda says, "and my cousin asked me, 'You know somebody named Swill? Somebody on Facebook is asking can I give them your contact.' I said, 'Yeah, I know Swill.' It was Frank saying he's getting out. Inside I'm thinking, 'Oh my gosh! This is real.'"

The romantic in Mecca sounds excited just remembering. "I was out on pass with Frank. He gave me the phone number, and I called her and we talked."

"It was so funny because I had never heard his voice in twenty–something years. Not since that visit at Nash, when we were in contact and we wrote. He told me about the MAPP and that he had a date to come home. I was extremely happy for him."

"Did you start to think at all of a romantic thing?"

"There's a small part of me that was like, hmmm? But then, more important, ninety percent of me was just happy for him. I felt like if anybody deserves to be free it was Swill. He didn't deserve that prison sentence, life. And there was also a part of me that knew that I still hadn't had that cry. I envisioned, when I saw him, that I would just bawl, because I just was so hurt by him.

"But don't get me wrong. Something bad happened to me, but he didn't deserve the time he got. I was happy that he thought enough of me, that he was saying, 'I'm calling to share this information with you.' We just picked up where we left off, really good intellectual conversations."

"And I must say this, on the tape," Mecca sits up straight. "The last thing I was looking for in all of my attempts to connect with Zelda was any kind of romantic relationship. Especially as I got closer to getting out. In prison your whole life is exposed. You butt naked in front of everybody. You have no privacy. The last thing I wanted to do coming right out of prison was, number one, to have to share my space with anybody, and number two, to be transparent. Take on a relationship with somebody, you gotta share your space, share some of yourself. You gotta be open and vulnerable. I didn't want to do any of that. Yeah, I like her, but I'm thinking, 'Heck no, I don't want to be responsible for nobody. I want some privacy. I want to come and go how I want.' I don't want, 'Where you going? Where you been?' It's too much like prison.

"Lo and behold, the more I talk to Zelda, the more I realize, 'You know what? More important than anything, more important than loving you as a person, I really like you.' And to me, that's important. You can love somebody, and still they can go way over there and you can go way over here, but when you like somebody, you want to hang around with one another. You like their company. I would tell her all the time, 'It's a good thing I like you, because I want you around me. I want to be around you.'

"We had some conversations about all this before she moved down here. Say me and Zelda married and we live in this house. There's a lot of rooms in this house. I want to go sit in that room all day by myself? Not talking to her? But to her, to a woman, she's gonna be thinking, 'What's that about?' But Zelda is so... she's always been so self sufficient that all the things I assumed would be a part of having a relationship, they weren't even there. I was kind of creating them. And I was like, 'Oh, this is much more low maintenance than I thought it would be.' I'm always hearing about guys come out of prison and relationships are one of the things they have forgotten how to do or maybe never learned."

"Being incarcerated," Zelda sighs. "I'm just imagining what that could be like, and I never want to replicate that. I have a feeling for what your life had been like... somebody telling you, 'Take all of your clothes off. Spread your butt cheeks.' I don't want to be anywhere near remotely reminiscent of that. So he asks, give me space, please? And I say, okay, 'cause I have things to do myself. I'm not here to cater to you and see what you're doing. I have a life too, before and after all of this."

Zelda looks straight at me. I remember her words to Bessie, her love and her determination to give this a chance. She says, "So far, it's the easiest relationship I've ever been in. He's a good guy. He really is."

Chapter 16: Processing Freedom: Emotional Side Trips

Going home after long years in prison is more like Rip Van Winkle waking up in Sleepy Hollow than it is like a high school reunion. At the reunion everyone is more or less in the same boat. Coming out of prison, you are on a raft by yourself. People have been living their lives, watching the world change at a commonly shared pace. That connection is not there if you have been locked away.

There are many rites of passage a person experiences after leaving prison. There are all the small things: getting a driver's license, figuring out how to scan a debit card, learning how to wrangle with cell phones, just getting used to walking around unsupervised, being free to make decisions on your own. Then there are the big ones: living in a "real" home, getting a job, and the emotional giant of reconnecting with the world, with places and people and experiences that have been distanced and mediated by time behind bars. I call these emotional side trips, and Mecca has taken me along on his big three: going back to New Jersey, visiting dad, and encounters with death.

Mecca is slowly settling into the outside world. He's gotten a driver's license and a car to drive. In the spring of 2016, while he is still on parole, Mecca is invited to go to New Jersey with Bessie and

Cheryl to attend his cousin Troy's wedding. If CV passes do not prepare you for the shock of getting out, they definitely do not prepare you for your return to Sleepy Hollow, New Jersey.

Mecca explains the logistics to me. He has a new, more relaxed parole officer who says he can make the trip as long as she has the exact dates and contact information. By the time that's settled and they're heading north, Mecca has missed the deadline for the wedding's head count RSVP. Just as well. Mecca explains to Troy that he's not comfortable being around a lot of people and definitely would not be comfortable drawing all that attention. It's Troy's wedding. Troy should be the center of it.

Mecca begins his narration at the point where Troy picks him up at his aunt's house so they can spend time together while Troy does some last–minute errands.

"Troy picked me up in East Orange, and once we hit the highway and started approaching Weehawken and Jersey City all of that, it just normalized. It was like old times. But here's the difference. Troy's older than me, but I lived faster than him. When we used to hang out, I was the one driving and directing where we were going. Now he's driving and he's dictating the pace. Kind of changing our places.

"See, I was the cousin that all my other cousins looked up to because I was in the street, living this life that they were scared to death to even think about trying to live. So they always deferred to me for some kind of excitement. Let's go to New York City. Okay, let's call Cousin Willie and he'll take us. We wanna go buy some clothes or go to forty-second street or Central Park? I tell them, I just come back from Central Park. Let's go there.

"Now, it's Troy who knows what's going on. He works on bridges, he hangs off bridges, and he says he can get me a job doing that. I don't want it, but it shows me he has some pull. Troy's been in the reserves. He has three kids – not from the lady he is marrying, but three kids. I knew about all of that through my mother, but to be actually with him was a little strange and awkward in the beginning. Then it normalized. We spent some one on one time. We hadn't done that in thirty years.

"And here's another thing. Going to New Jersey taught me about that how I remember or don't remember. Troy says the lady he's marrying knows me. We went to school together. I don't remember her. He showed me pictures of her, but I don't remember. That was awkward until we got past it.

"Since I'm also thinking about women, I asked him, 'Why now? What's making you get married now?' And he said, 'Time man, it's just time for me to do it. When *you* gonna get married?' I had to just laugh. I said, 'I don't know! It could be tomorrow, it could be later, but I want to talk about you getting married. Congratulations. I'm proud of you. Are you really ready?' And he's, 'Yeah.'

"I kept teasing him. That was like old times, good. But that ghost, the not remembering, kept sliding into view and right beside it, real places that had changed so much."

Mecca's friends from the hip hop group Naughty By Nature were playing a free concert in Newark. Kenny Gee (given name Kenneth Jackson) had kept up with Mecca and sent him those fine shoes while he was in prison. They tried to connect just after Mecca was released, but at the time Kenny was on a tour bus in Charlotte with no way to get to Durham, and Mecca was still bound to stay in the county. Now Mecca and his friend Demetrius head to Military Park in Newark for the concert. Demetrius is a steady friend who spent time with Mecca when he was on the run. He's doing okay, works at Tiffany's and, as Mecca puts it, has a side hustle buying Adidas wholesale and selling at retail.

"When we get to the concert it's overwhelming." Mecca rolls his eyes. "Look at it like this. Nobody's seen me in all this time, but everybody said it was easy to know it was me because I looked the same, 'cept that I'm heavier. Face–wise, I'm the same. When I get to the park, I see a few guys that I remember. They all say, 'When did you get out? When did you come home? How you doing? You look good.' But later, I'm walking in the park and I see several more guys, and they know me, but I don't know them. I just don't know who they are. They brought up things that I did remember, stuff from school, but I had to say, 'I'm trying my best man, but right now... there's a lot goin' on.'

"This started when I was on the run. I think I did an excellent job erasing, forgetting. That time on the run was like going through a tunnel, one that erases your memory. I willfully went through there, slowly, painstakingly. Every time I shut my eyes real hard it was like I was deleting something. Because the memories were too painful. I did that daily for that year and a half. I deleted so many memories, and the few that remained, I'm not really sure why. I haven't really explained that. I don't understand it.

"I do remember the last time I saw Naughty By Nature. I was in New York on the run, and they were there at the Apollo. I got word to them that I was outside, and they sent security out with this laminated pass. It was on a Wednesday night, which is when they film the Apollo. The band, they don't know anything about me being on the run. They keep saying, 'Come on upstage with us. Right here.' And the cameras are panning, and I'm like, 'I'm fine over here.' I'm trying to dodge those cameras.

"Same thing happened when I was in Atlanta and they were at the Armory with a bunch of other groups – Ice Cube, Ghetto Board. They kept saying, 'Come on. We're inviting you all the way to the table with us and you keep stopping there.' They don't know, and I don't want to put my friends in the place where they have to answer any questions about me. So I say I gotta leave.

"But now I'm out. I'm not on the run, and people are watching the security guard escort us to the tour bus. Who are these guys just cut through the crowd? What group are they in? We get on the bus and it's small. And being crowded, it's even smaller. You got guys in there and girls and guys smokin' weed and drinkin'... just like in a movie. I'm five months out of prison, Simone. Who's life goes like this? Who would believe this?

"Kay Gee was on his phone, texting or something. So I waved my hand in front of him, and he looked up. He just couldn't believe it, and he gave me the biggest hug. And his two little brothers and a cousin and the other two guys from the rap group and everybody were all around me.

"When the security guard came and said things were ready, the guys say to me and Demetrius, 'You all together with us.' And we get escorted on stage! And to me – I don't see a rap group that's really popular. I'm looking at friends I grew up with doing their thing. I'm saying to myself, 'How is a guy come straight out of prison and have these surreal experiences?'

"But it's just too much going on, so I exit the stage and join the crowd. I say let's see what it's like from that angle. I'm projecting myself away from myself and saying, 'Is this really going on?' Then people start coming up to me who I can't remember, and I tell Demetrius it's time. They want to go out to some clubs, but I tell them I'm going to bed. Had about all I can take."

The excitement of the concert started to wear off when Mecca took a short tour around his old neighborhood, starting with a trip downtown. Mecca's take on it was that it was more shock than familiarity.

"I dropped my aunt and uncle off in New Brunswick and kept trucking to East Orange where we lived with my grandparents. The houses seemed smaller and closer together. Maybe because I'm older, but all looking more rundown. All broken up. Kept going. Back on the highway, when I got to the Elizabeth exit, all my city instincts just kicked in. I can't even explain it. There was a buzz all the way until I saw the exit for my old neighborhood. I had total recall for a split second, and I said to myself, 'I'm home.'

"I felt that way until I got to the neighborhood. Right away that brightness, that vibrant feeling I had, was gone, 'cause what I saw was so heartbreaking. How the neighborhoods looked. How the people looked. The whole morale and the spirit of the place was terrible. What happened man? It was like a movie set for *Dawn of the Dead* or something. I would say to myself, 'Well this street used to be one of the really nice streets. And I used to love this street because it was really different from all these other streets.' Go down that street... gutted out again!

"I decide I'll move on to Irvington where we had such a nice house. Same thing. Who let this happen? When I was in prison, Cheryl told me – when they went to a funeral or something in Jersey – 'I'm telling you it's busted. You'll see when you go. It's gonna be heartbreaking. It looks like a third world country. It looks like ISIS has been through just ravishing it.'

"She was right. I texted her, 'Guess what, right now I'm on Eaton Place looking at the old house we grew up in and you wouldn't believe it.' And she texted, 'Oh yes I would.'

"And the house we were in before that, I went by there, too. I just took a glimpse. I couldn't give it my full attention; I was so hurt by how that whole street looked. That street was so special to me growing up. It nurtured an idea that there was a quality of life that was attainable. People left their garages open. Kids left their bikes and skateboards in the street. Nobody walked their dogs on a leash. It was called Park Place. When I was approaching that street, I sensed and I saw that it's not getting no better, and when I glanced down it, I turned my head away quickly. I know that stuff does happen, but when I saw it, it affected me.

"Next, final thing, I text Hakeem. He's out of OCC and he's married and working in New Jersey. He texts back, 'I'm heading to work. I'm doing home renovations. Here's the address.' Lo and behold, it's an address that I'm familiar with on the street where Keisha used to live. When I got there, I told him, 'See that house? I was there every day, all day for about four years. My ex–girlfriend used to live there.'

"Her family's gone a long time. Nobody's there now... Wow, one of the nicest streets ever, all busted up. I'm like, it's over with. My expectations just were gone. I say, 'Get it out of your head. Just take it for what it's worth. See it for what it is.' I just got this fake, Pollyanna idea that things were gonna be the way they were when I left them, and nothing is. Nothing is, Simone!

"When you take away neighborhoods, you take away a community mentality. People don't have that anymore and they move into that anti–social mentality. I felt that everywhere I went. It's better for me down here. I hated everything up there: the congestion, the potholes, the busyness, the pace of life, the way people are. Coming out of prison, it would be too much for me.

"I'm thinking if we had had enough time for that conversation, I would ask, 'Why do you want to be the last one standing on this dilapidated street? What is it that makes you feel you're going to be the last trooper to hold it down and represent your hood?' I don't want to be around that mentality. It about a lifestyle. Fast. Unconcerned. Busy. On my grind, doing what I got to do and blocking out everything else. Nobody cares about what's going on with anybody else."

It's a painful loss for Mecca, but I can't believe it's all bad. Troy is working on bridges. Demetrius works at Tiffany's. Not everyone is lost.

"Yeah, lot of the people do make that transition from drugs on the street to some kind of reputable business," Mecca answers reluctantly, not really convinced himself. "A little bodega. A club. A car dealership. Some guys tell me they got tired of going in and out of prison. So maybe they open a barber shop. That's attractive. All the hustles gonna come through the barber shop. All the boosters, people who got hot merchandise, they come in the barber shop to fence it. A barber shop keeps your ear to the street but it's legitimate. And 'cause it's cash, you can walk around with a wad of money and, in your mind, you can feel how you felt when you sold crack and had a wad of money from standing on the corner."

"Were there guys you knew who died?"

"Yeah. Several of my friends got shot and killed. I even saw places where shrines were for them. That was like a freeze frame over it. To drive down the street and somebody says, 'Slow down. That's where Chris Graham got killed. They took the shrine down 'bout two months ago.' That was very sobering. To know that had I not gone to prison, I probably could've been right there with them when that happened. Alleyways I ran through. Backyards I cut through. That was me. I was there."

"Have you ever been shot at?"

"Yeah, twice. One time a guy that was working for another guy I knew, he had some drugs. He didn't have the clientele I had, so he came to me and said, 'I need you to pause what you doing so I can get rid of what I have.' And I said, 'Man you gotta be crazy. It's open terrain. Do what you gotta do. I do what I do.' He didn't like my answer. He left and then came back and asked again. I said, 'You heard what I said the first time.' And this time he told me, 'Take your coat off.'

"All my drugs are usually in my inside coat pocket. But what he didn't know is that when he left, I stashed all my money 'cause already I'm thinking I don't know how he's gonna be when he comes back. We might get into a fight. He says, 'Take you coat off. I'm not playing,' and he pulls a gun out.

"I start to take my coat off, but then I threw it over his face and took off running. I'm laughing now, because it feels like that old cartoon trick, but at the time it's serious. He's running behind me shooting. I'm thinking I'm gonna die."

"When you heard the bullet go by, didn't it stop you in your tracks? Did the thought occur to you that maybe it's time to stop dealing?"

"No. Because dealing, the street life, it's a type of insanity. I went right back the next day. I never had a problem again with that particular guy, but I look back and I say it had to be some kind of insanity.

"There was a second time I got shot at. I was gambling, playing cards on the corner in Newark and some guys pulled up in an SUV, told everybody to lay down on the ground and a guy jumps out of the passenger side with his gun, scrapes up all the money. Then he kinda half–way pats everybody's pocket, but I had stuffed my money in the crotch of my pants. He jumps into the van and as they pull off you can hear gunfire. He sends off three or four shots and we keep our heads down until we hear the vehicle is gone and we know we are still alive.

"After that shooting, we just go and find another corner and start gambling again. It is a kind of insanity. But there is a difference between then and now. Back then, most of the time, the idea was not to actually shoot anybody. It was to know that the gun does work and will shoot, but to shoot around people. As time went on, younger guys missed that page in the book and actually started shooting people. I saw that things were heading that way before I got arrested."

I don't dwell on it, but in committing his crime Mecca himself did this kind of shooting to scare, and it got him a dead man and a life sentence. But we've already been there and back. I pivot the conversation and say that I heard from Scott-so that Mecca had make a New York City pilgrimage for him to Barclay Center and the Apollo Theater.

"When I knew I was making this trip up North, I asked Scott-so to tell me what to do. Picture–wise, video–wise. He told me, 'I want to see the Barclay Center. Get some of Brooklyn, as much as you can. Just give me the city.' I told Zelda that I was gonna do that for Scott-so, and she and her girlfriend said they would drive. That's like old times for me. I don't like to drive, so when I had a car, lot of the time I'd have someone else driving me. And here's this crazy thing about remembering again. We come out of the Holland Tunnel and it was like, okay, I know which way to go! I'm telling Zelda and Bridgett, 'Go left here. Now straight down there.'

"And they were like, 'You remember that? You don't remember who that guy is we just saw on the corner, but you remember how to get this way, that way?'

"I have Scott-so sittin' beside me in my mind while I'm doing this. I'm videoing with my telephone all the way across Canal Street into

Brooklyn by the Barclay Center and around Brooklyn. Back over the Brooklyn Bridge and we took, I think East River Drive. I wanted to give Scott-so the city vibe. And later I sent it to Tom, who shows it to Scott-so when they are out together on CV pass. Scott-so was overwhelmed. They called me and he said, 'That's my old neighborhood. I used to be on that street right there. Oh, man, that store's not there no more. Used to be Mr. So and So store.'

"Got off in Harlem. Harlem is something else. Never seen all these white people walking around Harlem on hundred twenty-fifth street, right across from the Grant Projects. When did that happen? You never see no white people here unless it was a police officer or somebody who owned one of the stores. That was the strangest thing to me. Rundown in New Jersey. White people in Harlem. I'm still processing. I've been processing since I got back.

"All around the trip was a multitude, a kaleidoscope of feelings and experiences and emotions. Not only did it make me feel like I been in prison a long time, but overall it made me feel like being down South is where I'm supposed to be. It let me know that that has run its course for me. Nothing about me wants any of that again. Nothing. The people. The places. The smells. Nothing. It's all like forty-second street with all the lights and the screens and all of that. It's not the same for me."

Prison is a form of death. Life as it was before incarceration has died. Each day happens... but it doesn't. The sameness puts time on hold. Even death is in a kind of purgatory. There is violence in prison and sometimes death, but day to day you are just wrangling with the over–arching business of doing time. If a parent or a child dies, depending on your custody level, you may be taken, in handcuffs, to a hospital or a funeral.

When Mecca emerges from prison, he steps into a world where he is suddenly hyper aware of life. At the same time, his freedom, his mobility, shorten his distance from death. For Mecca, who is carrying the death of another human being on his shoulders, this is serious business. What is this man's responsibility to those who are dying?

Darryl Hunt committed suicide in March 2016, three months after Mecca is released. Outside, most people never even graze up against the thought of suicide, but for men in prison there is a much narrower chasm between going on and giving up. But when a man has succeeded in beating the system, proving his innocence and winning his freedom, giving that up is an inconceivable choice. Darryl Hunt was a symbol, a man who fought and won and was known for his work advocating for the falsely convicted. He was an in–demand speaker, but behind the public persona there were troubling issues that came from his own mental health status, his life circumstances, and the pressures he felt from the world around him.

Hunt, 51, was missing for nine days before he was found dead in a truck at 12:19 a.m. March 13 in the parking lot of the College Plaza shopping center off University Parkway, across the street from Joel Coliseum. Winston–Salem police said it appeared Hunt had died from a self–inflicted gunshot.

> *According to the autopsy report, Hunt was found with a .38–caliber revolver on his legs. The truck's doors were locked and the ignition was still on, though the engine was not running, the report said.*
>
> *Winston–Salem Journal*
>
> *After 19 years in prison, Hunt was exonerated in February 2004 after DNA evidence led police to Willard Brown, who confessed to the killing. After he was exonerated, Hunt was pardoned by then–Gov. Mike Easley. He was awarded a settlement of more than $1.6 million in 2007 and founded the Darryl Hunt Project for Freedom and Justice, an advocacy group for the wrongfully convicted.*
>
> *But Hunt was also haunted by his experiences, said those who knew him. He would use ATMs daily, not so much to get money but so he could create a time–stamped receipt and an image recording his location.*

Mecca was upset but also philosophical as we looked at the clippings and he tried to puzzle it out.

"I met Darryl at Salisbury. He coached the basketball team and I was the scorekeeper. Bam. Pushed the button to start the game. Bam. Pushed the button to stop it. He's quiet, but he had a wild crazy basketball team. The Innocence Project hadn't taken up his case yet. He was just another guy who says he's innocent. Lots of guys saying that.

"When the game is over this day, Darryl was kind of leaning around, talking to everybody. I'm ready to go and kind of in a hurry, but he comes up to me and says, 'My guys crazy, ain't they?' That's a sign he wants to talk. Which he doesn't do a lot. I know about him, that he had a bad image, so I stop and chat with him for a little while.

"Salisbury has elevators. It's kind of rare, but every now and then you may end up with just one other person on the elevator. One on one in the elevator with him, sometimes he might say something about my working out like, 'What you workin' on tomorrow?' I would always let him initiate the conversation because you never know where he is at. And from there we started to talk when we were working out. Eventually he'd ask me about some particular exercise that I was doing – did it work? – and we got to know each other.

"He was kind of a depressed character, an alcoholic. He showed me pictures of himself before he got arrested, like that was who he really was, and he seemed to always feel out of place and insecure. I'm familiar with that because I saw that in my father growing up. And alcohol made him feel, you know, more satisfied. And I saw Darryl to be the same way.

"After he was exonerated, I took a re–entry class – this is when I am not even knowing a MAPP exists. I'm natural life. But I get in the class. I found out that Darryl Hunt was going to speak to the graduating class. I was pretty excited. His case was on the news and my mom had met him.

"When he came in the door, I was like, 'How is it for you, man?' He shook his head, and we talked briefly. He confided all of the things that I know now contributed to the end, to him committing suicide. All the money didn't help. It hurt. He was being pulled in every direction, and I could see the weariness of all that and that whatever he thought freedom was going to mean wasn't there. It was over–rated.

"He told me, 'I've been to Haj and I've been to Egypt. I been to California and all over the country.' But there was no sense of joy. It was just answering my questions. I thought maybe his personality is just like that, but when he got up to speak, I figured it was something about his life. He was so disappointed. The money, the actual experience of being free, that just didn't do it.

"His speech talked a little bit to the problems of getting out, spoke about education, different things he had done while he was in prison. But he said these things to encourage the men, because he thought it was appropriate. It was sad. I saw a guy that had been more in his element in prison than he was as a free person.

"Even back then I understood these things implicitly, and they make so much sense to me now, because as much as we hate prison, it's relative simplicity in there. Going out on CV passes required a part of my brain that had been unused, and it was stressful! Street clothes? I felt like I wasn't supposed to have on anything but what I was wearing for twenty years. I felt awkward and like everybody's staring at me thinking I look ridiculous. If I could have worn the prison clothes on that first pass? I would have! Because I was so in my head with everything.

"Honestly, I don't feel anymore like I don't fit in the outside world, but I do feel like the outside world doesn't fit with me! And I say to myself, 'Man, that place really played with your head.' Darryl got divorced and he had money problems from that and then cancer. That's not how you think of freedom. So when he died the way he did, I kind of understood how that happened. I felt real sad."

Mecca's connection to Darryl Hunt came from the past, but other men from prison and their families found their way into Mecca's post–incarceration world. One of the most intimate experiences starts with Mark, who was in prison with Mecca in Nash in 1993 and was moved to OCC after Mecca's release. A strange thread that will link Mecca to Niki, Mark's sister, starts unobtrusively at Whole Foods in Durham.

Mecca begins the story by saying excitedly, "I bumped into Niki at Whole Foods in Durham, and she was like, 'Oh my God. You are finally out.'" They recognize each other because Niki and her mom used to visit at Nash at the same time as Cheryl and Bessie. "Niki had been hearing I had a MAPP through both Mark and her parents, who kept in touch with my mother. We talked, and I told her I was personal training and she said, 'Great. I was just talking to my girlfriend about personal training. Gimme your contact information.'

"So, fast forward, I started training her, and one day her husband, Arthur, dropped her off to a training session, so I finally met him. Arthur was working for the City of Durham, but he had had a kidney transplant and wanted to earn some money while waiting for his disability to kick in, so I told him about Artistry in Plants – how I was working there part time – and he started landscaping with me.

"Niki asked me to keep eye on Arthur, saying, 'Arthur's a workaholic. Make sure he drinks his water, stays hydrated. He starts to look a little woozy, have him sit down, not do anything, because he just had a kidney transplant. He wants to work. That's his joy. He'll work his self literally to the bone.'

"She was right about his work ethic. As they say, it's off the chain. He would be mad at hisself because he didn't have the energy to do some of the things he used to do. At work, I ask what else he does, and he says, 'Man, I'm kinda like a jack of all trades. I could chainsaw trees. I clean floors at night in different restaurants. I work under the table. Waitin' for the disability to come.'

"Eventually him and our boss, Wendy, had some kind of conflict. I tried to mediate, but it didn't work, so Arthur left. About a week later, Niki called and told me he'd been getting depressed and his health had declined since he quit the job. 'We going back and forth to the doctor. He says he feels like something going on in his throat. He's having an ear problem.' Now we know that was the cancer starting up, and they gave him more medication, which did not help his mood.

"I talk to him on the phone and I can barely hear his voice. I found out that whatever it was was growing in his throat. He asks, 'What you doing today? Maybe just come pick me up? Get me out the house. Ride me around.' So we do that."

When he is talking about driving Arthur around, he and I are both also thinking about Darrell Davis, who was doing flips with his girlfriend's kids and broke his neck just a year or so after his release from OCC. It's a common nightmare: just when you finally get out, something horrible happens to steal your freedom. To Mecca's and my amazement Darrell recovered enough to use a wheelchair, and Mecca started to take him out and help him with physical therapy. When Darrell got a van with special equipment, Mecca coached him how to drive. Mecca is good at making time for himself and for others.

Mecca says, "I was taking Arthur around and then he got too sick for that even. And then he was in Duke Hospital and I went to see him and sat with him. And I'm remembering Darrell and his accident and saying to myself, 'Oh, here we go again. I was up here with Darrell. Now I'm back up here checking on my friend Arthur.'

"It's sad. But at the same time, Simone, for me personally it was... a necessary evil, a reminder how fickle life can be. How brief it is. How delicate it is. How much a person should invest in what it means to live your life each day. And that takes effort. You get up everyday. Go do your routine. Go to work. Come home. Cook. Clean. Go to bed. You do that so much you could do it by rote. But to really be present while you are doing things; that's different. I say this thinking of Darrell or Arthur right now, but there are a million of them, and all are reminders to just experience myself breathing, inhaling and exhaling.

"So every time I would go to see Arthur, much as I hated to see him like that, it was therapeutic to see it. Afterwards, Scott-so might call and I would tell him, 'You been sittin' in a stinking place eating processed food for twenty-five years, and you say, I gonna do this or that tomorrow. But who's to say, whether you were in prison or not, that something is or is not gonna happen. You gotta be mindful of that. Even sitting there in prison.'

"Every time I would see Arthur, it would put my reminder in a frame, and I would hang it on the wall in my mind to remind me, 'Hey man. Live your life today, 'cause you don't know what you might have to deal with for yourself tomorrow.' Don't do that, and you might as well still be in prison. Seeing Arthur kept me honest and it kept me able to see past my own suffering and to season my heart. The work I do with RSN, primarily mentoring kids that are dealing with opioids – that kind of stuff keeps me humble and honest. To see people in real time, dealing with their own demons."

We pause there. Mecca is famous for his bravura, his charm and his calm. I feel privileged but also a bit scared when he lets me see inside his head. Before Mecca got out, I was sitting with Bessie and she looked at me and predicted, "He's gonna have PTSD. He might not know it, but this is going to have damaged him." Listening to Mecca now, I hear that Bessie is correct; but no one should underestimate Mecca's ability to look himself in the eye and put that trauma to use.

He interrupts my reverie to get on with the story. After Arthur went home for hospice care, Mecca visited a few times but sensed that the family needed to be alone. Then, one day, Niki sent a text. Mecca places his phone on the table in front of me.

He has to go at this point... his kidneys have completely shut down and he's aspirating. So they will make him comfortable and we will allow God to handle the rest. I need this transition to be as smooth as possible in the morning. I was wondering if you could come and lift Arthur up and take him downstairs and put him in my car. My dad can't do it and he [Arthur] said your name. I said you want me to ask Mec? He said, 'Yes' and gave me a thumbs up. Let me know if you can do it. Please let me know. I will have him up and ready at 9am and all I would need you to do is take him from upstairs to my car.

Mecca tells me his grandmother used to tell him, "Gimme my flowers while I'm alive," and goes on to say, "That resonated with me. I never been really motivated to see a person post their inhaling and exhaling. I would rather carry Arthur in his life, in his living days, than to carry him as a deceased person, as a pallbearer or something.

"When I knocked on their door, Niki's dad was standing behind Arthur in the wheelchair and Arthur was kind of in and out of it. You couldn't be sure he knew what was going on. But I said, 'What's up, Art? What's goin' on? You ready?' And somehow, he would make gestures to say yes. So I said, 'If I do this wrong, somehow let me know. I don't care how – pinch me, groan, grunt. Do something.' And I picked him up and carried him to the car. Niki was in the driver's seat and his daughter was in the back seat, and when I put him in the back seat, he put his hand on his daughter's lap. And then I closed the door and said, 'Okay, Buddy.'

"I asked if I should follow them to Hospice and Nikki said yes. When we got there, Niki went inside to get a wheelchair. I got Arthur out of the back seat and I'm holding him, waiting on the wheelchair. His daughter was crying and just going in, coming out, moving around. I said to her, 'Do me a favor. Take a picture. Take this picture.' And Arthur, he kind of like faced the phone! That's the picture I sent you."

I was out of town when Mecca sent me the photo. Arthur is wearing a gray t–shirt and his thin arms are wrapped around Mecca, who has his signature baseball cap turned backwards, so you can see the clear solemnity of his eyes. It's there in both of them, a sense of honor and caring and love.

"I haven't been to his grave," Mecca answers when I ask. "I don't know if I will. When I carried Arthur to Hospice, I knew in my mind, 'I may never see you again. This is it for me.' I didn't go to the funeral, but I went to the wake, where they have the casket open. I stayed as long as I could. I was in a daze. I'm still in a daze about it."

I ask Mecca if he thinks that these losses have affected his sense of his crime, if all this was maybe sent to help him feel the enormity of death and loss.

He said, "I do and I don't."

It's a question we left hanging.

One big issue around doing time is how to manage relationships with the world outside. Your only control is your ability to make phone calls and write letters. On the phone, someone on the other side has to accept the call and your time is rationed to fifteen minutes. With letters you cast your words out, hope they reach the person you want to communicate with, and pray that person is willing to write back.

I've talked to a lot of people – prisoners, friends and families – who either did or did not stay in touch, and the reasons on both sides were rarely superficial. They dig deeply into feelings of loyalty, anger, fear, guilt, and profound sadness. Ava DuVernay's film *Middle of Nowhere* does a great job of showing how conflicted people on the outside can feel and how powerless a man on the inside can feel and how out of touch he can become.

When I asked a group of lifers in the workshop at OCC if they could talk about something they resent, some chip on the shoulder that doesn't go away, one man said, "It's a friend of mine. I have been in here for twenty years and I have not heard from him once. What makes that so hard is that I hear from my mom that this same friend always asks after me. 'How's he doing? Tell him I'll be in touch. Here's my number.' But when I call the number, he doesn't answer. I put him on my visitor list, but he doesn't come. Man, it's only a twenty–minute drive. That hurts. Keeps hurting. If he never saw my mom or never said anything, that would be different, but he's saying these things and then he doesn't come through."

There may be reasons for the silence. The years stack up and thinking about a visit or even writing a letter becomes too confusing. Where to start? It's easier to just go on being apart. And some people on the outside may simply be afraid of making contact. One day another man in the workshop asked me to call his brother, because he wanted to be sure the brother knew he was on the visitor list. This man was in a prison not too far from home, but his brother had never visited. I talked to the brother, a minister, a man with a clear moral compass who offers strength and solace to others, and he said, "I never told him this, but I did drive up there. I parked my car and I could see the gate. I looked at the fence and I couldn't get out of the car. I just didn't want to see him in prison."

Mecca had a strong support network. His family was fiercely loyal, and a lot of friends stayed in touch. But one voice was missing, that of Willie Elmore, Mecca's dad. His drinking and his anger when he was drunk were the catalyst of the explosion that tore the family apart, and he is deeply implicated in the events that sent Bessie, Cheryl, and William down the economic tunnel out of the middle class comfort of Irvington and back into tight financial straits. There is plenty of blame on the table there.

And then there is just plain confusion. Mecca's very direct about his disappointment with his father, and he knows that he's been on a long search for a replacement for that missing steward. It began with his grandfather, included the older guys on the street, swept up prison mentors like James Leone and his sponsor at OCC, Mr. Bill. He's also direct about his awareness that substitution is not the same as the real thing. As long as Willie Elmore is still alive, he is still Mecca's father and now he's living near Kansas City in Missouri.

August 2017, a year and a half after his release, is when Mecca decides to drive to Kansas City to see Willie, who is remarried and not in good health. We sit together on my porch not long after his return from the visit that had been looming since day one of his release.

"I been talking to dad since I got out," Mecca tells me, "and the whole time he has been asking what's my limitation with traveling. Early on I had the curfew. I told him I can't leave the house really. He's consistent, saying he really wants to see me. And I want to see him, too, but I am in that space where I'm not breaking my neck to see anybody. I'm moving at my own pace. Especially somebody I haven't seen in thirty years. Man, no, I'm not rushing into that."

Mecca explains to his dad that he's doing landscaping and working part time mentoring kids and says, "I'm not one of these people that have these jobs I don't like. I like my work. I like going to them."

To counter that, Willie Elmore started talking about his health, maybe he is face to face with his own mortality, and said, "I really would like to see you. I miss you."

"His health was getting a little worse," Mecca says looking down at his hands as if they hold the answer. "He has this breathing problem and he was coughing more. I could hear that on the phone. He has to be on breathing treatment 'cause of agent orange from Vietnam and he's got colon cancer and he had two strokes. All this had happened before I got out, but those conditions are getting progressively worse. He's getting older. He's seventy-one or seventy-two."

I remind Mecca that Bessie and I are that same age, but he has trouble putting that information together with the man wheezing on his phone. I know Bessie wants nothing to do with Willie Elmore, but she has also said, "It's William's father. I'm not going to get in the way of that."

Mecca looks over at his always–in–mint–condition Honda minivan. "I got this ultimate traveling vehicle and I was ready to put it on the road. I said to my sister, 'Look, here's the deal. Zelda and I are going to Kansas City to see dad.' I didn't say it to her because I thought she would come. I'd made my mind up that I was going, and I was just putting it out to her. And the dates that I picked to go were actually two days after she was coming back from New Jersey, so I didn't expect her to want to go. But she asked how we are going, and I said we were driving; the flights were way too high. I tell Cheryl, we not rushing going and we not rushing coming back. And she surprises me and says, 'Okay. I'm going too. Let me see if David wants to go. But with or without him, I'm going.' David said he would go, so now we got four of us."

I was surprised Cheryl had wanted to see Willie Elmore, but this family is all about surprises.

Four is not too many. Mecca is not a great one for distance driving, so having extra drivers is a good idea. He can sit in the back seat and coast out to Missouri and settle his mind.

"My dad didn't believe it when we rang the doorbell! I was telling him on the phone along the way, five hundred miles away, four hundred, two. Even with me calling, I guess he thought we would have some kind of reason not to come. I might say, 'Oh, we were gonna come today, but this happened and that happened.' When we rang the doorbell, he just burst out in tears. He was very overjoyed. He couldn't believe it."

"Did he understand that if you didn't come, he had created reasons for you not to come?"

"He said so in just so many words. He said that I had enough reasons to not come. I told him it was solely because I care enough about him that I wanted to visit. But that's easy for him to doubt, to be thinking, 'What the hell you want to come see me for?'"

"When I saw him, it was like going back in time. Yeah, he looks older. His movements are different because of his stroke. Personality wise, he's the same. He's active. I don't know how much of that was because we were there. His wife, Sheila, was saying, 'Oh, it's so good for him to have y'all here.' Like it brought some life back to him. My dad, he's always been like this, up and down. He can get really depressed and get sorrowful and drink. Or he can be real social.

"He still drinks. He's got one of those quintessential old school attitudes: Look, man, you gotta die from something and I ain't waitin' around for it. I'm gonna just live my life and drink and whatever. He don't smoke but his attitude is: I'm gonna live my life."

I want to know what they did to fill the time. I don't see Willie or Mecca diving right into the meat of the visit but more sliding in sideways with some generous meals and light conversation. Mecca paints me a picture.

"Everybody was all over his really nice, big house. Sheila, his wife, wasn't there a lot. She's active too, goes to kickboxing classes and bowls. I liked her. I liked her for him, because she seemed like she took good care of him.

"He has a pool table; we shot a lot of pool. He became Dad and I became Son. And it would go like this:

'Dad, in everybody else's estimation, I'm pretty good at pool. You taught me.'

'Yeah, I did.'

'Hey, dad.'

'Hey, son.'

'Hey, dad.'

'Hey son.'

"And then there were times it got a little harder:

'Why don't you stay?'

'I gotta go to work.'

'Man, just stay. I'll take care of you. You ain't gotta work.'

'No, man, I'm building my life. I can't do that, man.'

'I really wish you would stay.'

"It's a great thing to say, but I wouldn't have stayed if I could. Good part is – I don't know what he told people, but he was very happy to show us off. He took us to the bowling alley. I think for my dad – he's such a rolling stone experience – I think that when he tells people that he has a son and a daughter, people probably like, 'Where they at then?'

"Hey, look at this." Mecca's cell starts vibrating and dancing on the table. "How can that be? That's him right there calling.

"What's up dad?"

"Good morning. How are you?"

"How you doing, man?"

"I'm doing pretty good. I miss you."

"I know. You ready for us to come back?"

"Yes, sir. And stay a while. As long as you want to."

"Hey, look, you ain't ready for that, dad. You ain't ready."

"You know I am too. I need somebody to help me around the house sometimes."

Mecca laughs and points to the screen and winks at me.

"Okay, you like an old Ford truck, you finding a way to keep on trucking."

"Yeah, I can take a licking. I done pretty good though. You know what? I went fishin'."

"What'd ja catch?"

"I caught a crappy, about a pound and a half. Then got home and Sheila kept calling me the yard man. Boy it was hot out there, and I couldn't stay very long."

"Hey look, I'm in a meetin' right now. I'm gonna call you back soon as I'm done."

"All right. Love you."

"Wow. That's a trip. He always calls me same amount of time, short like that. Maybe twice a week.

"He's always talking about another trip, but I'm not doing that right now. Tomorrow is not really promised to anybody, but I don't feel like I need to hurry up and go out there again because I feel dad's going to die. That wasn't my motivation in the first place. I also know that even if he was a person in top shape – he can die. I can die."

Mecca falls silent for a bit. We listen to the birds, but when our talks start to probe more deeply, he likes to use the waiting time to just stare out at the world, like he is seeing it for he first time. I remember Scott-so and Frank describing their first sightings of Mecca by saying that he has this way of inhabiting even difficult thinking with a sense of wonder. It's very attractive.

"We had this one car ride. He was driving me around, trying to show me everything, and he just broke down and said, 'Man, I'm so sorry I wasn't there for you. I ask myself what I did wrong.' He went into that mode I seen him in before, after he would be drunk. Acting crazy at home. He would go into that mindset. Crying. Talking about himself in that way.

"I just sat there. I didn't feel like I needed to bail him out. I said, 'Yeah. I spent a long time wondering why you ain't come to see me or wrote me or anything.' And he was crying hard, but it was inaudible. I let him keep crying. I think it was good for him to get that out. Yeah. I left him to himself."

"When he came out of that, he called one of his friends and said, 'Remember I been telling you about that I had a son? Man, he's so in shape. You gotta see him. Man, he's beautiful.' He just kept calling me beautiful. And he looked at me and he said, 'Man you look so good. You look so strong.'

"I don't know. Maybe he thought... lotta people, it's hard for them to believe I did twenty-five years. Every time somebody says how good I look, I wonder what did they think should I be looking like?"

Mecca is a good–looking man, and he's also very deliberate about his training. He eats well and he never smoked, drank, or did drugs. He also looks like his great grandfather, Raspberry Johnson, who still looked way younger than eighty when Mecca was a kid visiting him in Alabama. It's like his temperament – some of it's a given and some of it is cultivated and cared for.

"There is a stereotype of people in prison working out, and most of the people in prison look pretty good for their age," I offer. "At the same time, people expect someone who is getting out of prison to look all beat up, unhealthy."

Mecca chews that over for a minute. "That's a paradox, people outside thinking those opposite things about people in prison." He takes another long pause and returns his thoughts to Willie Elmore. "Wow, it's funny my dad called. I do feel some sadness and some empathy for him. Even though he's married, he's lonely. I don't know *what* it is, but he's lonely for something. He's social, has friends, meets people. He's outspoken. He knows how to meet and mingle, but he's always been a lonely figure.

"Talking to my dad... it's a good feeling for me. I enjoy bringing people some kind of joy. As much as I can. Even him. There's a lot of sad people in the world, and that makes me sad. When I say that around my mother, she starts to get upset, and I say, 'Ma, it's not the kind of sadness where I just want to ball up in the bed and don't want to come out. I can function with that sadness. It doesn't make my days less sunny, but I'm aware of it.

"I'm not like Wendy, the lady I work for on landscaping, who hires all these guys coming out of prison. I don't feel like I need to fix that sadness. But when I am in the natural position to organically impart joy or some happiness to people... Man, I love doing that. I know my limitations. I know I can't change a person's life. Like you say about helping people getting ready to get out of prison – they have to help themselves. You can be on the sidelines and give them a little nudge now and then, but they gotta help themselves. That's how it is with my father. I want him to feel good, but I can't be making my life about that.

"Makes me think about my uncle Doug. He's someone could easily be real miserable. Looking at his life, lotta people think it's terrible. He works for minimum wage. On the weekends he buys him some beer and he's happy. He loves to watch sports and that's what he does weekend after weekend. Lives in these small places. Doesn't cost much, so that's how he does it.

"Doug's my mother's brother, so she and all of his sisters are working and taking care of their business. They always scratch their heads over him... 'I don't know what happened to Doug.' They don't see that that's all he wants. Whenever it comes around to me, I say, 'Doug has figured out how to be comfortable with that.' There are guys like that in prison. It's a personality thing.

"Some people can thrive. They don't need much. Me, I look at those people and say, 'That's okay.' Other people look at them and say, 'I can't believe that's all you want. Don't you want more?' Those people, they can get started and it don't never stop. There's always somebody else to say to you: You can be more. You should want more. If Doug is truly content living that way, then what are we talking about?"

This acceptance, along with having a way to get outside of bitterness, is a big part of what makes Mecca strong, not in body but in his mind. I had been wondering what would happen with his father – would it be about anger or would Mecca be looking for something there he couldn't get. It's a huge burden on both sides for people coming out of prison, the burden of owing and emotional debt. I ask Mecca if he had needed his father to own up to his failings. "Or, not owning up," I say, "that's some of your father's problem. It sounds like having contact with you and having you not have your life be ruined must be a huge relief to him."

"I'm sure it is. That's my mother's argument," Mecca says. His loyalty to Bessie is never to be questioned. "My sister said the same thing. 'Don't bail him out. You going all the way to see him! You should make him come here to see you.'

"I'm not about that. People gotta live with themselves. I'm not about trying to make them do that any more or less than they need to. He can never take back the time that he drank and how our family was. He has to live with that and with the idea that maybe he could have done something to keep me away from the streets, from that life, but he didn't. He's gonna die with that doubt.

"And I think life is too short to play that game, 'cause we could do it all day long with ourself and with other people. I said that to my sister and to Zelda, my desire to go see my dad was strictly my desire. It was for me. If we got all the way there and he opened the door or didn't open the door and we had to U–turn, I wouldn't have regretted it. I made up my mind about that before and said to myself, 'I don't know what I'm walking into. I don't know how this is gonna go, but I'm going. I'm open to however it goes. If it goes terribly wrong, I can live with that.

"Remember I told you the gambler's motto, don't bet any money you can't afford to lose? I take pride in that with my emotions and everything else. Don't invest nothing you can't afford to give. People might not give that back to you. I don't care who they are. You might not get it back.

"And when we were in the car and he was crying, I said to him, 'Look man, so you hear it from me. I don't know if you heard it from the family, if a little bird told you in a dream about it, but I want you to hear it from me. I don't hold anything against you, man. I forgive you for everything. I want you to know.'

"He said, 'Thank you, I needed to hear it.'

Mecca wraps up our session by looking straight at me and saying, "I had a lifetime to think about what forgiveness is. I got it. I got a second chance! How dare I walk around not wanting to grant that, or give that, or extend that to anybody else? Who the heck am I to live like that and decide? It doesn't just hurt you if I don't forgive you. It hurts me. I'm carrying that around. I don't want to live like that."

Chapter 17: This is a Movement!

For Mecca the common hurdles to post–incarceration employment don't pose a big problem. He wants a loose schedule and the freedom to choose what he does from day to day. He had been attending Straight Talk meetings with Bessie and Cheryl since he first got his levels and could go there on passes. So he already has some experience in the world of support networks for "justice involved" people and their families. He had offered to keep working at Neese's, but he was free to look for options more aligned with his desire to give back to the prison community. To understand how this works out, I'm going to step back to 2016 and look at the progression of jobs Mecca finds as he establishes his footing as a post–prison activist.

A few months after his release, Mecca accepts a job with RSN – Reintegration Support Network for Community Youth – a nonprofit founded by Tom McQuiston, an OCC community sponsor. Tom has had this offer in his back pocket for some time. He founded RSN in response to his own son's struggles with addiction and eventual suicide. At the time of Mecca's release, RSN is beginning to pull in grants that include funds to hire mentors. RSN does not do direct treatment. They meet with kids and their families and help route them to the services they need. Taking a job as a mentor for RSN is emotionally hot territory for Mecca, but it offers a flexible schedule doing meaningful work.

While some people need structure to manage their lives after prison, Mecca needs it loose. Not know exactly when you are going to be called to jump in? That's suits his style. He also mixes in some work for Artistry in Plants, the landscape business run by Wendy Gale that Mecca's already mentioned in other contexts. She hires a lot of people with a prison record, offering them a second chance at life and maybe a first chance to connect to nature.

Mecca loves the RSN job for the chance to catch kids heading in the wrong direction, but he may have underestimated the emotional draw–down of the work. He's going to have to deal with young people well on their way down the path he took if he's going to help them avoid it. Soon after he took that job, I asked Mecca to talk about working with his first client, C.J. "Does it give you just a little bit of a window into what it was like for Cheryl to watch you jump off into life on the street?"

He shakes his head and takes his cap off. That means we are serious. C.J., it seems, is not a mirror; he's a magnifying glass.

"Oh, man. Yes. There's a mother, but C.J. lives with the grandmother, so that's a problem. And he's up and down. More down than up. He takes two steps forward and five steps backward. He's on medication for real mental issues. So C.J. is like me but a totally different mindset. I want to say to somebody like C.J., 'Hey snap out of it. Knock it off. Just do what you need to do. What's the matter with you?' And maybe he would confide in me, and I would listen and say, 'Look man, you just got to get over that, keep moving, I'm serious.'"

I sense no small ripple of irony here. A friend told Mecca not to go out the night of the shooting, not to get sucked into it. And a quintessential picture in my mind, one that's at the heart of this book, is Bessie looking at Mecca as he climbs into her car, one hour early from the SATs. His ticket out for her. A ticket into nothing for him.

Mecca brings me back to his wrangle with C.J., and, as usual, he gives it a slightly different spin.

"I see now that would have be so unfair to say, because if he and I are friends or peers, for him to have confided that in me would have said he valued my opinion. He trusted me and I return with something that just made him feel stupider and more insecure. I'm gonna have do way, way more listening. It's a struggle for me, knowin' what I know about prison and seeing him heading that way.

"I'm learning that everybody's not like that, able to just change something. Experience in life has helped me to appreciate that it's really not like that. People need things, sometimes external things, professional help, to be persuaded to look at things differently. Might even need medication. Living in prison, in a place where I'm around a lot of guys who have mental health issues, real mental health issues. Some of them, I'm suspicious of the legitimacy; some I'm not. So I'm confused by both extremes. I meet C.J. and I'm having to examine myself.

"I had some conversations with the psychologists when I was in prison, trying to understand how that works. 'cause where I come from, I am very skeptical. I wanted to understand how they see my mind. What are they trying to do? And they all consistently said, 'Oh, you're fine.' What does that mean that I'm fine? Same thing, everyone I talked to, 'You have a sense of self and sense of accountability or responsibility for who you are in relation to everybody else. You will be able to negotiate traffic, your own trafficking in your head and other people's trafficking. You will be all right when you get released.'

"When I finally went to the psych, the person who has the real say so whether you get a MAPP, whether you are ready, he said the same thing, 'That's what it's all about. It's not about getting perfection. Everybody has problems, including me. It's how you negotiate them in relation to your existence.'

"I'm seeing with C.J. and with the other clients at RSN, that they don't have that ability to make choices. Way he sees it, everybody else has the problem. Makes it real hard to help him. Hard to see him going in another direction. Which is bad for C.J., because, prison or no prison, things are not going to work out for him if he has to stay this way, holding it out on other people. They can send him to prison or rehab and either way, nothing is happening. The school system is the same. School system doesn't see C.J. as somebody who doesn't know they have a problem. The prison system doesn't see C.J. as somebody who doesn't know he has a problem. He's just somebody who *is* a problem for them."

A couple of days later Mecca calls and says he's coming over "to do some oral history." C.J. is in jail and Mecca is upset for him and upset himself from having had to go inside the jail. When we sit down together, he says, "C.J. is in jail for fighting. Not sure why. Last time, they sent him to UNC hospital, and I visited him there, but now he's in jail in Hillsborough and I gotta go up there again. This is not something I am ready to do, go back into the system like that.

"And thing is, I saw him Monday, him and his mother at their home. And I told him, as I was leaving, 'C.J., I promised you that I was always going to be straight up and authentic with you.' He's very intelligent so I respect that when I talk to him. 'If we never talk again, I have to tell you this. There is a system in place to direct you to prison. If you keep screwing up in school or in society, they will herd you quick, fast and in a hurry to a confining institution. And in prison, they're not equipped to deal with people who have real issues. I've been in prison with a multitude of guys that have some real issues that they need real help for, and they kept getting in trouble, specifically for violent acts. Prison doesn't provide help with problems, it exacerbates them. You don't know what that means? It stresses it out and makes your condition worse, because inside, the answer is to restrain you and isolate you away from the population. Think about what that is, what that means. If I can't do anything else, I want you to be aware of this.'

"Lo and behold, on Wednesday he's in jail!"

When Mecca rides up to the jail in Hillsborough with C.J.'s grandmother and girlfriend, it turns out that the mother – whether she knew it or not – has used up all of C.J.'s visiting time. The officers are blunt with the grandmother, no breaks in the rules for anyone. Mecca is disturbed by this; it makes him think again of what Bessie and Cheryl had to go through year after year.

He says he tried to warn the grandmother to brace herself for the foolishness and explained, "You want to think they are professional people. They run a jail which is serious business so they should be serious about their business. That's not the case. They seen a million people like you, particularly women, women with bleeding hearts there to see boyfriends, fathers, sons, brother–in–laws, cousins. They watch these women come in like an assembly line and say, 'I'm here to see him. Please, let me see him. Oh please, oh please.' They don't care about that. Your problem, not theirs. I hear these officers giving their spiel, pretending like they care, pretending they're really listening, when really, they just want to go smoke a cigarette and joke about you."

With C.J. in jail, RSN is not just mentoring youth, it's mentoring parents and grandparents and siblings and girlfriends. They are all part of the picture. I ask Mecca how RSN sets boundaries.

"Tom meets with the family and he explains the boundaries. And whenever I meet with a family, I'm letting them know there is no way I'm gonna mentor this person that you are related to without you knowing exactly how that goes. I try to keep it open as I can to everyone involved.

"Then you have the real people. Now, with C.J., the mother is real young, more like a big sister Her words: 'He doesn't see me as his mother. We kinda grew up together.' So between son and mother, a boundary is not there, that place that stands between a son and a mother creating respect. Also, because the grandmother is the father's mother and the father is not in the son's life, there's some sticky stuff between them two. And the mother and the grandmother don't see eye to eye a lot. And C.J. is smart enough to play a game between them both.

"I've read about all of this stuff over the years in prison. Now I'm actually seeing it, the machine at work. It's like somebody's popped the hood and I'm actually seeing the working parts. School to prison pipeline. I'm watching it happen real time. That kind of takes my breath away. I see his life going through the wringer, like watching a train wreck in slow motion. Yeah. It's like, man, this is really happening."

Mecca also began working part time as an employment training facilitator with StepUp Durham. StepUp offers free employment readiness training, personalized job coaching, employer referrals, and supportive services. The organization focuses a lot of its work on people with barriers like gaps in their work history or a criminal background. Mecca works both in the community and in workshops offered inside the prisons. I laugh right out loud when Mecca runs down his experiences. He's amused and surprised to be giving advice, since his own job solution has been to juggle a mix of part–time jobs rather than get "stuck" in an office. But Mecca is good at the training and his own experience gives him credibility. He is good at seeing the issues beneath the surface. Time management is one of his favorite pitfalls to talk about. In prison, he explains, they do this for you. Getting out of prison you are going to have to do time management real time.

"In prison they tell you everything. I tried to have my own schedule as much as I could arrange it, getting up real early, going to bed early, but mostly everything gets set for you. Now I'm in an opposite situation. The people that we have meetings with, they're calendared in to meet with us. We got a meeting at such and such today. There's no chow call, but I'm not the only person involved so I gotta work it out.

"But, for me, it works because I can fit in these things how I want to. Call from School For Conversion about a meeting, going to talk to some church about re–entry. Great. I'm ready. Same happening with StepUp. They want me to teach some re–entry modules? I can work that out. And then, days when I am open, get outside and do landscaping for Artistry in Plants. Reminds me of the street – lot of things going on, but I'm deciding what I do when."

The job for the School For Conversion is part–time. They run a number of programs including Project Turn, which brought Duke students to OCC to take a philosophy class with people in the prison. Another program, the Church Without Walls, brings congregations together with currently and formerly incarcerated men and women. That's the program where Mecca works. He speaks to students or church groups who want to get involved in reentry and helps them see things from the incarcerated person's point of view.

Another important perk of the job is that the School selects Mecca to represent them at the 2016 national conference of the FICPFM, the Formerly Incarcerated and Convicted People and Families Movement, in Oakland, California. That meeting plants the seed for what is going to become Mecca's number one commitment: pushing forward for those he left behind in prison.

Mecca is allowed to take another person with him and invites me, but I can't make the trip, so he offers the slot to Zelda. She has moved to North Carolina and has been helping Bessie with Straight Talk, so she will take a high value perspective to the conference. Two flavors in one, a friend to see you through your first plane trip since Texas, and a partner who looks at incarceration and re–entry from the outside in.

Mecca explains the first hurdle without false modesty or manly pride and provides a good look at the Rip Van Winkle aspect of spending years in a prison cell.

"I'm going to tell you something up front. Having Zelda there, somebody familiar to really explain to me everything that's going on, that was very, very necessary. I can't imagine if I was on my own going all the way to Oakland. How I would manage that? It was too much critical thinking at one time. Terminals. All these different signs all over the place and, overall, the impatience of people that are supposed to be in a position to be of service to you as a consumer or customer.

"Right from the start, you are supposed to know everything. You have your tickets on your phone, so they need to see that the right way. Then the scanner thing. 'Put your phone right there. Like what's the matter?' They don't say that, but their disposition says it. You never done this before? The assumption is you done this before.

"Don't laugh, but it was just like prison. Never been to prison? You get there and nobody believes that you don't know how it goes. Gonna have to take your shoes off. Gonna have to put all your stuff in here. That book bag too has to go up there. Made me nervous. This technology was too much. I was in planes in the eighties. If they had anything then it was an unassuming metal detector set up in a way it looked like a door jam. You just walked through it. If it beeps, 'Step to the side, Sir.' If it didn't, you just kept going. Nobody took no shoes off! Zelda had been through it all before, so I tried to follow her.

"I had a lotion in my bag that was too big. Forgot it was there. So Zelda is going ahead, and they flagged me aside and they said, 'Sir, we saw something in your luggage that we need to look at.'

"I know there's nothing illegal in there, but I'm having this conversation with myself. Maybe it's random? Yeah, it's random. Maybe they know I've never flown before and they want to kind of set a precedent with me. I don't know, but I'm gonna go with it. Do what they say.

"So now, I'm wondering how long is this gonna take. I'm assuming that because they asked us to come through all that security, the plane is ready. They waiting for the people. Dang I'm gonna hold the plane up!

"So I'm hurrying because I'm thinking I'm delaying this plane. Zelda's like, "You got time. Relax.' I don't even tie my shoes. I want to get out of that area, 'cause that's high security, and I just want to get out fast as I can. That's too much like prison.

"Then there's these long walkways with all kinds of signs and there's the electronic billboards with gates and terminals and flights scrolling and changing all the time, real fast. How does anybody make sense of all this stuff? Then you got all the stores and you got all the people. And everybody in a hurry. Everybody's rude and moving fast but seem to be going nowhere but to get to another place to wait. Once again: too much like prison!

"And like in strip malls, everything starts to look the same. Example: I go to the bathroom and I come out kind of disoriented. Did I come this way or that way? I call Zelda on my phone and hers goes straight to voicemail and I almost panic. Did she get on the plane? She's assuming I know how to get there? It's very stressful.

"I took so long she finally called me, said, 'Where are you?'"

'I haven't moved. I'm right outside the bathroom.'

'I'm right here to your left.'

But you got a sea of people moving back and forth. 'How am I supposed to see you through all this?'

"Then we boarded the plane – flying, that doesn't bother me. Flying itself is exciting. It's just all that stuff that led up to flying." Mecca goes on to expound about the "baby–size seats" he's stuck in for five hours. "I never took my seatbelt off because I didn't have the space to take it off. And I'm self conscious. I'm thinking any movement I'm gonna hit somebody's knee. Only pseudo sleep. I'm just too wired up. It's too much like prison, transferring from prison. Those prison buses are set up like that, and you're forced to pack it in all the time. And I kept wrestling with that in my head."

Things finally felt better, "Much better," when they got to the conference site in a hotel near the Oakland airport.

Mecca and Zelda make a side trip into Oakland to visit Mecca's cousin who lives by Lake Merritt. Mecca is shocked by the rent but loves the place. He sends me a photo, arms open, facing the sunset over San Francisco Bay. He goes running early in the morning with his cousin – just at the right moment to see a stream of hundreds of costumed runners for Gay Pride Week flash past. Opposite of the airport. Nothing like prison.

Gay Pride Week is something new, but it fits right in with the crazy air travel and the drop into a world of eucalyptus trees and soft sunlight, but the real stunner is the conference itself.

"FICPFM, the Formerly Incarcerated and Convicted People and Families Movement," Mecca repeats the name twice as if savoring the flavor of it. "That's the name of the conference and the group. Very spirited. Very energetic. Very vibrant. Very serious. Very intent. Very structured. They had lectures. They had groups. They had over four hundred people, and ninety percent of them were formerly incarcerated people. Zelda was the exception, along with others who came with someone like me."

In classes, I try to give the men in prison some sense of what the prison reform and rights movement outside is like, but they find the idea of people organizing outside to be very abstract. I bring in my copy of the *New York Times* every week and flag the articles about incarceration. Once few and far between, now there's something to highlight every week. I download Bryan Stevenson's TED Talk describing his experience working with men on death row, trying to reverse cases for the innocent or reduce extreme sentences.[19] We argue about the relationship of innocence to the conditions for men who are guilty of a crime. The men are interested but skeptical. They get the feeling that it's not really about them; it's all about entertainment for people on the outside.

Mecca is not above such suspicions. The kids who come to RSN seem to be spinning in place. The numbers of men and women trying to navigate reentry are high, and the ability of support teams to push beyond compassion, to get practical problems solved, is woefully inadequate. Jobs? There's a move to get employers to interview first and ask about criminal records later, to eliminate that box that says, "Check here if you have ever been convicted of a

---

[19] Bryan Stevenson, *We Need To Talk About Injustice*
(https://www.ted.com/speakers/bryan_stevenson), posted March 2012.

felony." But in most places, it's business as usual. Criminal record? Forget the job. Felony? Don't even think about moving in with your mother or your wife in public housing. Rental application? Check the box all over again. With this in mind, it's no surprise that Mecca is stunned by what he sees in Oakland.

"Everybody was very impactful, talking about what this movement had done with voting rights, ban the box, housing rights, employment. Trying to change laws. The school to prison pipeline. Everybody was on point. Many of the people there had been all the way to the White House with their issues. And one thing I can say, one of the things that stood out to me the most, was that they were battle–tested for meeting opposition. They had seen it. They had shared it. They had testified to it. Obstacles? That did not phase them one bit. They were in for the long haul and knew that this issue is a lifelong issue. It's not overnight. And they were ready for the fight.

"They are challenging the system. We are people who've been in prison; what you gonna do? Lock us up? That don't phase them. Man, we all been to prison, so let's go, full speed ahead. They were ready. All the spectrum of time they had done! A lot of Spanish people. A lot of women. I had never seen any women that had been incarcerated. With the prison thing, it's mostly men. But women were there, full charge. All ages. Wow, you get a real glimpse of how big a deal this incarceration thing is. How vast the net is. It gets everybody. It doesn't care. It's a machine that will eat anything that's in its way. And all kinds of people locked up. Dang. You really locking up people like that?

"And it was very structured. Everybody was on cue. When you had breakfast and lunch, that was the time you mingled and networked. For me, it seemed everybody that was there had been there before. They just fell into it. I felt like I was the rookie, despite the time I spent in prison. They were initiating me, asking me, 'Where you been?' and then telling me, 'This is what we do.'

"It made me feel like all the while there's been a real movement against mass incarceration and the school to prison pipeline. A *real* one. Not just people talking about it. It's one thing to see something like that on the news, but when you out there amongst them, you experience the energy. That's something else. That's what they had, energy; and they weren't just talking.

"I kind of went into it like, okay, you gonna hear a lot of stories. Everybody gonna have this testimony about what the system did to them when they were locked up. War stories. Nobody was talking like that. It was very focused on the problems *now*.

"And guys that had been to the White House to see this woman in the Office of the Attorney General, to talk to her about these issues and ask her to come speak at the conference. They won her over. She testified to that. She was there because of seeing the commitment, the relentless commitment of the people who had traveled to D.C. and demanded to meet with somebody in the justice system, not allowing themselves to be run off. That forced her to really pay attention and listen to what they were saying."

Mecca stops to catch his breath.

"One more thing. At the conference, they had a mock prison set up that they hooked to a pickup truck and they took it around. Inside there is a cell, segregation, and visitation and you can go in. It's just about as big as this room here. And I couldn't get myself to go in. Zelda went in and took pictures. I told her, 'I can't do it. I just can't.'

"She wanted to understand what was in there, so I peeked in for a second and then told her, 'That's lockup. And that's visitation. And in some prisons, there's one of those behind the glass. That's a holding cell right there.' But I had to tell her I couldn't go in there. I'm done with that. I'm done with that.

"FICPFM, it's probably the most significant thing I've witnessed in real time. In real time as opposed to seeing something like that on the news. It motivated me to speak a little louder when I can and where I can about these issues. And it helped me realize my job with the School For Conversion, my work for StepUp and RSN, it's more significant than I thought it was.

"I also want to say again that the women were the most impressive. They were strong like the men. They were vocal. They weren't just there sitting around. They were hands on, involved. I've never seen women as assertive, or as affirmed. And there were a lot of them – mothers that had been to prison. They all helped change laws about when you are handcuffed to the bed while you are giving birth; they changed those laws. In prison where I was it's just men and you don't know anything about women who are in prison. You don't think about it.

"When I went into the School For Conversion office to give my report, I told them I had never seen such a large amount of people all in accord, working in an organized, civil, intelligent way. There wasn't none of that whooping and hollering or just making noise. They were focused on their agenda about trying to end this mass incarceration epidemic. In prison, nothing's moving. The time is not even moving. So people talk about it, say there's a movement going on out there, but in prison, I don't feel it. I don't see it. I don't even sense it. Now I have seen it and it's energizing me.

"I was looking around at the crowd a lot. Dang, all these people – which is probably a drop in the bucket – that have been incarcerated and dealt with the issues. Maybe they couldn't get a job or a house or medical care or health insurance just because they'd been in prison, and they heard about an organization that would stand up for them and they got involved. They heard about an opportunity to be a voice, along with and alongside an organization that was willing to go all the way to legislation about getting that stuff changed. They got people to listen. That was very impressive.

"In prison people have legitimate issues, but the way they want to present it... nobody is gonna listen to that mumbo jumbo. Never get anybody's attention with that. The people at this conference were informed, knowledgeable, and intelligent about how they went about doing it. They're not just whining and complaining. They are saying it in a way that matters: we know our rights. They did it in a way that was very respectable – where people had to pay attention. They knew how to start this movement, and I see that this movement is going to keep getting bigger. It's in motion. It's in motion.

"For me personally, it let me know that what we are doing here has to be done a lot better and more effectively, 'cause what we are doing can complement what I saw. It's up to us to make that happen. However we can. Movements start small in what seem like insignificant ways and get to what I saw in Oakland, and they can go way past that. For me, seeing this was a necessary brick in the wall. It says to me that there's a lot more to be done in relation to what I'm doing here and what they're doing there. For me this was a giant step."

Several years ago, back at OCC, I encouraged – you could say bullied – the men in the workshop to sign up for a public speaking course being offered by UNC inside the prison. "When you get out," I said, "you need to be speaking up to other people." I'm excited and proud that Mecca has stepped up to this challenge. In addition to his talks at churches, community groups, and organizations, I have added to my archive a speech Mecca gave at a conference on incarceration and re–entry hosted by the governor of North Carolina and the state's attorney general. They sat, fully engaged, while listening to Mecca. More important, when he speaks, he does not mince words. He calls out the self–limitations and hypocrisy of providing "support" to people in prison and people re–entering that skips across the surface of the problem.

"I made a vow," Mecca said at that conference, "that once I was out of prison, I'm not going to tell my story no more. I did my time. But as I walked around this room and I saw some of my friends, I'm reminded it's not just all about me. It's about representing people that don't have a voice...

"The support that I received in prison, the people that gave me a sense of dignity, that made me think differently about myself were key. Because, in that environment, there's not a lot of reason or incentive to think different about myself – especially as someone who had a natural life sentence. Why read a book? Why take a class? Why try to better yourself? What's the point? You're bettering yourself to be a better inmate?

"When I wanted to think that way, my mother's hope was transferred to me and it said, 'Listen. You never know what might happen. Your life still has value.' And I had the courage to buy into that. And weekend after weekend, letter after letter, I started a new paradigm in my thinking. I started to re–indoctrinate myself about who I was as a man...

"Upon my release, all of those tools that I bred, have served me well and put me in rooms like this. If you notice, in my talk, I've come full circle. I started with asking, *How the heck did I get here – Why am I standing in this room talking to you?* I end with saying, *Now I understand exactly why I am here.*"

Chapter 18: Biophilia: Prepare the Soil, Treasure the Harvest

What we did was humanize [prisoners], just by telling their stories. Once you commit your crime, people think that's what it is, but individuals change. They don't stay the same people that they were when they committed their crime. They grow up — literally.

Earlonne Woods, co-host of Ear Hustle[20]

Incarceration is the sound of a collision between the rigidity of the prison system and the flexibility of the human mind. Some authors listen from the side of policing, courts, and laws and write valuable books advocating different strategies for reform. We, however, have been listening from the inside out, writing about the need to understand what to do to make it possible for people to be released from prison with a reasonable chance of doing good. For that to happen, something has to change inside the minds of the prisoners, their families, and all of us. When Mecca and Bessie exchanged that promise in 1993, they may not have realized how much it would change them; but it has. It has changed their lives for the better. It has made their family whole.

---

[20] Sarah Ruiz-Grossman, "Earlonne Woods, Co—Host of Ear Hustle Podcast, Has Sentence Commuted." *Huffington Post*, Nov. 26, 2018.

It's now 2020, and Mecca has built a good life for himself. That life includes a wealth of actions that back up the commitment he made in Oakland to use his own experience to repair the damage done to other human beings by the justice system. Always a man with a taste for variety, Mecca has successfully skirted the 9–to–5 world. While his favorite gig is working as a personal trainer, he is also still doing outreach for at–risk youth, teaching classes that prepare people for re–entry, recruiting church and community teams who will provide support to individuals when they are released for re–entry, as well as participating in conferences, on boards, and at speaking events, and always reiterating his message: prison can be an opportunity to grow.

Mecca and I talk a lot about the commitment he made in prison never to forget the people who are left behind. He is constantly gathering new information, honing his ability to clarify how to get people to understand what happens when you put a person in prison and what it is going to take to recover those people when they are free. That's what is on his mind when Mecca calls me up on a Saturday in January. He announces, "I'm understanding something about all this, and I want it on the record."

Mecca picks me up and we drive to see Wendy Gale, Mecca's boss at Artistry in Plants beginning right after his release. Even after he secured enough jobs doing outreach, he stayed on with Wendy for the challenge. It was like unloading the corn at Neese's – very physical and very satisfying. Most of the men who work for Wendy have a prison record, and she feels she has a mission to help them, but she also wields a lot of power.

"I have other jobs," Mecca told me once when he came by after a clash with Wendy. "I can tell her I don't want to do this, or I can't work that day. Other men don't have that choice. Wendy doesn't like that. She wants to be in control."

I'm curious what can be important enough to hustle us to Wendy's. She is a slim, tough–looking woman in her sixties but strong from physical work. Her house is small and surrounded by green, and inside, there's a big dog settled on the rug and a cage of songbirds in the kitchen. First, Mecca explains our oral history project, then he says he wants to say something and wants her to be a witness. He is going to record it. Wendy looks wary but also amused. I press record and Mecca begins.

"When I go jogging, I look for different places. Yesterday I ran past a street called Denada – we did some landscaping at a house on that street. And I had this epiphany. And it's relevant to you, Wendy, because you are the person who told me about this word, biophilia, that describes how we connect with nature. That word, while I was running, it came back to me and it opened up for me what happens in prison and what it meant to work for Artistry in Plants when I got out.

"Coming out of prison to a strange environment, getting a job doing landscaping and riding in the truck, going to different streets, different homes, different demographics, meeting different people – to me that was one of the most therapeutic experiences that someone coming out of prison could have.

"While I was running and saw Denada Street, I had this idea. I wanted to say to you, Wendy, how grateful I am for the opportunity to unlock and open up a part of my mind that I craved for twenty-five years. Being around nature. Working in yards in all these different places. That was a priceless experience. I held on tightly to all of that and I still do. So this is my opportunity to give you your kudos and to also say we need to continue to let people have that experience. Trauma, drug abuse, incarceration, it stifles people. To allow them to experience freedom in nature is what they need.

"This is not just my idea. Everybody that I talk to who did this work, they say, 'I felt the same exact way.' Doing the work with the plants, putting them in the earth. That's what everybody in prison craves. To actually put your feet on the ground. To smell the air. To touch the earth. You don't get to do that in prison.

"After prison lots of people get jobs they hate. Prison prepares you for that. It teaches you how to do something you hate over and over again over a long period of time. Say guys get out of prison and they get a job at a laundry; they tell you all day 'I hate my job,' but they'll get up and go to it. You learn that in prison. I gotta get up and go to work – to the clothes house or to the kitchen, canning plant, road crew. Then it's the same after prison. You wear different clothes, but it's the same. But with plants, doing landscaping, you have to be doing something different all the time. Each house is gonna be different. Each day the weather is different and the problems with the plants are different. That's a healing experience.

"So I want to say, for the record, that I loved my work for Artistry in Plants. It gave me a sense of my true self, and that had to do with being around nature. When you told me that word, biophilia, that right there put it in a context that I didn't know one word could capture."

Wendy looks genuinely surprised. While she and Mecca have had their battles, she is also fully committed to her ideas and her post–incarceration work crew. She's very excited to hear those ideas coming back from Mecca.

"Biophilia is just like he said," Wendy turns to the window and gestures toward the trees outside. They are bare, but it's sixty degrees out there, the sun is shining, and even in January we feel spring getting ready to happen. "Biophilia is about people's innate attraction and connection to everything wild. And it goes beyond that. Biophilia incorporates a spiritual element that a more scientific term would not necessarily include. I believe that we each have God in us, my dog over there and my birds and the plants outside. That is what makes up God. The better each of us is, the more powerful and wonderful God is, because you reach that little self deep inside."

Mecca looks at the dog, and as if on cue the birds tune up their song. Mecca lets us sit with Wendy's words and then picks up the thread.

"This is relevant to all the work I do, not just landscaping. I learned from Wendy you don't just dig a hole and put the plant in there. I started doing it that way, but she showed me how you gotta pick the spot and prepare the dirt. It's a little different for each plant. Before that all plants were the same to me. Now, in my work with youth, with reentry, I can see that each person is like that, a plant. You gotta prepare the soil and they gotta be in the right place with the right light.

"So I bring this full circle to say this was my revelation in running and this is my ode to you, Wendy, thanking you for the opportunity. It's not just that you are a second–chance employer; you help us be better people by way of what we do. I attest to that."

I look up biophilia afterwards. The term was coined by Erich Fromm in *The Heart of Man: Its Genius for Good and Evil* (1964) to mean "love for humanity and nature, and independence and freedom." It was extended by Edward O. Wilson in *Biophilia* (1984)[21] to mean the rich, natural pleasure that comes from being surrounded by living organisms, the nurturing affinity between all living things.

This makes sense to me. It makes sense of what Mecca has been teaching me. It is the practice that Mecca and Bessie and Cheryl have been cultivating: if you are not going to lose everything, you need to be working the soil, even the concrete soil of a prison cell. Sometimes, scraping around in the bad dirt of the prison yard may seem futile, but growing is happening and life is there, ready for release, ready to prosper.

After the visit at Wendy's it was clear that Mecca was feeling good about his life. I wanted to know if the whole family felt this way. As Mecca said, the plant does not grow on its own. I invited Bessie, Cheryl and Zelda to join Mecca and me to talk about how they felt about this journey.

Bessie begins the conversation by taking us back to the source: her determination not to accept the verdict, not to see her son spend the rest of his life in prison. She says, "The sentence didn't mean

---

[21]   Edward O. Wilson, *Biophilia* (Cambridge: Harvard University Press, Reprint edition, 1984)

anything to Cheryl and me. Okay, that's what the court says but now we are just gonna pull ourselves together and beat this. My father always told me, if there's a way in, there's a way out. That was my job. Finding the way out. I didn't have time to hear anybody talk about negativity. 'Well he shouldn't have been involved with those people.' I didn't have time for any of that. Stay focused. Meet the people I needed to meet to help me get the job done. That was it.

"I went to speak with Susan Edwards [the district attorney] because I wanted her to see my face. I wanted her to remember my name. I wanted her to know that what she did was wrong. I said, 'When you wake up at night you are gonna see my face, and I want you to remember my name because you are going to hear it.' This is not over. You didn't win."

Cheryl is even more defiant. Thinking back to that courtroom, she tells us she raised her fist in the air. She remembers, "I was extremely angry, and I expressed my anger with the fist, the same fist that was at the Olympics. Straight Black Power. Total defiance. Injustice." Lowering her arm and quieting her voice, she collects herself and continues, "We see on the news that people of color are disproportionately thrown in prison, given lengthy sentences. You never think it is going to happen to you. And when it does, it's injustice. I wanted the court and whoever was there to know what I felt about it." She laughs, "We were quickly ushered out of the courtroom."

Mecca listens carefully. Remember, after his sentence was read out, he kept his head turned away, looking down, as the bailiff ushered him out. He's seen his mother and sister in action, but it's not part of his courtroom memory. Maybe he lost something by not looking back at them.

"Listening to this, it makes sense to me now. My sister is a rebel. If somebody said to me, 'Do you know your sister is a Black Panther?' I would say that makes sense, because she's always been aware of the injustices and the Black plight. I recognize that now, and I can picture her raising her fist. My mother, she's the same way, angry, but right away she is strategizing on the come back. Always thinking and contemplating. How to either get through it or around it or over it."

He pauses to consider how to express what he needs to say.

"But, for me, my mother was also in denial about my sentence. She was saying that we are not going down like that. You not gonna be here the rest of your life. It wasn't Lala Land, but she was not accepting the gravity of that life sentence. For me, there was no way to deny it. The smells. The look. The feel. The bed. The soap. The shower. The phone. The TV. The lack of fresh air. I could go on and on. All reminding me that this is really prison and you are really here. There was nothing about the place that let me think for one second that I wasn't locked up. Nothing. And from what I knew, locked up meant forever.

"At the same time, hearing them, I know that their refusal to accept the verdict helped me keep my sanity. Maybe be like those plants, sun moving in different places at different times of day or putting different stuff, nutrients in the soil. I would think about it from the mind of my mother, my sister, my aunts and uncles. I would think about myself from the side of my friends who had no idea that I was even out of state, and then they heard that I got sentenced to life in prison. I would go into these different rooms in my mind and that would help me. I was fighting for my life. And spiritually... I went to God because He is the only one who could convince me what's really right and what's really wrong. There were people in powerful positions who had put me in prison. I would have gone crazy if I had of stayed in that lane, always thinking about them."

Bessie listens and considers this. "Yes, my faith in God increased too, but that is because it was tied to my fight. Natural life? Are you kidding me? No. Um hmmmm. I was all about faith *and* focus. Faith *and* focus."

Mecca's comment about his aunts and uncles, his friends back in New Jersey reminded me that shame shines on the family as well as the convicted. I asked Cheryl how this affected her. What did she say when she first met her husband and they got serious?

"When I met David and I told the story, he said, 'Life sentence? You gonna get him out?' And I said, 'Yeah.' He probably didn't think that could happen. He probably just thought that I'm on this crusade, and maybe Willie will get out and maybe not. But I never changed my thinking. I never changed my desire to support my brother and my mother. We knew, without a doubt: he's not gonna spend his life in prison."

William watches his mother's face, watches his sister's eyes flash. He must have seen this a thousand times – across the table at visits, at Straight Talk Support Group meetings, watching them speak at public events – but something about the closing of the circle, the completion of this book, has given their words added force. He gives us his take.

"Listening now, I'm hearing this and putting my mind as if I've never heard it before. Never witnessed it before. I'm thinking how it's sad to know that there are many people out in world today, people I have met in prison, who come from families that are more whole, less broken than my family, but someone in that family could still have gotten a life sentence and got left inside a prison with nobody on their side. That blows my mind. I come from a family that was fractured, that has had big problems, but my mother and my sister decided to lay it all down for me one thousand percent.

"In prison, I didn't start dealing with my feelings until I got a good grip on theirs. Once I got the visits and the letters and they told me how they felt and I sensed it, it made me stronger. Then I could start dealing with my own feelings. When I meet other people and they say how awesome and how rare and how unusual that is, it makes me turn my head aside. I wonder why. Why? It don't have to be a life sentence, could be six months to go to prison for whatever the reason and nobody is going to support them? I see that a lot. So for my mother and my sister to say, 'Hey man, we got you. It ain't over.' – my sister's words, verbatim – it was overwhelming. But also it is sad, because it highlights that other people don't have that type of support."

Zelda has been quiet, but I can feel her listening, moving this around in her mind. Because of Mecca's decision to hold her at arms length while he was in prison, she was not directly involved in his case, but now she has definitely become the fourth Musketeer. I ask her how she feels about this.

"When I moved down here, instead of feeling like I was in a strange place I felt like I was at home! I was quite frankly impressed and influenced by Mrs. Elmore and Cheryl. They way they were sticking by him. We share the same values in terms of how we view the world, how we view the justice system. And even though people of color predominate in the prison system, they don't have the kind of support that Mrs. Elmore and Cheryl showed for Swill."

She and I share a laugh, because even though Bessie says she doesn't ever want to hear that street name, when Zelda talks about Swill it summons up a form of affection that makes us all a little bit nostalgic for that bright eyed young man. Zelda holds a key to a magic connection.

"I think that when it comes to Black men getting locked up, too often there's a normalcy to it. You think, 'Okay, maybe I'll write once in a while, but he'll be home.' And like me with Swill, it goes in and out. But Mrs. Elmore and Cheryl, they show what support looks like: sending books and supporting other people that were Swill's friends inside prison. Black women... we want to support our men, but we don't always know how, and they detail how it should be done. I've learned a lot! And it has influenced some of the directions that I move in now."

Mecca is leaning into this, almost reeling with the spirit. "I'm grateful! As much as I believe in myself, I believe in the power of support. I believe life is about momentum. Momentum and energy. You set out on a mission all by yourself that could seem crazy and unrealistic to everybody else, but if you keep at it, you start attracting people, places, and things that support your mission and add to it. I believed in myself, and that attracted other people, but getting a natural life sentence made me question my self value. Believing in myself had a lot to do with my mother and my sister, the way they showed up for me reminded of my value.

"The same way, after all of these years, having dated Zelda before I went to prison and pushed her away sometimes, and then twenty some years later she's right down here with me for the rest of my life! That lets me know, that reminds me that wow, I do have some value! I did take somebody's life, but I wasn't just a liability. Man, too many people sit in their cells and act like they never need a second chance for anything. I saw that a lot in prison, and I seen it now when I teach reentry classes for StepUp. That feeling works against them. But maybe they don't have anybody to tell them they are worth a second chance. We all need second, third, and fourth chances. I'm grateful that I understand that, and I try to surround myself with people that understand that."

"I remember when we used to teach at the Troy House," Cheryl says, her expression alternating between a big smile and a frown. "The guys in the classes, people that had make mistakes, could be very resistant to the idea of reconnecting with their families. They are in a transition house, between prison and home. Maybe there were bad feelings on both sides. I would say to them, 'We make mistakes every single day. You made a very big mistake, and that mistake is not going away. But don't you want a second chance? Don't you want a chance to connect with your family? Who else better in the world is there that you want to be connected to when you get out of prison? You can apologize. Sincerely apologize. Tell them you didn't mean to cause that to happen.' In their eyes I saw it: 'Wow, I could do this.'"

Bessie steps in, seeing Cheryl and raising her one, getting right to the heart of why we wrote this book.

"This book is about empowerment, for the people who read it in prison and for their families and for anyone who wants to do something about mass incarceration. When people read this book, I want them to see me as just an ordinary mother who was determined to make something happen and willing to stick to it and go the distance. I think everybody can be empowered. People do look for a hero. They like the image of the hero. But when you really can touch somebody who's been through something, like we have in our story, that can encourage other people. It says, 'You can do the same thing!' I want to open people up, open their minds up to believe that they can do the same exact thing. To empower them. To free them. To break the chains off of their minds. That's what my hope is for when I speak, for the Straight Talk Transition House and for this book."

We sit with that for a moment. Parts of this book have been very hard for Bessie to read. As Mecca has said, a lot of his life on the street was invisible to her. In prison they sometimes spared each other talk about who really had a handle on what was going on. And maybe not everyone is up to the job of full throttle support. I ask Bessie, "Do people ever say to you that you are giving people false hope?"

"No. No. *No!* Number one, I wouldn't give anybody false hope. No one ever said that to me. But you do have to be careful about who you are empowering and how you go about empowering that particular person. And with some people you can waste your time. If a person isn't thirsty enough, they are not going to drink. But you can work with a person. You can intrigue them to want to drink. And that's when you open up their minds.

"There's one person in particular that came to our support group, and she was so timid and so shy, but she kept coming! She had her little note pad and she was taking notes and she began to use what she learned to find ways she could support her son in prison. She was empowered. We get so many thank–yous from people who come to the support group and learn what we did for William. Then they come back and share what they did and what they learned. That is awesome. Empowering people is very important to me."

Cheryl nods. "When you talk about giving people false hope... Our situation on the outside, by the letter of the law, was hopeless. But I would never say the words natural life. I didn't accept it. Maybe that helped me. But even if a person does have the same exact sentence as my brother, and the family can say the words, and they accept it, they can still support their loved ones. They can still have hope and pass that hope to their loved one."

For Bessie and Cheryl and Zelda, the fruit of that hope is sitting in the room with us. Mecca has not just survived prison, he has used prison to thrive as a human being. When I ask them if they have any regrets, Mecca's got his answer ready.

"Yeah, I have things I wish I would have done differently. But in a lot of ways that's not a fair question to ask me now. The quality of life and the value of life that I discovered while I was in prison erases the regret. I learned how to live while I was in prison. Natural life taught me how to live. It made me ask, 'What kind of life is it if you are not going for what you believe in and what you love? What kind of life is it to live not discovering who you are as a person?' I found all that out by getting hit in the head with the natural life stick and bouncing back, waking up to my mother and my sister wrapping my head with bandages – man, I wouldn't forsake that for nothing.

"I don't say that I *wanted* to go to prison to get it, but I got it, Simone. And it's a priceless jewel and that erases all the regret. All the people I lost. All the time I lost. I could have gone to Seton Hall, could have gone to college. But I ask myself, how much would those things have helped me advance myself, learn the quality and value of what it means to really *live*? I don't think any of them would have, because they provide too many perks, and that can distract you from what it means to really live. I went through the fire. You don't know what you made of 'til you get burnt real bad. Any regrets? Naw."

Cheryl has a similar take on the issue of regret. She laughs and says, "I think the only thing I would say about regret is when I was late to visit! I hated being late. I was always running. The visits were hard for me. I wasn't like Mom. Sometimes I didn't want to go, but I knew I had to and then I would stall.

"And I did a lot of things because my brother was in prison here. People would ask me, 'How did you do this or that? You just came to Durham and just started singing in a band? You were vying against a hundred forty-three other people to get that job at UNC. How did you get it?' I did things because I needed to keep busy and I needed to show my brother, look, I'm not just sittin' around. I'm in a band. I'm in Connecticut. I've been to Alaska. And I'm doing all these things because I want to motivate him as well."

I know Bessie doesn't spend much time on regret and she confirms this.

"I don't regret the journey. I don't. It made me into who I am now. What I do regret is that there are people who were along with me that didn't get to see him released, who died before we got where we needed to go. I regret that. But I do not regret what I learned doing this. I told myself, 'Stay focused, Bessie.' I don't care where I was, I was gonna make the visit. I don't care what I had to do, I was gonna get my son out of prison. Those people at those prisons were going to know who I was and who my son was. That's one of the things I convey over and over to family members: write letters to the people in charge. Write a card. Let those people in Raleigh know this person belongs to you. You have the power. Utilize it."

Zelda thinks about the question of regrets for a moment before answering in a soft voice that is thick with concern.

"I wish that I had had a little more courage to resolve some things that we left unresolved. And I wish I was more mature and could have been the *bigger person*. That's probably the only regret. The major regret. I think that this book will lay a blueprint for people like me and for families, so they won't make the same mistakes. A lot of times you're programmed into a way of how things should be, and you don't do what you could have done. This book can be a blueprint to change that."

Bessie is all in. "It was like William invited Cheryl and I on this journey, and we were like the old *Mission Impossible* and came out on top. And during the journey we have learned that we have an obligation to give back, to reach back to help somebody else. William does it his way. I do it my way. Cheryl does it her way. And when you put it all together, it's awesome. And now that Zelda is on our team, we are a force. We are a force for good."

Which brings me to the end of our journey. We have moved from the inside out, and Mecca has hit the ground running. He gets the last word.

"I believe in the redeeming value of human beings. My jobs give me the opportunity to share that with people. Sometimes it's directly a spiritual sharing and sometimes it's camouflaged. I might be talking about reentry or my life in prison or just doing personal training, but all of that is an exemplification of decisions I made about myself while I was in prison. Landing in prison reflected the culmination of decisions I made about myself on the street. The quality of my life now is a direct reflection of the decisions I made about myself while I was in prison. I started by doing that work on myself and then with the people I had to live with in prison. Now, as a free man, I get paid to reach out to all kinds of people. That's the end of my story. Like my mother says, we won big time. Salute to y'all – Mom, Sis, Zelda! We won!

Photographs

Cheryl & William with
Bessie's mother,
Rosa Della Steel Johnson

Raspberry Johnson,
Bessie's grandfather

Cheryl, "Willie" and Bessie

"Swill" (upper left)
and friends
1986

"Swill" the dealer
(left) In
New Jersey

Keisha's Prom

On The Run
(lower left)

"Mecca" on visiting
day with
Bessie and Cheryl
Salisbury/Piedmont
Correctional Institution
12-09-2006

January 1,2014
Mecca's first
CV Pass
with David Bellin
(and Simone
not pictured)

Mecca's first day
in his new home
with Cheryl
Dec. 21, 2015

James leone, Bessie, & Mecca at the Straight Talk Annversary Celebration

Frank Walls & Mecca cycle on the American Tobacco Trail as free men

Mecca & former public defender Joe Knott

Mecca, Cheryl, & "Dad", Willie Elmore Sr.

Mecca Carries
Arthur into
Hospice

Mecca & Scott-so
form Community
Landscaing
after Scott-so
gets his MAPP
and Release

Mecca &
Zelda
take a
cruise
to the
Bahamas

Appendix 1 List of Prisons

Central Prison, Raleigh, NC: Admitted for Processing, May 1993

Eastern Correctional Institution, Maury, NC: Transfer, June 1993

Nash Correctional Institution, Nashville, NC: Transfer, October 1993

Limestone Detention Center, Groesbeck, Texas: Transfer, August 1996

Lumberton Correctional Institution, Lumberton, NC: Transfer, November 1996

Nash Correctional Institution, Nashville, NC: Transfer, November 1996

Odum Correctional Institution, Jackson, NC: Transfer (Hurricane Floyd), September 1999

Piedmont Correctional Institution, Salisbury, NC: Transfer, February 2000

Brown Creek Correctional Institution, Polkton NC: Transfer, January 2011

Johnston **Correctional** Institution, Smithfield, NC: Transfer (Evaluation), May 2012

Caledonia Correctional Institution, Tillery, NC: Transfer, May 2013

Orange Correctional Center, Hillsborough, NC: Transfer, February 2013

Johnston Correctional Institution, Smithfield, NC: Transfer (Kitchen Fire), June 2014

Orange Correctional Center, Hillsborough, NC: Transfer, November 2014

Release: Probation (5 years), December 21, 2015

Probation Ends: December 21, 2020

Appendix 2 Not All Prisons Are Alike

North Carolina houses more than 31,000 incarcerated men and women in fifty-five prison facilities across the state. Mecca was a resident in eleven of these in addition to the year he spent in the Wake County Jail awaiting trial. As he moved through the system, Mecca had to learn a critical lesson: Not all prisons are alike. When a person is shipped to a prison, there is no promotional literature with photos of the accommodations or information about job options. In theory the rules are determined by the security level of the prison or the custody level of the prisoner; in fact every prison has its own character, its own culture, its own path to survival.

After conviction men are *processed in* at Central Prison in Raleigh. There are separate facilities for women in North Carolina. Most are housed in the North Carolina Correctional Institution for Women (NCCIW) in Raleigh where there are close to 1800 women at all custody levels including three women on death row.

Mecca got a preview of Central Prison (CP) when he was moved there from Wake County Jail for his protection during his trial. Two of his former street partners had been brought from federal prison to Raleigh to testify against Mecca and were housed at Wake County Jail. However, in temporary custody Mecca was not in the belly of the beast. As a convicted murderer, he went into the heart of the prison.

Central Prison is a vast facility located just west of downtown Raleigh. Originally constructed by prisoners in the shape of a large castle, it opened in 1884 with a $1.25 million dollar price tag. That number is not adjusted for inflation. It has been expanded over the years to include a complex of sturdy cinder block and concrete buildings spread over twenty-six acres. There is a prison industries building (state license plate fabrication and a complete print shop), an acute care hospital with wards, operating rooms, X–ray laboratories and a pharmacy, two mental health wings, a custody control and administration building, a building with single cells for those who are assigned to jobs within the boundaries of the prison, and a maximum security housing building that includes death row and safekeeping. Mecca only stays at CP for a month of intake, but it's a difficult month in which the full meaning of being incarcerated hits him hard.

North Carolina prisons have five custody levels: close, medium, minimum I, minimum II and minimum III – the last three are referred to as honor grade. The men usually talk about *close, brown clothes*, and *green clothes*. The names come from the tight conditions in maximum security and the color of the prison–issued clothing for medium (brown) and minimum (green). In prisons or *camps* for close custody movement is heavily restricted. There are guard towers, gates, doors, locks, visits through glass or mesh partitions – just as in the movies. Medium security prisons have the same guard towers and armed officers, but there is more freedom of movement, more opportunity to attend programs (education, Narcotics Anonymous, Alcoholics Anonymous) and therapeutic activities, better work opportunities, and face to face or *contact* visits.

Minimum or honor grade camps are the most relaxed. In many of them, there is an open picnic area for visits, a more easy going yard culture, and people who are either close to release or older and less involved in contraband activity. Officers are not armed. There is razor wire on top of the fences but no guard towers around the yard. The exception to the rule would be a camp like Johnston Correctional Institution where a medium security facility has been reassigned to hold minimum level prisoners but the old facility design stays in place. Many minimum custody camps in North Carolina have community volunteer programs that allow men and women to earn the privilege of going out *on pass* to church or a restaurant meal. Privileges are earned as an a person moves from minimum I   (no offsite privileges or work) to minimum II (community volunteer passes one on one with a volunteer) to minimum III (offsite work as well as community volunteer passes with a group of up to three).

Prisoners who violate regulations at any level can be placed in *Seg* or segregation also referred to as *the hole.* They are in a cramped cell for twenty-three hours a day – leaving only for a shower and/or recreation in a small fenced area. One doesn't need to master the intricacies of custody to understand that as a person passes through the system they must stay up–to–date on all of the regulations in order to weigh the benefits of education, work, and good behavior, against the risks of committing an infraction. In close custody, for example, a person might feel that making a phone call home on a contraband cellphone is worth the time spent in segregation if they are caught. Conversely, for a person with a fixed release date or someone hoping to earn parole, avoiding infractions is very important. Despite his natural life sentence, the slim chance of freedom and his family's faith in that possibility made staying out of trouble worthwhile for Mecca.

When people are transferred from one prison to another it is referred to as shipping, and Mecca was shipped frequently. I have met lifers who have spent twenty years in the same facility, but most are moved around to make it more difficult to build personal connections between the incarcerated and staff, a situation seen by administration as rife with opportunities for bending regulations. At the same time, staff turnover and transfers can also make it harder for administration to keep the place running smoothly.

Prison is all about weighing options.

Administration can ship someone in their custody for myriad reasons or no reason at all. They can be juggling occupancy and staffing. They can move someone who has been a problem (wide definition here). Or they can ship in response to a change in custody level. An incarcerated person can also request shipment to a prison closer to their family or to a camp offering a service or program they want to take advantage of, such as learning cooking or carpentry. Mecca is in medium custody until he receives his MAPP, so he is usually shipped at the discretion or caprice of the administration or, in the case of transfer to Texas, by orders from the Department of Public Safety in Raleigh.

For the transfer, people are loaded into white security buses with mesh over the windows and *North Carolina Corrections* stenciled on the side. Smaller white mini–vans are used to transport prisoners to another camp, a medical facility or a work site. Most of the time, even for a medical visit, they are shackled wrists and ankles. Even during a hospital stay, a person will be handcuffed to the bed.

The transfer bus usually takes the men to Sandy Ridge, a transfer site near Winston–Salem, where they are placed in holding pens. I've been told it feels like a pen in a stockyard. There they wait to hear their name called for the transport bus heading to their new camp. While Sandy Ridge is not a pleasant place, it offers a time to catch–up with men you knew at another camp, people you may not have seen in a long time. The irony does not escape the men. Sandy Ridge is depressing and social at the same time. Moreover, an individual may or may not know exactly where he is being shipped. There is even an informal form of punishment where a man is loaded onto a bus and left to ride from facility to facility with no idea how far or how long the ride will be.

After processing at Central Prison and evaluation at Eastern Correctional Institution, Mecca is shipped to Caledonia, the farm. This is the second oldest facility in the state. Much of its 7,500 acres is active farmland. The incarcerated population is a mix of brown and green clothes (medium and minimum custody), and many are lifers or serving long sentences, hard time. Correction Enterprises manages the farm and describes itself on its website as providing "rehabilitative opportunities to inmates" and producing "high–quality merchandise at a savings to the taxpayer". The farm includes livestock, row crops (including cotton and soybeans) and three hundred acres of vegetables, which are grown in greenhouses in winter. A huge cannery can put up about 500,000 gallons of produce per year. For men who grew up in rural settings, this landscape at Caledonia is familiar. For a street dealer from New Jersey, it is alien territory. While the Department of Public Safety website describes Caledonia's original intention as "meaningful work in a healthy farm setting", today the farm and nearby camps like Odom call up too much of the old southern plantation to be dismissed lightly.

After not much more than a year, Mecca ships to the Nash Correctional Center. It was renovated in 1992 to serve as a medium security facility. With its many single cells and work options, Nash is a palace compared to Caledonia. Correctional Enterprises has a canning factory there and, for many, this is a best case alternative to working for seventy cents to a dollar a day in the kitchen, as a dorm janitor, or in the clothes house. Workers in an industrial plant can make a regular wage and save money to use at the canteen, for phone cards, or to send home. Because Mecca had family support, he does not work in the factory, which isn't his style anyway. But doing nothing can get boring and it does not earn points toward advancing his custody level or, for a lifer, attaining the holy grail of honor grade. So Mecca works as a janitor and in the clothes house. A work assignment also earns him the privilege of a single cell. In some facilities there are only dorms, but at Nash and at the next prison, Piedmont Correctional, there are both dorms and single cells.

In 1996, when overcrowding inspires North Carolina to set up an prisoner leasing program, Mecca is shipped from Nash to Texas. Thanks to Bessie's persistence, he is in Texas for less than five months before he is returned via Lumberton Correctional to Nash. His next long stop is Piedmont Correctional Institution in Salisbury. It's an oppressive setting with big, multi–story cell blocks. But veterans learn to manage and Mecca finds a job as the score–keeper and set–up man for the gym. Then he is forced into the kitchen. Some jobs like the kitchen are so essential that a man can be pushed to do them whether he wants to or not. Rescued from there by a sympathetic staff member, Mecca gets a job in the clothes house. He is also able to earn a single cell with his jobs. It is important to understand that a single cell does not provide peace and quiet, but it is a place a person can, to some extent, make his own. The guards do periodically *toss* a cell looking for specific contraband or just on a general search and destroy mission, but other people are not in your face the way they are in the dorms.

When Mecca is shipped out of Piedmont, he goes to Brown Creek, a medium/minimum facility. It's up in Anson County and a long drive for his family but the contact with men at minimum provides the grapevine that alerts Mecca to the MAPP system and a route to parole. On the downside, Brown Creek has gangs and coded behavior. Prisons like this can be a minefield for someone like Mecca who is still trying to reach minimum custody or honor grade.

Mecca is sent back to Caledonia to wait for the decision on his MAPP. When he receives a MAPP, Mecca is moved to Orange Correctional Center, the last stop on his prison tour. It is interrupted briefly by a kitchen fire that necessitates a move to Johnston Correctional Institution where Mecca had stopped briefly earlier on for an evaluation. That's a jolt because even though Johnston has recently been reclassified from medium to minimum security all of the trappings and culture of medium custody remain in place. There are guard towers and armed officers and a bullying culture among the staff. Fortunately the kitchen at Orange is repaired and the men return.

The MAPP contract includes specific dates for progressing through the three minimum security levels, so Mecca is not left guessing when his next level of privileges will be approved. The camp at Orange has an open yard, strong volunteer programs, a cook school and carpentry shop, and a relaxed atmosphere. Visits in the warm months take place at picnic tables with a playground for the children. Even among the minimum security facilities in North Carolina, Orange has a reputation for being well run and low stress. There is a low flow of contraband from cigarettes to drugs and home brew, but a man doesn't need to carry a shank or look over his shoulder. It's a good place to finish a stretch and get ready for release.

On Our Bookshelf

Michelle Alexander, *The New Jim Crow: Mass Incarceration in the Age of Colorblindness*

Laura Bates, *Shakespeare Saved My Life: Ten Years in Solitary With The Bard*

Morrie Camhi, *The Prison Experience*

Tessie Castillo, *Crimson Letters: Voices From Death Row*

Joshua Dubler, *Down in the Chapel: Religious Life in an American Prison*

Viktor E. Frankl, *Man's Search For Meaning*

Anthony Ray Hinton, *The Sun Does Shine: How I Found Life and Freedom on Death Row*

Bruce Jackson & Diane Christian, *In This Timeless Time: Living & Dying on Death Row in America*

Jodie Michelle Lawston & Ashley Lucas, editors, *Razor Wire Women: Prisoners, Activists, Scholars, and Artists*

Bo Lozoff, *We're All Doing Time: a guide to getting free*

Jarvis Jay Masters, *Finding Freedom: Writings From Death Row*

Christina Rathbone, *A World Apart: Women, Prison and Life*

Behind Bars

Jeffrey Ian Ross & Stephen C. Richards, *Beyond Bars: Surviving Prison* and *Beyond Bars: Rejoining Society After Prison*

Mark Saltzman, *True Notebooks: A Writer's Year at Juvenile Hall*

Bryan Stevenson, *Just Mercy: A Story of Justice and Redemption*

Timothy B. Tyson, *Blood Done Sign My Name* and *The Blood of EmmettTill*

Malcolm X, *The Autobiography of Malcolm X: As Told to Alex Haley*

Acknowledgments

This book could not have been written without the participation of all of the people whose voices and stories we recorded over the past six years. While not everyone we interviewed is quoted directly in the book, all of you have contributed critical insight that resonates in the depth of the story we have told: Chris Agoranos, Chris Chambers, Bessie Elmore, Norman Bishop, Zelda Everson, Wendi Gale, Tuywn Huynh, James Langston, James Leone, Cole McCauley, Cheryl McDonald, Thomas McGarity, Andrea Neese, Michael Thumm, Edward Scott, Lucas Vrbsky, and Frank Walls. Without your words, we would not have a story to tell.

In the writing of the book, heaps of appreciation to our editor, Jill Hannum, and to David Bellin, for his patient work on the manuscript. Thanks also to Cindy Waszak Geary and Anne Tazwell for many monthly conversations about words and writing. Also thanks to Brandon Proia at UNC Press. Even though you could not publish our book, your knowledge and encouragement were important to shaping the final text. For inspiration in the use of oral history, Tim Tyson stands at the top of our list. For the call to make noise about mass incarceration, Bryan Stevenson has been a guiding light. For introducing Simone to the universe of prison outreach and writing, all praise and respect to Marsha Warren and the Paul Green Foundation, and to my co-teacher for many years, the poet Jaki Shelton Green.

And top of the list – for compassion and respect in shaping our narrative and helping see us to publication, we thank the Human Kindness Foundation, Sita Lozoff, Catherine Dumas, and the entire board.

Finally, we offer praise and thanks to all of the incarcerated, the people and the families whose struggles and triumphs are the subject of this book. Everyone of you is part of us. In particular, Simone would like to call out to the many men who have attended her weekly workshop at the Orange Correctional Center and to the men, some free, many still behind bars, who have offered friendship and support and companionship to Mecca during his journey. Your stories are embedded in our story.

About the Authors

"Mecca" – William Elmore

In 1993 Mecca was convicted of first degree murder and sentenced at the age of 23 to spend his natural life in prison. He had been dealing drugs, shot a gun and a man had died. Mecca fired in self–defense, but the jury disagreed. Before trial, Mecca was offered a plea that required he plead guilty to murder with intent. Mecca refused to sign. For the next 24 years he lived as a "lifer" in eleven North Carolina prisons.

In 2011, Mecca learned about the MAPP, a program that offers offenders who committed crimes before October 1, 1994, the opportunity to be granted a parole. In 2012, Mecca was granted a MAPP, awarded honor grade and moved to the Orange Correctional Center, a minimum security prison. On Dec. 15, 2015 he was released.

Since regaining his freedom, Mecca has committed himself to outreach. He works with youth through RSN, a support network for young people with problems related to addiction. He is involved in prison ministry, mediation, arbitration support, and teaches job–readiness workshops at Step Up Ministries in Durham. Mecca is a founder and lead facilitator for Wounded Healers, a program that brings together people who have been released with the incarcerated., and a member of the board of The Human Kindness Foundation. Outside of work, Will is an avid athlete and a certified personal trainer.

"Simone" – Susan Simone

Simone is a documentary photographer and oral historian. Her documentary projects include: We Are All Housekeepers (an exhibition about labor history on the UNC campus), Fotos del Pueblo (an early look at the emerging Latinx community in North Carolina), Habitat For Humanity: Celebration 2000, and Nepal and Tibet: The People Who Live in Shangri–La (a collaboration with renowned Nepali poet Manjul).

In the 1990's and early 2000's Simone served as the coordinator of the Prison Pen Pal Project for the North Carolina Writer's Network, pairing professional writers with aspiring incarcerated writers. She also taught creative nonfiction in the North Carolina Correctional Center for Women. In 2009, Simone began offering a workshop at the Orange Correctional Center in Hillsborough, NC, incorporating writing, film, art, and spoken word in an eclectic weekly learning circle.

When she is not doing her part to stop mass incarceration, Simone works as a technical writer, editor, and yoga instructor. Her previous written work includes numerous short form fiction and technical publications and the books "The CRC Card Book" (Addison Wesley) and "The Structured Systems Development Manual" (Prentice Hall).